"What is success and how do I achieve it? Plenty of authors have offered answers to those questions. But only Richard Shell has taken a hard look at the questions themselves. In this insightful book, Shell offers a new way to think of success—as a way to live rather than a goal to achieve—that can transform your own life and the lives of those around you."

—DANIEL PINK,
author of *To Sell Is Human* and *Drive*

"*Springboard: Launching Your Personal Search for Success* is a rare find—like one of those special mountaineering guidebooks about a challenging assent that captures the wisdom and experience of generations of climbers. But the Wharton School's Richard Shell has a very different climb in mind: he wants you to find your way to a successful life based on self-understanding, meaningful work, and deeply rooted human relationships. Lace up your boots and get out your ice ax. You will not find a better guide to overcoming the obstacles ahead on this all-important journey."

—JOSH LEWIS,
Founder and Managing Principal, Salmon River Capital

"Richard Shell is an award-winning teacher and the well-known creator of the Wharton School's only course on the meaning of success. Having attended the course myself, I'm thrilled that he is now sharing its tremendously valuable insights with readers. Although there are hundreds of books about 'how to succeed,' Richard helps you think through what success actually is—and he is one of the most reliable guides I know to help you figure this out for yourself."

—ANGELA DUCKWORTH,
Associate Professor of Psychology, University of Pennsylvania,
winner of the Joseph E. Zins Early Career Award, and
codeveloper of the GRIT Scale

"Richard Shell has written a book that is at once wise and practical, attentive to the scientific literature and full of gripping stories of individual lives. This is a book every college student should read."

—BARRY SCHWARTZ,
Darwin Cartwright Professor, Swarthmore College,
author of *The Paradox of Choice: Why More Is Less* and
Practical Wisdom: The Right Way to Do the Right Thing

Springboard

Springboard

Launching Your
Personal Search for SUCCESS

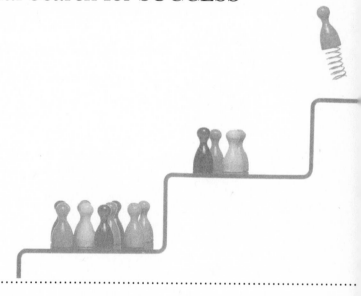

G. RICHARD SHELL

PORTFOLIO / PENGUIN

PORTFOLIO / PENGUIN
Published by the Penguin Group
Penguin Group (USA) Inc., 375 Hudson Street,
New York, New York 10014, USA

USA | Canada | UK | Ireland | Australia | New Zealand | India | South Africa | China
Penguin Books Ltd, Registered Offices: 80 Strand, London WC2R 0RL, England
For more information about the Penguin Group visit penguin.com

Library of Congress Cataloging-in-Publication Data
Shell, G. Richard, 1949–
Springboard: launching your personal search for success /
G. Richard Shell.
pages cm
Includes bibliographical references and index.
ISBN 978-1-59184-547-8
1. Success. 2. Self-realization. 3. Satisfaction. 4. Job satisfaction. I. Title.
BF637.S8S464 2013
650.1—dc23
2013017451

Printed in the United States of America
10 9 8 7 6 5 4 3 2 1

Book design by Elyse Strongin

For my students, past, present, and future.

In gratitude

for teaching me so much.

A man saw a ball of gold in the sky;
He climbed for it,
And eventually he achieved it—
It was clay.
Now this is the strange part:
When the man went to the earth
And looked again,
Lo, there was the ball of gold.
Now this is the strange part:
It was a ball of gold.
Aye, by the heavens, it was a ball of gold.

—STEPHEN CRANE, 1895

It is only when we have the courage to face things exactly as they are, without any self-deception or illusion, that a light will develop out of events, by which the path to success may be recognized.

—*I Ching* Hexagram #5—Waiting/Nourishment

Contents

Springboard

Two Big Questions

RALPH WALDO EMERSON: Harvard teaches most of the branches of learning.

HENRY DAVID THOREAU: Yes, indeed. All of the branches and none of the roots.

As a senior faculty member at the Wharton School of Business, I am best known for my work in negotiation, persuasion, and interpersonal influence. I have written two popular books on these subjects and teach MBA and undergraduate courses. I have also coached everyone from Navy SEALs and FBI hostage negotiators to top executives at Four Seasons Hotels and managers at Google.

Given what I do now, most people are surprised to learn that I did not start my academic career until I was thirty-seven and spent most of my twenties unemployed, much of the time deeply uncertain about who I was and what I wanted to do. But I count those years as the most important in my life. It was during that intense period of living with failure that I gained my first insights into the meaning of success.

Here is what happened.

I was admitted into college on a full military scholarship. In exchange for this completely free ride plus spending money, I agreed to become a naval officer at graduation and to spend at least six years in military service. At the time, this seemed natural because I came from a military family. My father, a retired general in the

U.S. Marine Corps, was the leader of a military college, the Virginia Military Institute, and both of my grandfathers had been career military men.

So far, so good.

But it was the Vietnam War era. Troubled by vivid images of the horrors of battle, convinced there was no justification for the war, and surrounded by classmates and teachers who were protesting against it, I surrendered my scholarship and handed my draft card to the university chaplain. I committed to becoming a pacifist. My family's military traditions were no longer a source of pride. Instead, they became a source of crisis and conflict.

Don't let anyone tell you that symbolic actions are unimportant. On the day I turned in my draft card, I severed the narrative thread of my life. While I continued to function on the outside—now studying literature and creative writing—I no longer recognized who I was. I graduated and, instead of putting on the uniform everyone expected, I became a social worker for families living in condemned buildings without heat, water, or electricity in Washington, D.C. My new clients taught me how people survive even the most desperate living conditions, but they could not tell me what I was supposed to do with my life. Unable to imagine my future, I quit and became a part-time housepainter. I stopped speaking with my parents, refusing to go home even for Christmas. My life as an "achiever" was shattered. I had no idea how to put it together again.

So began the journey that led to this book.

ODYSSEY YEARS

Sociologists have identified a relatively new, distinct stage of life in Western societies—the "Odyssey Years" between twenty and thirty-five (i.e., roughly between college and marriage)—when men and women set out to discover their own values and goals. Odysseys can also begin later in life with an unexpected layoff or divorce, or as people near retirement. The work on an Odyssey is to discover what the next stage of your life will hold—to find out what's ahead, sometimes in the face of conflicting family, cultural, or economic pressures. Each person's journey is, by definition, different, and you can never be sure exactly where it will end.

My Odyssey started with magic. I sought out self-help seminars where I learned about affirmation, visualization, autohypnosis, and mind control. I progressed from magic to the mantras of Transcendental Meditation, and from mantras to psychotherapy. Between house-painting jobs, I did some acting in local theaters and even toured the country with a ragtag, left-wing theater group: the People's Revolutionary Road Company.

But underneath all the activity, I was living a life of quiet desperation. Painting houses gives you plenty of time to think and I spent much of mine in culturally inspired success fantasies. I became a world-famous poet. Then I was an important member of Congress. Then it would be time to paint the trim on another window sash.

One especially vivid daydream dominated all the rest. I had an impressive office on K Street, Washington's central artery for lobbyists and consultants. In my office, a big, leafy potted plant stood next to an equally imposing window that looked out at the people, buses, and cars rushing by. I felt very important because I had a professional office with a potted plant.

It must have been a powerful vision because, in a roundabout way, it eventually came true almost exactly as I had imagined it. Tired of painting houses, I launched a search for a white-collar job by answering newspaper employment ads. One day, my search took me to a suburban office park where I was interviewed for a time-share real estate sales job by a well-dressed man who was eager to know what my "five-year plan" was. Of course, I did not have a five-year plan. I did not even have a five-day plan.

But he asked me an obvious question I had not thought about before: what could I do better than most people? My college major was in English and I could definitely use words better than many of my classmates. This insight changed my job search.

I started calling every number in the Washington, D.C., yellow pages related to a job that might require writing skills: magazines, newspapers, trade association newsletters, public relations firms, fund-raising groups, and so on. I finally hit pay dirt when I talked my way into an interview with a fund-raising consulting firm. They needed someone who knew something about social work (they had a new client in that field), and I passed the writing test. Miraculously, when they ushered me into my new office on my first day at work, I discovered that I had a potted plant and a window looking out on K Street.

I learned three important career lessons from this episode. First, fantasies are fun, but taking action is what gets you a job. Second, it helped to be looking for work doing something I did better than most people. That gave me a story to tell.

The final and most important lesson came soon after I started that job.

I learned that success is not a place.

My new job was no better for me than painting houses had been. I got a bigger paycheck and had a recognizable professional "role" to talk about when I met someone at a party. But the potted plant in my office had no answers to the inner questions I was asking. I felt like an impostor—an actor posing as a professional.

So in June 1976, I quit and left America altogether, setting off to travel the world with my life savings of $3,000 and a backpack. I did not know if or when I would return. All I knew was that I longed to feel confident again, to have a direction in life I could believe in.

I started in Greece, sleeping as often as possible in cheap hostels, hotels, and even public parks. I trekked from the Orthodox monasteries of Mount Athos in northern Greece to the hillsides overlooking the Sea of Galilee, reading the Bible as I went. In that great crossroads between East and West—Istanbul—I learned about a hippie express called the Magic Bus that left every day to go overland to New Delhi, India. For thirty-five dollars, you could get off anywhere along the route, and get back on a day, a week, or even a month later. So I climbed aboard, traveling in stages from Istanbul to Iran and from Iran into Afghanistan.

It was in Afghanistan that my Odyssey ran completely off the road.

HITTING BOTTOM

I vividly recall the particular day my journey changed because I kept a journal of my travels. I had just finished a grueling two-day bus trip, inhaling dust across the entire length of Afghanistan, from Herat to Kandahar to Kabul. Every two hundred kilometers or so, as the bus rumbled along from one warlord's territory to the next, it stopped for what amounted to a changing of the guard. Everyone got out; the local men, women, and children who were riding on the roof scrambled down; and we all sought shade under a tree or inside a tin-roofed hut to take tea. The rifle-toting militiaman who had been riding next to the driver departed, and, eventually, a new guarantor of a new warlord's protection showed up. At the driver's signal, everyone would pile back into and onto the bus and we would rumble off. As we pulled into Kabul, rain had begun to fall. I was dimly aware of feeling dizzy as I stepped off the bus and into the mud that passed for a street.

Then I remembered what day it was: Christmas Eve.

"Hotel?" I asked the driver, and I followed the arc of the man's finger to a set of low-slung buildings nearby. With the rain soaking both me and my backpack, I made my way to Kabul's version of skid row and checked into a cheap hotel, getting the last remaining bed for fifty cents per night. It was a cot in a hallway surrounded by a soiled sheet as a makeshift curtain.

I put my gear down and headed back outside to make my way to town, but my dizziness increased with every step. Before I had gone more than fifty yards, I blacked out, collapsing on the side of a street.

When I came to, I was lying on my back in some mud and looking up at a ring of dark-complexioned, curious faces forming a tight circle around me. A man in a dirty Afghan army uniform bent over, hands on knees, and peered into my face. A young boy offered his hand to pull me up. I was sure I was going to be sick, but I managed to get to my feet.

It isn't often that you know exactly—to the second—when you have hit the bottom of your life. But I knew that morning as I stumbled back toward my hotel that I was very close to being at the bottom of mine. A few minutes later I learned from some pot-smoking Australian travelers in a nearby room that my dizzy feeling had a name. One of them led me to a mirror and told me to look into my eyes. They were both a dull yellow.

"Hep," he said. Hepatitis.

If you had told me that night that I would one day graduate from law school near the top of my class, clerk for a federal appeals court in Boston, and become a professor of law, ethics, and management at the Wharton School, I would have questioned your sanity. But something shifted in my life that day. I had pushed myself to my psychological and physical limits and had ended up alone, filthy, sick, and no closer to finding my direction than I was a year earlier. A sense of deep despair crept over me.

Sometimes it is only when the status quo becomes intolerable that change happens. As I lay in my hallway cot that night, the status quo of my life on the road became intolerable. I did not know what sort of change was coming, but I knew that continuing to travel aimlessly around the globe was not going to solve my problem.

And, as fate would have it, I turned a corner before the night was out. It started with a midnight visit from two European teenagers who belonged to a religious group called the Children of God. They poked their heads around my curtain and bore a brown paper bag with the words "Merry Christmas" written on it in crayon. Inside were two fresh-baked cookies and a tangerine. They left this gift along with some literature by their prophet, a man named Moses David.

They also left behind, I wrote later that night in my journal, a vivid impression of what life looks like when it is motivated by a sense of purpose rooted in deeply held beliefs. The apocalyptic religious teachings of Moses David did not win me over. But the power of these two young people's beliefs—no matter what the content was—set me thinking. They had traveled the same roads as I to the same back-street hotel in Kabul where I had landed. We had shared something on a Christmas Eve. Only I was in a pit of despair while they were cheerful, energetic, and generous. What was I missing?

These two "angels" (I could not help but think of them this way) had caught me just as I was falling into a very dark place. And they lit a small spark of hope, kindling a desire to look inside myself and see if I could discover a point of view I could call my own. I was still sick, but I woke up the next day with the sense that it would be better than the one before it.

The French novelist Marcel Proust once wrote, "The voyage of discovery lies not in seeking new horizons, but in seeing with new eyes." It was in Kabul that I began to understand what Proust meant. I was no longer interested in the stark, beautiful mountains that surrounded the city. Instead, I was looking inside for a hint as to who, exactly, was looking out at those mountains.

A FORK IN THE ROAD

It took me a few weeks to get my health back, and after that my journey changed from a road trip to a more focused quest for inner experiences. Making my way through the Khyber Pass to Pakistan and India, I learned contemplation techniques at Hindu ashrams and finally took up residence in the Kanduboda Buddhist monastery in Sri Lanka. Under the patient guidance of a wise monk there, Venerable Seevali Thera, I sat and walked through eighteen-hour days of insight meditation, coming to some direct realizations about perception, the nature of beliefs, change, suffering, and death. I also saw how distressingly easy it was to get caught up in the bustle of day-to-day striving and forget everything I had learned. Slowly, I began to understand myself, my family, and my emotions more clearly—goals I hope I can help you achieve for yourself in this book.

Having learned the basics of Buddhist meditation practice, I next sought to learn more about the Buddha's life. I made pilgrimages to the holy sites in India where he achieved enlightenment (Bodh Gaya) and gave his first sermon on his insights into life and death (Sarnath). Over the ensuing months, I made my way to Nepal, Thailand, Hong Kong, Taiwan, and, eventually, Korea. There, at a beautiful monastery in the southern mountains called Songgwang-sa, I met a Zen master named Ku San Sunim. Master Ku San, as I described him in my journal, was "an energetic little man with dancing eyes and a very direct way about him" who presided over a large community of monks. At first glance, he looked more like a farmer than a Zen master. A French nun named Song-il, who now helps to lead a meditation center in England, served as his translator.

Master Ku San invited me to stop traveling and live there at Songgwang-sa, become a monk, and dedicate my life to the search for enlightenment. He advised me to consider carefully because "the most useful life is led by one who is fully awakened and who can share that equally with all. One who attempts to help others without being enlightened," he said, "cannot do so well as one who is awake."

I stayed in Songgwang-sa for a while to think it over. I faced a fork in the road. One way led to a lifetime investigating the deepest layers of inner truth—a search that I had come to respect and admire. The other led back home, where I would get a chance to test whether the limited understandings I had gained about perception, emotion, and my own inner resources could help to resolve the personal conflicts I had left behind when I began my Odyssey.

At length, I decided to take the path that has led me to where I am today rather than the one toward the meditation hall. Three considerations—only one of which is easy to relate in words—tipped me toward home.

First, the easy one. My meditation practice had taught me something blindingly obvious about myself (which I was, of course, the last to know): I am basically a practical person. Seeking challenges and solving problems suits me better than sitting in stillness.

The second factor had to do with something invisible that I had acquired and that answered the question I had been asking since Christmas Eve in Kabul. The intense, direct experience of my own inner world had fundamentally anchored my sense of identity. I had learned to watch and observe the moment-to-moment parade of impulses, insecurities, memories, plans, fantasies, and fears that made up my mental reality. The "self" inside me that did that observing was something different from—and stronger than—the thoughts, insecurities, and fears themselves. Ironically, a religion that teaches there is no self had helped me to find my identity. I now had a point of view about the world and my place in it—a point of view that supplied for me what the cult-based belief system had supplied for my two midnight visitors in Kabul. Unlike them, however, I was capable of living with uncertainties, mysteries, and doubts without needing to resolve them into a single truth or ideological belief.

Finally, I had come to terms with a fundamental, hard-to-face fact of life. I understood that suffering and death are not exceptional conditions that afflict the unfortunate. They are the essential challenges around which every worthy life is built. I knew and accepted how my story would someday end. My task was to write a purposeful narrative using the life I had left in front of me.

I went home because the quest that had started in Kabul was over.

FROM THE MONASTERY TO THE CLASSROOM

The poet T. S. Eliot once wrote that "the end of all our exploring will be to arrive where we started and know the place for the first time." So it was for me. By the time I returned home, I was in my late twenties and still had no idea what I would do with my life. But I was in the right place with the right people.

A prodigal son, I reconciled with my parents and moved into their spare bedroom in Lexington, Virginia—the small rural town where I had grown up after my father retired from the Marine Corps. I got a job selling home insulation door-to-door. As I visited all the familiar haunts of my childhood, I was astonished to find that everything was almost exactly as I had left it years before. Only I was seeing it— as well as my parents, old friends, and grade-school teachers—with a new kind of clarity.

As the next year passed, I zeroed in on a vocation by thinking (once again) about what I could do "better than most" and surveying professions that depended on writing skills. I discovered that law was such an occupation and applied to the law school at the University of Virginia, which was just up the road in Charlottesville. I also fell in love all over again with a woman from my college class whom I had dated back when we were students. We married.

Then, during a law-school class one day, lightning struck. I was sitting in a classroom with 150 other students, all primed and ready to talk about that day's legal topic. An especially gifted professor had me riveted to my seat, anticipating what question he would ask next and hoping he would call on me to answer it. The energy and intellectual excitement of that moment sent an emotional charge through me that delivered a realization: I wanted to be the person in the front of that room. I wanted to create that kind of excitement and insight for others. I wanted to be a teacher.

The classes that followed confirmed my insight and provided me with a concrete occupational goal. But lots of hard work lay ahead to achieve it. It would take another six years—spent finding role models, finishing law school, clerking for a federal appeals court judge, and working as a lawyer—before my Odyssey Years finally ended at the age of thirty-seven with the beginning of my teaching career at the Wharton School.

After joining the faculty in 1986 and advancing from the junior to the senior ranks, I discovered a secret of academic life. Working as a professor allows you to create, not just follow, your passions. I started out teaching law but soon launched the Wharton School's first class on negotiation and conflict resolution—a course that required me to read deeply in social psychology and that allowed me to help mentor students in the kind of emotional self-awareness I had picked up on my travels. As I spoke with more and more students about their careers and aspirations, I discovered that examining the idea of "success" provided an even more meaningful way to help them reflect on their goals and identities.

My academic environment also exposed me to many colleagues who were a lot smarter and more accomplished than I was in subjects I wanted to learn. For example, my study of success led me to Professor Martin Seligman, a world-famous University of Pennsylvania researcher who established the field of positive psychology in the late 1990s. Then, with the help of Marty's top graduate student, Angela Duckworth (who is now a star scholar in her own right), I established a university-wide success seminar in honor of Benjamin Franklin's three-hundredth birthday. Franklin's *Autobiography* was the first how-to-succeed book in American history, and we invited leading academics in psychology, philosophy, and religion to give talks on the meaning of success today. Needless to say, I was taking a lot of notes.

Finally, in 2005, I created and continue to teach a popular course at Wharton called The Literature of Success: Ethical and Historical Perspectives (we will call it "Success" for short in this book)—a course that distills my study of hundreds of how-to books, philosophical works, biographies, and psychological research papers on success, extending from ancient to modern times. Aristotle, Plato, Dale Carnegie, Charles Lindbergh, and Steven Covey share top billing with Benjamin Franklin on the reading list for my Success course.

The author of *Walden*, the philosopher Henry David Thoreau, once commented to his friend and mentor Ralph Waldo Emerson that Harvard had taught all the branches of learning but got to "none of the roots." My goal in Success is to get to some of those roots by allowing students and faculty to talk directly and candidly about life goals and success concepts in a classroom. As my work in this course has become known, I have been invited to give school-wide lectures as well as lead sessions on the meaning of success for top leadership teams and executives.

What have I learned teaching this fascinating subject? That Ivy League students and organizational leaders are no different from the millions of other people who look to success guides for counsel. All alike are seeking help to solve some fairly complicated problems: how to get along better with others, get ahead in their careers, and find meaning in their lives. They need just a little help—as I did so many years ago when I painted houses in Washington, D.C., and attended courses in local hotels on mind magic. In the Success course, and now in this book, I hope I can provide a few shortcuts through the maze that popular culture has made of the "quest for success"—and to do so in a uniquely open and interactive way.

THERE ARE NO SECRETS

How does this book differ from other books about success? First, I am not a hard-charging entrepreneur, media celebrity, or motivational guru who wants to tell you how I have succeeded so you can apply my "system." The story you just read about my Odyssey is the most you will hear about my life in this book. And I can tell you right up front: there is no foolproof system that always leads to success. Instead, I want to give you the benefit of what I have learned as an avid student of this subject for over four decades. I have set the book up so you can craft your own goals and devise your own success system based on your unique skills and personality.

Second, I want to take some of the mystery and anxiety out of success. There is no "secret" you need to discover. And you do not have "one true purpose" for your life that it is your duty to find or die trying. The raw materials for success are tucked away inside you and your next big goal is probably within arm's reach—if only you have the clarity of mind to see it.

Third, I want to offer hope. Malcolm Gladwell's book *Outliers: The Story of Success* stood the world of success studies on its head, arguing persuasively that world-class performance in any field is often a matter of good fortune combined with innate talent, lucky genes, sociological advantage, good timing, and obsessive work. The "story of success," he concludes, is usually just that—a tall tale we make up after the fact that (falsely) gives the starring role to the individual rather than to luck and circumstance. I agree with Gladwell that the small subset of the population we label "extremely successful" (people such as Gladwell himself) are, almost by definition, unusually talented, very lucky, and blessed with favorable genetic predispositions and relentless personal drive.

But I think there is still hope for the rest of us.

This book will help you do two things that are firmly within your grasp: clarify your goals and understand better how to make progress achieving them. *Outliers* explains how Bill Gates, the Beatles, and various Nobel Prize winners scored their remarkable achievements. This book has a different goal. I want to help you start where you are today, regardless of your current advantages or disadvantages. Then you can use this book as a springboard for launching your search to find a truly personal vision of success. From what my students tell me, this work can change your life.

TWO BIG QUESTIONS ONLY YOU CAN ANSWER

Students and executives frequently ask me how I came to be interested in success when my main fields of interest are persuasion and negotiation. I tell them that my study of success came first. By investigating the meaning of success, you begin the lifelong process of deciding what is worth doing. Your skills at influence, persuasion, and negotiation can then help you to achieve those goals.

In this book I will challenge you to answer two questions I ask my students to confront throughout our course.

- The First Question: *What is success?*
- The Second Question: *How will I achieve it?*

To help you address these issues, the book is divided into two parts that take up these questions and provide ideas and exercises to help you answer them. Every now and then I will give you my own opinion about a success topic, but you and only you can answer the two success questions for yourself. Moreover, as your life progresses, you are sure to encounter both predictable and unexpected challenges that will force you to revise the answers you give the first time you read this book. What makes sense at one stage of your life may not make sense later on. As Harry Potter tells his friend Hermione (in the film *Harry Potter and the Deathly Hallows—Part 2*), "When have any of our plans actually worked? We plan, we get there, all hell breaks loose!" Jobs come and go; accidents happen; careers change; retirement looms. The questions raised in this book are useful to consider now—and may be worth revisiting down the road.

Throughout the book, I will present a series of exercises and assessments I have created in my work with students and executives. These are based on well-researched psychological principles as well as insights from religion, literature, and philosophy. As you will see, success is never simple. It always involves hidden assumptions and trade-offs. Cultural beliefs, amplified by family expectations, can operate like automatic pilots, steering your intuitions, emotions, and actions even when you are only dimly aware of their influence.

WHERE WE GO FROM HERE

Here is how the book is organized. Part 1 consists of four chapters to help you answer the First Question: What is success? We will start with a success values survey I use in my training programs. Then we will proceed to look at some of the answers commonly given to the what-is-success question: happiness, family, professional status, fame, fortune, and a "calling"—or what I refer to as meaningful work.

Chapter 1 gets you started by allowing you to choose your own life. It features a self-assessment I call the Six Lives Exercise to help you take a snapshot of your current success attitudes. If you had a free choice in the matter, would you live a life devoted to happiness or aim at some significant accomplishment? It is easy to say "both," but there are always trade-offs. This chapter will probe how you are thinking about those trade-offs today.

Chapter 2 examines the most obvious answer to the success question. Try asking random people you meet during the day what "success" means to them. You will find that most have a simple, immediate answer: "happiness." But when you ask them what they mean by happiness, they are not so sure. For some it is family; for others it is pleasure; for a few it is doing God's will. Thanks to Marty Seligman's positive psychology movement, there has been an explosion of research on happiness in recent decades. We will look at some of those findings, and you will get a chance to figure out for yourself what you mean by this all-important but elusive word.

Chapter 3 examines the roles that family and culture play in establishing your ideas about success. Your family may not have demanded that you become a doctor or a lawyer, but you probably got the message that your parents wanted you to "be somebody." What exactly does that mean? In addition, our celebrity-dominated culture provides two compelling anwsers to the what-is-success question: fame and fortune. We'll look closely at why so many people in our modern, media-saturated world are drawn to these success measures. Even if these specific goals do not appeal to you, this chapter will help you better understand how the social world surrounding you has influenced your success goals.

Chapter 4—"An Inspired Answer: Find Meaningful Work"—focuses squarely on success as it relates to your professional aspirations. There are at least three different ways to think about work: as a job, as a career, or as something that has special meaning beyond either of these. Interestingly, research shows that the meaning in work comes from *within you*—not from the occupation itself. When I was living in South Korea's Songgwang-sa monastery, for example, jobs as menial as washing dishes and cleaning toilets were considered meaningful. They gave the monks opportunities to practice mindfulness and attitudes of service to the community. By the same token, you may know people who are nurses, social workers, or teachers—occupations that look, from the outside, to be meaningful. But when you ask them about it, they may see what they do as just paycheck-oriented jobs.

With your ideas about what success is in mind, consider the Second Question in the book: How will I achieve it? The five chapters in part 2 are designed to help you figure out the special combination of talent, experience, and drive you are bringing to your success journey.

Chapter 5 addresses your unique capabilities and asks you to think about the question that got me my first professional job and launched me on my current career: what do you do "better than most"? We will survey your unique aptitudes, passions, and skills. In addition, I will ask you to complete a personality profiler to determine your personal strengths in terms of social skills, achievement drives, intellectual/creative impulses, and emotional temperament. One of the great ironies in the study of success is that many people believe the secrets to achieving it lie "out there" somewhere—in a far-off, hard-to-find place. The truth is much simpler: the answer lies within yourself. Your task is always to discover (and rediscover) your own innate abilities.

Chapter 6 investigates the motivations that power your success engine. We all run on our own favorite fuels. But I have found that people who motivate themselves through a combination of seeking both inner satisfaction and outer rewards can often stay with a single task longer and get a stronger sense of having "succeeded" than those who rely on only one or the other. You may discover that you have some important energy sources you have neglected.

Chapter 7 explores a critical success factor: self-confidence. It investigates the role of failure as a factor in your achievement and examines whether you have the kind of "mindset" that allows you to take risks and that researchers have shown can help you to get ahead in life. Norman Vincent Peale's classic *The Power of Positive Thinking* (1952) launches with the exhortation "Believe in yourself!" This chapter will help you discover the unique sources for these beliefs in your own life.

Chapter 8 looks at one of my favorite subjects in the success field: the powers of mental focus that help you achieve things. There is a lot of hocus-pocus and magic associated with this topic. So we will use the real-life, remarkable story of how Charles Lindbergh made his historic flight across the Atlantic Ocean in his tiny aircraft, the *Spirit of St. Louis*, to track how the four genuine powers of the mind—passion, imagination, intuition, and reason—can work together to help you accomplish your most important goals.

Chapter 9 wraps up the second half of the book by exploring how your social skills affect success. Having written several earlier books about the arts of persuasion and negotiation, I have a theory that what matters most in your social life is your ability to exert influence through credibility and an art we will call "dialogue." The challenge in social interaction is figuring out how to maintain your sense of personal authenticity at the same time that you make the adjustments needed to work with a variety of other people and personalities. This chapter will give you the chance to look at the science of impression management as well as the practical steps you can take to gain people's trust and cooperation as you move important projects along.

The book's conclusion, "The Right Answers," reviews the major themes and lessons that I hope you have taken away from our work together. I will challenge you to list the actions you need to take in your personal as well as your professional life to further your personal concept of success.

You will be reading about a lot of people in the pages ahead—some famous and many you have never heard of. Almost all of them will have stories about how they overcame hardships, corrected mistakes, set their sights on what they believed in, and achieved their own version of success. But, ultimately, this book is not about any of them. It is about you.

As Apple's cofounder Steve Jobs said in his famous 2005 commencement address at Stanford University, "Your time is limited, so don't waste it living someone else's life. . . . Don't let the noise of others' opinions drown out your own inner voice. And, most important, have the courage to follow your heart and intuition. They somehow already know what you truly want to become."

I hope this book with help you hear your own inner voice more clearly so you can discover what you should do next with your life.

Then the fun begins. You get to do it.

| PART ONE |

THE FIRST QUESTION

What Is Success?

The first four chapters give you the chance to examine your current assumptions and beliefs about success. Once you begin to think about it, you may be surprised at how many of your ideas about success originate from your culture, family, friends, and exposure to mass media. As you become more aware of these sources for your beliefs, you can decide whether to embrace, reject, or integrate them into new and more creative ways to approach your life.

From a distance, success may appear obvious. Put simply, successful people already have whatever it is that you want—fame, wealth, happiness, fulfillment, professional status, or a life of leisure. The closer you get to achieving any or all of these things, however, the more complex and elusive they turn out to be. For this reason, some people end up deciding that success is less about the goals you should strive to achieve and more about the way you should live your life.

In this part, you will look at some of the most common answers to the what-is-success question: happiness, fame, fortune, professional status, and meaningful work. It would be great to have it all, but life usually demands trade-offs. Where do you set your priorities?

The First Answer:
Choose Your Life

There is no one who, if he listens to himself, does not
discover in himself a pattern all his own, a ruling pattern.

—MICHEL DE MONTAIGNE

I met Eric Adler when he was in his first year of Wharton's MBA program taking a required law course I was teaching. Sandy-haired and slightly older than the average student, he was the kind of person every teacher loves—prepared, eager, smart, and full of good questions. One day he dropped by my office to talk about a question he had raised in class. He had never had a course on law before and he was excited by the challenges posed by the material. Before long, however, the conversation turned to deeper, more personal issues. "I'm not sure yet what I want to do," Eric confided. "I love business school, but I don't know where it is taking me."

Two kinds of students attend graduate business school. By far the majority are "Quants." These are the students who studied economics, math, or engineering in college; got their first job in some sort of business-related field; and can do complex calculations of net present value in their heads. They know what they want: the excitement of doing big deals, investing big money, or advising the world's biggest companies as strategy consultants. I respect the passion that many of these students have for the world of global business. They are combining their genuine talents with the excitement of vying for some of the most important and influential jobs in the world economy.

But every class also has a group that we call the "Poets"—people from a range of backgrounds that include former professional athletes, military veterans, Peace Corps volunteers, and journalists. For them, business school is a pathway to entirely new opportunities and careers. Classes on statistics and finance can be a little harder for the Poets because they have to compete with the Quants on materials the Quants can master without opening a book. Being the faculty version of a Poet myself, I try to offer them what comfort I can.

Eric was skilled in math (he had majored in economics and engineering in college), but he still profiled as a Poet. He was a graduate of one of the best liberal arts colleges in the country, Swarthmore College, and had been a teacher and an administrator at a well-known private high school in Baltimore for eight years. He loved his classroom teaching, but it had become routine. He was looking for something with more of an "edge"—the kind of competitive, every-minute-counts energy that he thought a career in business might provide. He had enrolled in business school hoping the experience would help him discover what he should do next. Now, midway through his first year, he was just beginning that search.

"You could always combine what you are learning about business with your knowledge of education," I suggested. Eric agreed, but he looked dubious. "I don't want to go back to what I've done before," he said. "I'm looking for a change." We chatted for a few more minutes before he had to leave for a class. I invited him to check back and talk more anytime he wanted. And over his two years at Wharton he did just that, even taking another course with me—this one on negotiation.

To tell the truth, however, I became increasingly worried as Eric moved through the program. Business schools have very distinctive, career-oriented cultures. Everyone agrees on what the high-status jobs are. Pretty soon everybody—even those who privately harbor doubts—gets swept up into the technology-finance-consulting whirlpool funneling students into these prestigious industries. Eric's situation left him vulnerable to these cultural forces, and it was not long before he was succumbing to them.

Soon after the beginning of his second year, Eric stopped by my office to make an announcement: "I've figured out what I want to do!" he said excitedly. "I want to become a consultant!" Inwardly, I had my doubts. Outwardly, I congratulated him and wished him luck.

A few months later, Eric achieved his goal and landed a consulting job in Washington, D.C. When I saw him just before graduation, however, he was having second thoughts. He had been turned down by his first-choice firm. The position he was taking was not the one he had dreamed about. "I'm pretty sure this company isn't where I want to spend my career," he said. "But it is the right thing for me to do now."

For many, that would be the end of the story. I might have caught up with Eric ten or twenty years later at a reunion, and I would have been curious about how it had all worked out.

But that is not how Eric's story ends—and that is why I am telling you about him to start our work together on your success. Less than a year after Eric graduated, I ran into someone from his consulting company at Wharton's executive conference center, and I asked her how he was doing.

She looked uncomfortable. "Eric was not really cut out to be a consultant," she said. "He is no longer with us." She had no idea what he was doing. My heart sank.

Not long after that, however, I learned that Eric's story was turning out to be much more interesting than I had expected. He had figured out even faster than his firm that he was not cut out for consulting. One of his first projects involved an elaborate, time-consuming analysis for a large corporate client about how to save money. The project ended in a recommendation that the firm print its customer invoices on two-sided rather than one-sided paper. He had not gone to graduate school so he could do that kind of work. He had to get out immediately. And his dissatisfaction threw him back into searching for his real interests and passions—only now with more urgency.

As the French philosopher Michel de Montaigne noted in the quote that opened this chapter, when you stop and listen to yourself, you are likely to discern "a pattern all [your] own, a ruling pattern." This is exactly what happened to Eric.

First, he realized that he wanted to be his own boss, to build something that would be important and that would use his unique combination of talents and knowledge. "What can I start?" he asked himself. His parents had both been entrepreneurs who had launched and sold a successful company—and then started another one. He had grown up in a home where entrepreneurial spirit and risk taking were normal aspects of family life and dinner-table talk.

The business-school culture had framed his career problem as a recruiting question: "Where should I work?" When he asked, "What can I start?" his mind immediately started buzzing with ideas about what he knew best: education.

In rethinking his experiences as a high-school teacher, he reviewed an old puzzle: why did at-risk teenagers who had been given scholarships to attend his elite private school so often struggle? They were smart enough to do well, but they lacked the social foundations and study habits their better-heeled classmates brought with them from home. To solve this problem, Eric began kicking around a crazy idea to create a first-of-its-kind "public education boarding school" that could provide some of the missing elements these kids needed to thrive. The school would create a safe environment for study, a peer group devoted to academic achievement, adult role models, and a culture of accountability. As he developed the concept, he envisioned a 24/7 high school with a rigorous curriculum and a staff of teachers as committed to excellence as he was. Their common goal: to show the world that these young people, given the right circumstances, could succeed.

Before long, Eric was talking about his dream to anyone who would listen. And during his last few weeks at the consulting firm, one of the newer partners suggested he meet a young Princeton graduate named Rajiv Vinnakota. Raj, it seems, had been talking to people at *his* consulting firm about a very similar concept.

Eric and Raj soon met for a life-changing, three-hour dinner at a local fast-food restaurant in Washington, D.C. They decided then and there to join forces.

Within two months they had written a full-blown proposal for their model school. And within eighteen months they had raised $2 million, renovated an old building in Washington, and opened their doors to forty sixth graders—all admitted based on a lottery for local children from Washington's toughest neighborhoods.

The first School for Educational Evolution and Development (SEED) was born. It would grow to encompass grades six through twelve—roughly fifty students per grade—with a clear goal of sending as many inner-city students as possible to college.

The rest is history. Eric and Raj received a Use Your Life Award from Oprah Winfrey on her television show in 2002. Appearances on ABC's *Nightline* and a special segment on CBS's *60 Minutes* followed— and additional SEED schools have opened in other cities. Most important, Eric and Raj have proved that their model can deliver dramatically different educational results by creating the learning and psychological conditions needed for inner-city children to flourish.

In 2010, every single one of their SEED graduates—all coming from poor neighborhoods where only 33 percent of students even graduate from high school—was admitted to college, including such schools as Duke, Brown, and the University of Maryland. And the outlook for them there is excellent. Nearly 70 percent of SEED students who start college end up graduating—a graduation rate six times higher than that of the public high schools in the at-risk neighborhoods SEED draws from.

Did Eric need to spend two years of his life obtaining a business degree to discover the SEED concept? Probably not. But by asking the question "What can I start?" he found that he had acquired a powerful set of capabilities to apply in answering that question. He was able to combine his business knowledge with his unique educational experience to make SEED a success. When he and Raj needed to raise $14 million through a Bank of America bond offering to complete the SEED School Washington campus, Eric had the knowledge, skills, credibility, and experience to attract investors and close the deal.

Just as I had hoped the first day we met in my office, Eric had put it all together and found what I'll refer to in chapter 4 as "meaningful work"—a sweet spot of success that appealed to his entrepreneurial motivations, made good use of everything he knew, and advanced a goal he believed in. In the process, he and his partner helped establish a new and exciting kind of career: the public education entrepreneur.

FINDING SUCCESS: FOUR THEMES

Eric's story illustrates four important theories about success we will explore in this book. Keep these in mind as you dive into the pages to come.

First, finding out what success means to you often involves trial and error, not just theoretical contemplation. You have to take risks, try things out, and experiment. As Eric's example shows, your search may involve flashes of insight such as his "I want to become a consultant!" that will turn out to be false signals. But you must nevertheless summon the courage to try out new roles, admit they do not suit you, and return to the search process.

Conventional success stories often feature heroes who know exactly what they want to do and then overcome enormous odds to achieve it. But the story reads this way because it starts only *after* the heroes have gone through the messy and uncertain process of finding their targets. For most flesh-and-blood people, the harder question is discovering what they want to do. In chapter 7, we will meet a man named Bill Richmond whose life included careers as a fighter pilot, a big-band drummer, and a prizewinning comedy writer in Hollywood. His philosophy expresses the improvisational spirit that many successful people bring to life: "Do it, then learn how."

Second, your goals do not just appear out of thin air. You need to become aware of the success values your culture and family endorsed. That way you can be sure the ideals you are shaping your life around truly reflect *your own, freely chosen* values. As the eighteenth-century philosopher Jean-Jacques Rousseau once noted, individuals take their cues about what is "good or desirable" in life from what they think their culture judges to be good and desirable. The Roman emperor Marcus Aurelius noted this truth in his *Meditations,* nearly two thousand years ago. "I have often wondered," he wrote, "how it is that every man loves himself more than all the rest of men, yet sets more value on others' opinions than on his own." For better or for worse, most of us seek to achieve things that will prompt someone, somewhere to think well of us. An important aspect of getting clear about success, therefore, is breaking free of those assumptions and looking inside to discover what you, yourself, genuinely esteem.

Eric Adler came from entrepreneurial parents, but he did not follow in their footsteps blindly. He tried other lines of work before creating his own, highly original version of the entrepreneurial story. Moreover, he won high social acclaim in the best possible way: without seeking it. Others—those who seek success primarily to bask in its limelight—often end up addicted to fame and fortune in much the same way drug addicts need daily fixes. We will see some examples of such people in chapter 3. Buddhists have a name for them: "Hungry Ghosts."

Third, success is a multidimensional concept, not just a work-related one. You may have noticed that my story about Eric emphasized his career. But before this chapter is over, you will see that this book makes no such assumption. I will share some further, more personal information about Eric's life later on. And shortly, I will give you your own personal success values assessment, called the Six Lives Exercise, to help you begin thinking about the balance you want in your life between inner, emotional aspects of success and the outer, achievement-related ones. This exercise will also give you a chance to begin understanding what motivates you—a topic we will cover in more detail in chapter 6.

Fourth and finally, success is not a single, once-and-for-all destination. It is a journey with way stations, stopovers, and campgrounds.

You can get to one place, enjoy it, and then move on. Chapter 4, which introduces a concept I call "meaningful work," will give you a chance to explore this idea in more detail. Eric's story illustrates how life can provide you with chances to discover different ways of enjoying success at different times in your life. Eric loved teaching high school—until he sensed it was time to move on. He is enjoying his entrepreneurial SEED venture now and has no plans to step away from it. But a time for change may come. What is sweet when you are in your twenties and thirties may lose its savor in your forties and fifties. The same can happen at each stage of your life as you learn, grow, and mature. The good news is that you bring new capabilities to each stage of life—a topic that chapter 5 will expand on. Your changing combination of abilities and experiences will offer new opportunities. New paths to success can then emerge.

In the sections below, you will take the first step of your journey by discovering what you think about success today. In the following three chapters, you will get a chance to drill deeper into the ways happiness, family, culture, and work have influenced your success beliefs.

This chapter is your alarm clock. It is time to wake up.

YOUR SUCCESS VALUES

To help you understand your own intuitions about success, I have devised a values assessment called the Six Lives Exercise. This diagnostic will help you investigate where your ideas about success come from and lead you to more detailed reflections on all the topics ahead.

Here is how it works.

Read through all six of the following biographical sketches. Then go back and think more carefully about them. Finally, rank them in order, from most to least "successful," giving your top choice the number "1" and your bottom choice the number "6." No ties are allowed. Try to respond as honestly as you can.

Once you have ranked them all, we will see what your choices may reveal about your current success thinking.

THE SIX LIVES EXERCISE

YOUR RANKING

_____ **Teacher.** *Patricia Kelly teaches physics and serves as head coach of the women's lacrosse team at a suburban high school (children ages fourteen through eighteen). Her spouse manages a chain of retail stores his family founded thirty years ago. Pat has led her school's Science Olympics teams to three regional championships and one national title over the past ten years. Under Pat's guidance, the high school has placed a number of students in the country's top scientific universities (places such as MIT and Cal Tech). Pat has two daughters, one of whom earned a Ph.D. in artificial intelligence and is now working for a high-tech company. The other ran into trouble in high school, never graduated, and lives in a distant city. She has rebuffed all attempts by the family to stay in touch with her.*

_____ **Banker.** *Jane Rule has worked for her entire career at a global bank in a large city, where she has risen through the ranks to become a regional vice president for private wealth management, serving high-net-worth customers. Jane is also an accomplished marathon runner and a single parent with a daughter, Julie, who suffers from severe learning and physical disabilities. Friends and family members have encouraged Jane to find an institutional home for Julie so she can "get on with her life," but Jane responds that "Julie is my life—I would never dream of letting anyone else take over her care." Indeed, she has been active in raising money for research into learning disabilities. Last year, Jane raised over $25,000 for her cause by running the New York City Marathon while pushing Julie in a specially rigged carriage—a feat that earned her and her cause a segment on an international news television program. She has dated several men over the past few years, but she has never believed in marriage—in part because her own parents were so unhappy together.*

_____ **Wealthy Investor.** *Peter Taylor is a private-equity investor who balances his mostly single life (he married once but divorced four years later) between homes in London, New York, and Bermuda. He made his first fortune guiding a start-up Internet company through its early stages and then selling it to a large competitor. His $240,000 investment turned into a handsome payoff of $50 million. It has been all "upside" since then. A leading business magazine recently published a cover story on Peter, revealing him to be an avowed freethinker, a lover of freedom, and a committed libertarian. In the article, he said, "I love the excitement of placing a big bet and seeing it pay off." His passions outside the office include parties in far-flung* *places ("I like to work hard and play hard") and hang gliding ("being in the air alone gives me a sense of freedom"). He donates generously to conservative political causes and is consulted by influential politicians across the globe for his opinions regarding the world economy.*

_____ **Stone Mason.** *Fred Hampshire is a stone mason who has lived his whole life near a large city. A passionate student of historical architectural design, he has been married to his wife, Mary, for fifty-two years and he has three children (a lawyer, a banker, and a homemaker) and seven grandchildren. "Every piece of stone you pick up is different," he once told a news reporter. "In my work, I can see what I did the first day I started and watch it grow. And I go back years later and it is still there to see. It's a good day laying brick or stone. It is hard work, but you get interested in fitting each piece in just its right spot and the day is over before you know it." Hampshire admits that money has sometimes been a problem, but he proudly points out that he personally helped to build homes for each of his three children.*

_____ **Tennis Pro.** *Janice Chung is a hardworking, professional tennis player who has won four major tournaments in her career and finished in the top fifteen money winners in seven of the past ten years. She started playing tennis with her father at the age of five, and, as a result of the relentless drills her father insisted on, she perfected her game. Tennis has dominated her life since then. A few years ago, she founded the Chung Tennis Institute, a group that provides free tennis instruction and "life skills training" to young women who live in poor urban neighborhoods. She is married to a real estate developer and, unable to have children herself, has adopted three Korean kids, now aged two, six, and seven. "It's a tough life on the tennis circuit," she told a tennis magazine recently. "You don't get as much time with your children as you would like."*

_____ **Nonprofit Executive.** *Bill Paulson used to be an award-winning investment adviser for wealthy families in a major city, where he was well known for his ability to manage the complex estates of entrepreneurs after they died. He has been married for twenty years to his wife, Terry (a child development counselor), and they have four children. Five years ago, Bill quit his job and took a huge pay cut to become a top administrator at a fast-growing nonprofit service organization founded by a charismatic religious leader from South Africa. "I heard God's call," Bill told the local paper, "and I answered." Bill's main project has been to carry out the group's "international mission" helping rural African villages secure clean water supplies. Bill helped to organize a coalition of religious charities to fund this work, and his investment skills have doubled the investment value of the money raised to* *date. The family is planning to take the next two years off to go live and work in a rural community in an impoverished African country, where they will run one of the coalition-funded water projects. Bill and Terry's four kids range in age from eight to sixteen, and all of them are strongly opposed to going to Africa. But Bill and Terry are determined to take the entire family.*

SIX LIVES: A CLOSER LOOK

When I give the Six Lives Exercise in classes and seminars, an interesting pattern emerges. Every life receives some votes as "most successful" and "least successful." And I am also frequently surprised by how often one life in particular attracts votes for number one or number two in terms of success: the Stone Mason.

Why do votes for the Stone Mason surprise me? Because my audiences are often Wall Street executives, doctors, pharmaceutical researchers, business students, and top government officials. These people lead lives considerably more complicated than the Stone Mason's. The gap between the Stone Mason's life and the lives they are actually living is striking.

I often challenge them with a question: if the Stone Mason represents success to you, what steps might you take *right now* to move your life closer to that ideal? For example, perhaps you need to focus more time on your family or loved ones. Or perhaps you should recraft your workday to emphasize activities you control so you can take more genuine pride in your results. The same question applies no matter which life you picked as number one. Take a minute and make a list of what you could start doing today to bring your life more closely into harmony with the one you picked as your top choice.

That list of action items alone may be worth the price of this book.

Whichever lives you ranked highly, these choices reveal something important about your motives, aspirations, and fears when it comes to making real-life decisions. Let's take a closer look at the factors that probably weighed in your decisions.

THE TWO SIDES OF SUCCESS

If you are like most people, you probably measure success in two different ways. The first is the private, "inner" perspectives of fulfillment, satisfaction, and happiness. Each person profiled in the Six Lives Exercise has some claim to inner fulfillment. But most also have something missing. The Wealthy Investor has no family. The Tennis Pro's work takes her away from her children. One of the Teacher's children won't speak to her. The Banker's disabled child dominates her life, and she seems unable to commit to a long-term relationship. The Nonprofit Executive's children are in rebellion about leaving their friends for an isolated life in rural Africa.

Against these compromised claims to inner harmony, the Stone Mason appears to "have it all." He has a stable, loving relationship with his wife of fifty-two years. His three accomplished children and seven grandchildren live nearby (a fact suggested by his help building all of their homes). And he takes a sincere, craftsmanlike satisfaction in his work—a job that he controls and which enables him to see the fruits of his labors every day. His work appears to be meaningful to him. As he puts it, "It's a good day laying brick or stone. It is hard work, but you get interested in fitting each piece in just its right spot and the day is over before you know it." There is almost a Zen-like, spiritual dimension to the Stone Mason's life.

Thus, people who pick the Stone Mason's life as number one or number two are usually voting for a life with more of this "inner" dimension of success. There is quite a lot to be said for this point of view. Most of us would be hard put to define anyone as "successful" whose life lacks joy or satisfaction. And extensive research on happiness (more on this in chapter 2) confirms the importance of these inner positive feelings to your ability to function effectively.

But there is a second, more public "outer" perspective on success that (like it or not) motivates many of our day-to-day actions and decisions much more than the quest for inner happiness. These are desires for achievement, social recognition, and respect.

Seen from this perspective, the Stone Mason's life is missing something that all the other lives seem to have: a notable accomplishment that has been recognized by his society or his peers. All the other people profiled have achieved something that a broader social group has taken note of, ranging from quasi-celebrity status (the Wealthy Investor and Tennis Pro) to international media attention on behalf of a worthy cause (the Banker), good works on behalf of the poor in Africa (Nonprofit Executive), and professional awards from knowledgeable peers (the Nonprofit Executive and Teacher).

The Stone Mason has not even been profiled in *Masonry* magazine, much less *The New York Times*. Moreover, he admits that money has sometimes been a problem.

People who rank the Stone Mason near the bottom of their Six Lives list may admire the Stone Mason's devotion to the satisfactions of a craft and a family, but they see overall success in life as including more emphasis on that outer-achievement perspective. After all, it feels good to achieve something notable and be recognized for it.

In other words, whatever our professed desire to "feel fulfilled," most of us are also moderately excited when we receive praise. As we will see in chapter 6, on motivation, the brain releases some very pleasant chemicals into our system when we are rewarded by our social circle. Even within Buddhist monasteries, as I learned firsthand, some less-than-enlightened monks seek the winner's circle. They want to beat out their colleagues to become a Zen master.

So I will ask you to reflect back on your choices one more time and see if you identified the values and goals that actually motivate you when you make real-time decisions about what to do. To help, I have provided an explanatory chart describing some career motivations that may be underlying each life. See if you recognize your own motivations in the rankings you gave. It is also worth noting what parts of your life—your hobbies, career, passions, interests, volunteer work, or family—informed the "inner voice" that spoke to you as you ranked each life. If one of these lives spoke much more clearly to you than the others, that may be telling you something about the direction you want your life to take and what, for you, constitutes the true measure of success.

Life	Achievement Motivation
TEACHER:	Organizational Excellence. A life devoted to leading and helping teams achieve at high levels. Success resides in a career built on group accomplishment and recognition. This person also develops the talents and abilities of others and takes satisfaction from their achievements.
BANKER:	A Life of Loyalty and Commitment. A life characterized by a strong sense of duty, loyalty, and personal commitment to specific people and organizations. These may be close friends, family members, or work partners. Success springs from maintaining and nurturing these loyalties.
WEALTHY INVESTOR:	Power, Glamour, and Variety. A life that takes on high-stakes, publicly visible challenges. Success comes from winning through the creation of a successful enterprise, the use of individual skills, strategic acumen, and competitive energy. Pleasure, variety, and sensation are high priorities.

Life   Achievement Motivation

STONE MASON: Craftsmanship and Family. Recognition, fame, or fortune means little. Intrinsic motivation is sufficient to give you satisfaction. Success is measured by creating your work, completing defined tasks to the best of your ability, and devotion to your family.

TENNIS PRO: Individual Excellence. A life of disciplined practice and hard work within a defined career that measures success through recognized, individual achievement.

NONPROFIT EXECUTIVE: Answering a Spiritual/Values-Based Calling. A life characterized by work that embodies core beliefs and values. Success comes from using one's best abilities to serve a higher cause.

Before we leave the Six Lives Exercise, I have one final challenge for you. Think about the six profiles again and imagine you had one (and only one) child. Then imagine that you must pick one (and only one) of these lives for that only child to live out.

Now—choose which life you would bestow on your only child.

Does that put a slightly different spin on your decision? When I offer this choice to executives, as many as one third of them change their vote for number one when they think about their selection this way. Putting the question in this frame may help you assess how you are actually living your own life as opposed to what set of ideals you currently associate with success.

You would want only what is best for your children—and your picture of "what is best" tends to be a clearheaded balance between survival needs, life ideals, and what you actually think an interesting, productive life is all about. Thus, whatever you would choose for an only child may be what you are already unconsciously working toward yourself.

Are you happy with that choice? Is there something you should do to begin improving on that life? Because there is good news: you are not limited to any of these stories. You have the power to take whatever your life is today and start writing a new story about what it will be tomorrow.

BACK TO ERIC ADLER
....

Before we conclude this opening chapter, I want to return to Eric Adler's story for a moment. First, he is, in fact, very happily married to his wife (a physician) and they have two children and three dogs. So if you wondered how to rate that element of the inner dimension of his success, his family gives you a bit more data. Second, tracking his motivations through the lens of the Six Lives Exercise, I would say his life has exhibited the drives of three of the people featured in that test: the Teacher, the Stone Mason, and the Nonprofit Executive. He has been able, in his choices, to expand his abilities for building organizational excellence while attending in a craftsmanlike way to the details of his social entrepreneurship work—all while answering a values-based calling.

But his life has also had its share of challenges. A few years after starting the first SEED school with his partner, Raj, he confronted a world-class personal crisis. He discovered he had pancreatic cancer—a lethal disease with long-term survival rates below 5 percent. "I stopped work immediately," Adler said. He then underwent surgery, followed by a grueling regimen of chemotherapy and radiation. He lost fifty-five pounds in the process, though he kept his spirits up with twice-daily doses of the comedy television show *Seinfeld*.

Battling cancer of the pancreas is a you-bet-your-life version of the lottery—there are extremely long odds, but if you win, you get something even better than riches. Eric won. He has been cancer-free for over a decade. And his battle with the disease has given him, he reports, a new and even more profound respect for the preciousness of both life and relationships. The aftereffects of the cancer treatments he received, however, have continued to present him with a full measure of health challenges. These have become and will remain a regular part of his life.

I asked him what he might do if, someday, he steps aside from the SEED schools. "Something new and entrepreneurial," he said. "That's what I love about what we are doing with SEED." He also reminded me of the first class I had taught him. He has always been fascinated by the law, he said. He might want to go to law school and find out how that knowledge might help get even more things done.

CONCLUSION

This chapter has given you a first look at what your success ideas are and where they come from. Culture—even the culture of a single school—can act like a gravitational field on your goals, making it difficult for you to set a truly independent path. In Eric Adler's story, you got a chance to see how this subtle process can work. He was briefly drawn into work he thought he "should be doing," but by being honest about his own sense of dissatisfaction, Eric kept himself alert and in motion. Eventually, he was thrown back to considering what he could truly do better than most people. It was then that he remembered the legacies of his entrepreneurial family and his passion for education. He asked the key question: "What can I start?" From there it was a short hop to the idea for the SEED schools—an idea that changed his life and has improved the lives of hundreds of young inner-city students.

The Six Lives Exercise gave you a chance to "choose your life"—assessing the balance you are now striking between the inner and outer aspects of success. But in a larger sense, you have also begun the important process of clarifying and choosing the success values you want to embrace for the next stage of your life. It is your life story you are writing, after all. So you get to select the character traits and motivations for the person playing the central role.

With this foundation to work with, you are ready to dive deeper. In the next chapter, we will look more carefully at happiness and inner satisfaction as the truest measures of success. And from there, we will work our way to the outer dimensions where the promise of fame, fortune, and professional status beckon to us.

The more you study success, the more you will find that cultural forces are at work everywhere you turn. And if you think you are immune from these forces, think again. Even the brainiest research scientists battle each other for their fifteen minutes of fame, and few people would give the money back if they won the lottery.

Our first stop explores the most common response to the question "What is success?" Most people's answer is swift and sure: happiness. But it turns out happiness is just as hard to define as success. Let's see why.

BALANCE THE TWO SIDES OF SUCCESS

Some people think of success primarily in terms of outer achievements. Others think of it as mainly about inner satisfaction and fulfillment. Think about your own balance between the inner and outer dimensions of success. Consider where you are striking that balance today and then answer the following questions.

1. Do you need to make some adjustments between the inner and outer dimensions of success to get your balance right?

2. What are two or three specific steps you could take in the short term to make these needed adjustments?

3. Can you identify at least one specific longer-term goal that would help you keep the balance where you think it ought to be?

4. Ask yourself: "What is stopping me from taking action on these steps and goals today?"

Balancing the inner and outer sides of success is not always an either-or trade-off. If you pick the right work, for example, you can gain inner satisfaction from the activities that result in outer achievements. And if you seek the right inner satisfactions, work sometimes takes care of itself. But as the rest of the book will show, this is not as easy as it sounds.

An Easy Answer:
Be Happy

Those only are happy who have their minds fixed on some object other than their own happiness.

—JOHN STUART MILL

A few years ago, an elderly man showed up at a research seminar at the Wharton School about income and happiness. He came in a bit late, when the presentation was already under way, and sat down next to me near the end of a long conference table. I immediately noticed his rough, calloused workingman's hands. He sat quietly while the presenter clicked through his PowerPoint presentation on how national income levels related to aggregate data on reports of "subjective well-being." The presenter concluded with a few summary thoughts about the ways his research connected to the overall topic of happiness. When he called for questions, the man raised his hand.

"I am just a member of the public," he said slowly, "and I don't know much about what you have been discussing here. But you mention the word 'happiness' and I am confused. What has that to do with anything you were saying about income? As I see it, happiness is just three things: good health, meaningful work, and love. You have that, you are happy."

The room became dead silent. The heavy shroud of academic life had, for that moment, fallen away under the weight of these few simple words.

After a couple of seconds, the presenter thanked the fellow for his comment and went on to answer a question about the methodology of the study. The man eventually slipped out the door. I never saw him again.

I sometimes think of this man as a kind of Wise Angel, sent to tell us what is really important. Like many such messages, this one fell on deaf ears. The seminar went on and the discussion went back to average income levels and the measurement of life satisfaction.

But his comment left a permanent impression on me. And I told his story that year at the Wharton School graduation ceremony. I like to think one or two people took it to heart.

As we shall see in this chapter, money and happiness have complex connections to each other. But I think the Wise Angel was basically correct: although earning a lot of money can be good for your sense of pride and self-esteem, money has very little effect on the amount of day-to-day joy you experience and none whatever on the larger, more spiritual dimensions of happiness that many consider the most important parts of their lives.

In my work with students and executives, most realize intellectually that success is more than just a list of achievements. When I press them to say what that something is, they almost always say, "It's about happiness." Then I push them to go one step further and define what they mean by happiness. And that is where it starts to get really interesting.

In this chapter, I will help you write your own definition of happiness. You may be surprised, once you start to think about it, at how hard happiness is to pin down. In his book *Thinking, Fast and Slow*, Princeton's Nobel Prize–winning psychologist Dr. Daniel Kahneman, who has conducted cutting-edge research on this subject, concluded, "During the past ten years we have learned many new facts about happiness, but we have also learned that the word *happiness* does not have a simple meaning and should not be used as if it did."

As this chapter will show, people use the word "happiness" to describe at least three different things:

- a momentary, positive emotion,
- an overall evaluation of the past or hope for the future, and
- a deep sense of joy, connection, and meaning.

Near the end of the chapter, I will ask you to take what you have learned in the sections below on each of these three meanings and come to your own conclusions about what happiness means. After that, you may be in a position to decide what, if anything, it has to do with success.

THE HAPPINESS PUZZLE
....

In the Six Lives Exercise in chapter 1, you balanced the inner and the outer dimensions of success to select which life appealed to you most. Now we are ready to explore that inner dimension in more detail.

We will start with a couple of questions.

First, have you ever had a conversation with your parents or a trusted relative that went something like the dialogue below?

You: What do you think I should do next in my life?

Parents: We'll support you no matter what you do. We just want you to be happy.

If so, I am sure you appreciated your parents' support. But what did they mean by your being "happy"?

Now, with that conversation in mind, answer the next questions.

Read the following sentences, then put the book down and note what comes first into your mind.

During the past week or so, you probably had a moment or two when you felt happy. Think of one of those moments now. What were you doing? Where were you? What did it feel like?

Here are some examples of answers I have received to this question:

- I was biting into a soft-serve vanilla ice cream cone that had been dipped in chocolate sauce.
- I was holding hands with my boyfriend while we sat on a bench on a sunny day.
- I was playing poker with some friends late at night and I was winning.
- I was planning a surprise birthday party for a friend.
- I was out running in the early morning. I went into the "zone" and felt I could go on running forever.
- I was on the phone with my aunt and she was telling me that the latest tests showed her cancer had disappeared.

By comparing what your parents meant when they said "We just want you to be happy" with your answer to the short quiz above, you can understand some of the definitional problems we have with the word "happiness." When your parents said they just wanted you to "be happy," they were talking about a special, positive quality that would describe your life *as a whole*. The word "happiness" referred to a career, good health, finding the right life partner, or having stability in your cultural, religious, or family life.

The second, "ice cream cone" concept of happiness, by contrast, has to do with immediate moments of pleasure, satisfaction, love, or fun. This kind of happiness is a momentary, positive emotion.

In addition to the two meanings suggested above, happiness has also been thought of as having a larger, almost spiritual quality that goes beyond both momentary feelings and reflective thought. Philosophers have talked about this third kind of happiness in terms of the fulfillment that comes from exerting the right kind of effort on the right kind of task (for you).

The Hebrew word "simcha" has been used to capture this sense. There are many translations of this word into English, most of them related to ordinary feelings of happiness associated with celebratory events such as weddings or births. But one of my students told our class about an expanded definition used by Rabbi Akiva Tatz—an Orthodox rabbi from South Africa—that I like a lot. Simcha, Rabbi Tatz said, is "the experience of the soul that comes when you are doing what you should be doing." Simcha can encompass everything from taking time to comfort a sick friend to the joy of practicing your profession at a high level of skill. Positive psychologists have used words such as "flow," "flourishing," and "meaning" to describe this deeper sense of happiness. The Greek word Aristotle used in his work *The Nicomachean Ethics* to describe this ultimate form of happiness was "eudemonia"—which literally means "spirit of goodness."

So I have bad news and good news for you. The bad news is that defining success as simply "being happy" does not really solve your problem. It merely shifts your investigation of success over to a new mystery.

What is the good news? If you can come up with your own definition of happiness that is as eloquent as the Wise Angel's, you may be well on the way to getting clear about what you mean by the word "success."

In the sections below, I will help you develop your ideas about happiness by exploring (and offering some guidance on how to increase your experience of) the three different types of happiness we identified above. I will also offer a word of caution.

The first of the Buddha's insights when he achieved enlightenment was that life is, by definition, an experience marked by suffering and dissatisfaction. People get sick and die; they are injured; they have physical and psychological pain. For that reason, most of the world's great art, music, literature, and religious wisdom investigates how we cope with and transcend this situation—not by seeking to escape it into a land where everyone is always "happy" but rather by confronting this reality head-on and learning from experience. In addition, negative emotions such as frustration, righteous anger, disappointment, and sadness often spur us to reexamine ourselves, press for social justice, reach out to others, and make needed changes in our lives.

Defining success entirely in terms of "happiness" may therefore leave out most of the things that make life interesting and meaningful. As the chapter concludes, we will take a brief tour of the world's great religions to see what light they can shed on whether happiness is the right word to use when you describe the inner dimension of success.

MOMENTARY HAPPINESS:
THE VALUE OF MINDFULNESS

We start our tour of happiness with the most direct, pleasant, and sensory form of it. The Roman philosopher Epicurus said, "Everything we need to be happy is easy to obtain." At the simplest and most immediate level, happiness is one of life's great positive feelings, an emotional experience of joy, love, warmth, rapture, pleasure, tenderness, intimacy, or exhilaration. If you think that success is about being happy, is this what you are talking about?

The cartoonist Charles Schulz, creator of the comic strip *Peanuts*, gave the world one of its most memorable definitions of Momentary Happiness in his April 25, 1960, comic strip. The crabby, cynical character Lucy, who was usually terrified that the family dog, Snoopy, might give her a kiss, dropped her guard that day and, in an unbridled moment of affection, hugged Snoopy. Lucy's final words have found their way onto countless posters and coffee mugs: "Happiness is a warm puppy." According to the blog *Escape*, Schulz himself believed in this definition: "It's not sentimental. It's a statement of truth. Can anyone come up with a better definition of happiness?"

When I asked you to think back over the past week and recall a happy moment, I was helping you identify this sort of experience. I call it "Momentary Happiness." Daniel Kahneman has defined this as the happiness of the "Experiencing Self"—in contrast to the "Remembering Self," who evaluates how happy you were in your last job or on your vacation last year. Momentary Happiness comes in bursts. It makes gloomy days brighter and sunny days sweet.

No matter how you define success, Momentary Happiness ought to play some role in it. In my research, I have come across two simple ideas for increasing your weekly supply of it that might be worth considering: pay more attention to the pleasant aspects of your experience and reframe your expectations for the future.

Slow Down and Pay Attention

Modern psychologists study Momentary Happiness by giving people beepers and asking them to record their emotions on a "happiness scale" whenever the beeper goes off. They also ask their subjects to do the same on a daily basis, hoping that memory will not distort reality too much over such a short span of time. The ancient sages studied Momentary Happiness through meditation—a practice that can strengthen your powers of attentive mindfulness. Both systems are attempts to help you gain entry to the Experiencing Self so you can identify what is actually happening moment to moment inside your head and heart. Whether you prefer a beeper or a meditation cushion, you can often increase your experience of Momentary Happiness through one simple adjustment in your life: pay more attention to the pleasant aspects of it.

A research study showed that French and American women spend about the same amount of time each week eating. But French women pay roughly twice as much attention to their food—and receive a corresponding increase in their daily allotment of Momentary Happiness.

The Vietnamese Buddhist teacher Thich Nhat Hanh tells a story in his book *The Miracle of Mindfulness* about a friend who was excitedly talking about his plans for the future. As he spoke, he was popping sections of a juicy tangerine into his mouth. The faster he spoke, the faster he swallowed the tangerine sections. Thich Nhat Hanh gently pointed out what was happening, prompting his friend to notice the sweet taste of the tangerine that had been there all the time. That reminder refocused his friend's attention and created some tasty units of Momentary Happiness.

The award-winning American poet Wallace Stevens was a high-ranking executive for the Hartford Insurance Company in Connecticut. Instead of driving to work every day, he walked. And while he walked, he paid attention to what was going on around him and sometimes thought of words to express his experience. He converted his commute into a poetry workshop. "It seems as though Stevens composed poems in his head, and then wrote them down, often after he arrived at the office," one of his biographers noted. "As for his commute, he enjoyed it profoundly. It was his only time out of doors, alone, thinking, receptive to the influx of nature into all the senses." If you go to Hartford, you can actually follow the route of Stevens's daily commute, the stages of which are marked by thirteen granite stones engraved with the verses of one of his most famous poems: "Thirteen Ways of Looking at a Blackbird."

As you consider the role of Momentary Happiness in your concept of success, ask yourself if you could use a little more mindfulness of the kind that Thich Nhat Hanh and Wallace Stevens have demonstrated. You are probably missing a lot of Momentary Happiness in your hurry to "get somewhere."

Reframe Your Expectations

As I mentioned earlier, some forms of Momentary Happiness have cultural rather than sensory roots. Evidence for this can be found in the studies that Professor Dan Gilbert at Harvard has done demonstrating how often people are poor predictors of what will make them happy in the future. His book on this subject, *Stumbling on Happiness*, is one of the best (and funniest) books in the success literature.

For example, the *Peanuts* cartoon I mentioned above played a pivotal role in how one of my students, Kathy, learned a sad truth about Momentary Happiness. She encountered her first, clear, objective definition of happiness as an eight-year-old child when she saw a "Happiness Is a Warm Puppy" poster of Lucy and Snoopy hugging. Unhappy at the time, she latched onto the idea that a puppy would bring happiness and begged her parents to give her one.

They did. She was then "crushed" (her word) to learn that, even with a puppy in her life, she was still unhappy. She later told me, "I have come to understand that I'm just not the kind of person who experiences a lot of happy moods. Even today, I am not a particularly upbeat person." As an adult, she has learned to reset her expectations about how she will respond emotionally to future events. Expecting less, she now has more pleasant surprises in her life—and fewer dashed hopes. Even better: she no longer fantasizes that a single solution can solve all of life's problems.

Gilbert's research reveals that expectations surrounding events such as weddings, graduations, and birthdays that are grounded in cultural assumptions about what is "supposed" to make us happy often interfere with experiencing Momentary Happiness. When expectations run high, future events seldom measure up. As Carol Ryff, the director of the Institute of Aging at the University of Wisconsin, has commented, obsessive desires for any single aspect of life to bring happiness often backfire, becoming "a psychological burden" to everyone concerned.

Another force that can reduce Momentary Happiness is what psychologists call "adaptation." Something good happens—you get the new job or relationship you wanted—but then you rapidly adjust to your new circumstances, and these become the new baseline for judging how you feel. The glow of the new job or relationship fades, and you start to focus instead on the annoying way your boss talks or how your new romantic partner texts people while you are having dinner together.

Just as mindfulness helps you focus more on the pleasant things that are already happening, it can also help cure you of unrealistic expectations and adaptations. As you experience your life more directly, moment to moment, you are less likely to build some future activity into a "happiness dream." In addition, as you spend more time in the present, you will tend to appreciate the little ways your life is working. You can count your blessings instead of adapting too rapidly to some positive change.

Gilbert's discoveries take us back to the point I made earlier: your day-to-day experience of life consists entirely of what you pay attention to. If you are in an accident and have to use a wheelchair to get around every day, you will eventually stop paying attention to your disability and start paying attention to the other parts of your life, which will contain many moments of happiness. So long as you are paying attention to a tangerine's taste, it is just as sweet no matter where you are sitting.

To sum up: the positive emotions relished by the Experiencing Self are a good place to start your quest to understand how happiness fits into your definition of success. And it is reassuring to know that you can increase your allotment of Momentary Happiness by doing things as simple as slowing down and paying more attention to managing your expectations.

The elusive quality of Momentary Happiness, however, suggests it should not be the end of your search. We still have two more forms of happiness to consider.

Next stop: something I call "Overall Happiness." Can you restructure your life to make it "happier" as a whole—not just filled with a few more pleasant experiences? And if so, does this make you more successful? You be the judge.

OVERALL HAPPINESS: JUDGING
LIFE AS A WHOLE

Meet Gretchen Rubin. She's a mother, wife of a wealthy Wall Street private equity investor, Yale Law School graduate, and former law clerk for Supreme Court Justice Sandra Day O'Connor. Her husband is the son of the former Goldman Sachs cochairman and U.S. Treasury secretary Robert Rubin. With all this going for her, she would seem to have most of life's big problems solved. Nevertheless, she was dissatisfied enough to set out, by sheer force of will, to raise her level of Overall Happiness. Her journey has inspired hundreds of thousands of people to start their own happiness quests.

Riding a New York City bus one rainy day and feeling a little blue, Rubin had a startling insight. "What do I want from life?" she asked herself. "Well . . . I want to be *happy*." Thus began a yearlong program to make her life happier, an effort she turned into a bestselling book called *The Happiness Project: Or, Why I Spent a Year Trying to Sing in the Morning, Clean My Closets, Fight Right, Read Aristotle, and Generally Have More Fun.*

She read all the happiness and self-help books she could lay her hands on. Then, inspired by a similar plan for "moral perfection" that Benjamin Franklin had laid out three hundred years ago, she devised an elaborate, lawyerlike "Resolutions Chart" to implement the advice she collected—day by day, week by week, and month by month—for a full year. She found herself paying more attention to everything she did, from exercise to expressing gratitude and from cleaning her house to shopping. At the end of her happiness-project year, she tried to put everything she had learned and practiced together so she could experience one solid month of what she called "Boot Camp Perfect" happy days. She fixed the clutter in her closets, sang cheerful songs in the morning, laughed out loud as often as she could, focused on acknowledging other people's feelings, practiced more silence, left potentially hurtful things unsaid, wrote every day in her private journal, met more often with her writers' and children's literature groups, listened more carefully to hypnosis and relaxation tapes, and ate better food.

Did Rubin succeed in her quest to find perfectly happy days? It is hard to say. On the one hand, she never had even one "Boot Camp Perfect" day, much less a month of them. But I think she nudged her level of Overall Happiness up a notch from where it stood the day her project began. I say this because she reports that she made progress on something extremely important that we will explore later in this book—her character. Her biggest "happiness boosters," she said, came from reining in her habit of criticizing other people and from finding the self-discipline to clean up the clutter that had taken over her home. Both of these items had been bringing her down, and improving both lifted a load of guilt—especially her habit of criticizing others. "It made me happier to be in better control of my sharp tongue," she said. Thus, she gained valuable insights into her personality. Her husband, Jamie Rubin, described her victory this way, too. "I think this happiness project is all about you trying to get more control over your life," he told her.

As Rubin's story shows (although she does not make this distinction), raising your level of Overall Happiness is not the same thing as increasing the number of Momentary Happiness experiences you have on a given day. Gretchen Rubin set out to have more fun, but underneath she was on a quest to improve her overall attitude about herself and her life. Increasing Overall Happiness, it seems, may not be much fun, but the effort can pay meaningful dividends.

As you think about Rubin's story, ask yourself if you are at a stage in your life where your success depends more on the inner work Gretchen Rubin set out to do or the kinds of outer career goals that Eric Adler was concerned with in chapter 1. Rubin considered herself successful in the outer sense—she had achieved a lot; she had a stable marriage, children, and a degree of wealth. But with all that, she still felt unsatisfied with the quality of her inner experiences of satisfaction and joy.

Measuring Your Overall Happiness

When psychologists measure Overall Happiness they do not give people beepers. Instead, they give them surveys and ask subjects to reflect on their lives and evaluate them in globally oriented terms. Here is an example of an actual question from one of these surveys. You might find it interesting to answer this survey question yourself.

···

Overall Happiness Scale

···

Please imagine a ladder with steps numbered from 0 at the bottom to 10 at the top. The top of the ladder represents the best possible life for you and the bottom of the ladder represents the worst possible life for you. On which step of the ladder would you say you personally feel you stand at this time?

0   1   2   3   4   5   6   7   8   9   10

How did you rate your Overall Happiness? Momentary Happiness probably factored into your ratings. People in better moods tend to rank their Overall Happiness higher. You also may have quickly scanned your memory for evidence that recent positive emotions outnumbered, or outweighed, any negative ones. Research shows that people, when deciding how to rate an experience in the past, tend to scan for memories of "peaks" (that visit to Disney World was great because of the unforgettable Space Mountain ride on your second day) and "ends" (the family reunion carries a warm glow because the toasts at the final dinner were so heartfelt and moving).

But there is more at work than memories of Momentary Happiness. Happiness researchers report that people look to see if there is a "gap" between the life they actually have and the life they hoped to have. If the gap between these two is getting smaller, their Overall Happiness is higher. If the current situation falls far short of the one they hoped for—or if the gap is widening in the wrong direction—Overall Happiness falls.

My guess is that Gretchen Rubin launched her happiness project in response to what she perceived to be a widening gap between the level of satisfaction she had expected to feel at her stage of life and the actual satisfaction she was experiencing. Her project helped her in two ways. Some of the mindfulness exercises increased her level of Momentary Happiness. But perhaps more important, after a year of relentless self-help she made peace with a few of her expectations. Overall Happiness responds well to the famous Serenity Prayer to accept the things you cannot change, change the things you can, and gain the "wisdom to know the difference."

In general, most people rate themselves in the range between six and ten on Overall Happiness scales. Is that where you fell? According to one of the world's top scholars in the happiness field, University of Illinois professor Ed Diener, surveys show that "most people are mildly happy most of the time." Of course, loss of loved ones, poor health, unemployment, lack of a safe environment, and social isolation all cause great unhappiness. But happiness usually reasserts itself one way or another. Positive evaluations of our lives seem to be nature's way of helping us survive in a sometimes hostile, unpredictable, and stressful world. We are not happy all the time; neither are we sad all the time. Like the earth's tides, feelings of overall satisfaction ebb and flow.

Interestingly, Professor Diener and his colleagues have confirmed that people who score a perfect ten on the Overall Happiness surveys pay a price on the achievement side of success. Reflecting their don't-worry-be-happy attitude, they accomplish less, earn less, get lower grades, and earn fewer advanced degrees than people who score an eight. Perhaps this helps to explain Gretchen Rubin's modest results on her yearlong happiness project. She was shooting for a perfect ten, but she may have discovered that being "perfectly" happy involved achievement trade-offs she was unwilling to make.

Finally, her instincts about where to set the balance between Overall Happiness and achievement had a genetic foundation. Biologists have demonstrated that the single most important predictor of your Overall Happiness score is your genetic map. If you had an identical twin from whom you were separated at birth, the chances are excellent that the two of you would rate your Overall Happiness at roughly the same levels as you moved through adulthood. Thus, Gretchen Rubin never really had a hope of turning herself into Little Miss Sunshine. Her achievement-oriented genes would not allow it. As my student Kathy discovered after her childhood "warm puppy" episode, some people are just more innately cheerful, positive, and satisfied than others. It is their nature.

As David Lykken and Auke Tellegen, the two scholars who conducted the key studies linking genes to happiness, put it, "making the team, being promoted at work, or winning the lottery tends to bring about an increment of happiness." But the effects of these events "appear to be transitory fluctuations about a stable temperamental set point or trait that is characteristic of the individual." They conclude that around 50 percent of the variance between people's Overall Happiness is set by genes and the other 50 percent is the product of environment.

We will go into more detail about the role of genes in success in chapter 5's treatment of your unique capabilities. Until then, Lykken and Tellegen's research is another bad news/good news part of the happiness story. The bad news is that your Overall Happiness levels appear to swing within a range that is out of your conscious control. The good news is that it is still possible, within that range, to follow Gretchen Rubin's example and work to improve your Overall Happiness.

Here are four ways that researchers have suggested may help you raise your score by a point or two. Interestingly, they affirm both the Wise Angel's advice—to pursue good health, meaningful work, and love—and the findings of the scholar he challenged, who argued that income and happiness are connected.

1. Make Your Health a Priority

I think the Wise Angel was right to list "good health" first in his lineup of happiness factors. Gilbert's research shows that you will probably adapt if you have an accident and end up in a wheelchair. But illness, disease, and pain can wreck anyone's Overall Happiness score. Be grateful if you are in good health. And do what it takes to stay that way.

At the same time, if ill health strikes, as it did in Eric Adler's life when he was diagnosed with pancreatic cancer (see chapter 1), take steps to maintain your inner balance. First, you can follow Eric's example and do everything in your power to maintain some Momentary Happiness in your life (Eric watched marathons of his favorite comedy show, *Seinfeld*, from his hospital bed). Beyond that, the next two items become even more critical to your Overall Happiness: exercising control over your life by setting and marking progress toward long-term goals (in this case, ones related to your recovery) and opening yourself to the care and concern of people through your relationships.

2. Achieve Some Long-Term Goals

Research suggests that achieving long-term, difficult goals increases your Overall Happiness. If you set out to be a doctor or a lawyer and achieve that professional status, your Overall Happiness will probably benefit. If you set out to be a ballet dancer or a movie star and fall short, your Overall Happiness will suffer—until you adjust your expectations and set off in a new direction.

What is important is not the fame, fortune, or professional status itself, but rather whether you achieved whatever you set out to achieve. As we will see in the coming chapters, however, these achievements will mean more if they are based on goals you yourself have set. If you are living your life mainly to please other people, your achievements may not give you as much personal satisfaction. The solution is to achieve things you find genuinely meaningful—a topic we take up in chapter 4.

3. Invest in Your Relationships

I agreed with the Wise Angel when he said that love was a big part of happiness. If we interpret this to cover all of your close relationships and not just the romantic ones, research confirms his intuition. Summing up the research findings on this aspect of happiness, Daniel Kahneman has commented, "It is only a slight exaggeration to say that happiness is the experience of spending time with people you love and who love you."

One of the most comprehensive studies about success ever conducted followed 268 men who entered Harvard College in 1937 and tracked their lives for seventy-two years. It was called the Harvard Study of Adult Development, or the Grant Study. There were a number of factors that characterized the men who made it into middle and old age as both "happy" and "healthy": (1) mental adaptability to changes in life, (2) advanced education, (3) a stable marriage, (4) not smoking, (5) not abusing alcohol, (6) getting some exercise, and (7) maintaining a healthy weight.

The most important factor of all, however, was attention to relationships. The psychiatrist George Vaillant, the main investigator on this study for over forty years, was once asked point-blank, "What have you learned from the Grant Study?" His answer, swift and sure, was that "the only thing that really matters in life are your relationships with other people." It was the social life of these men, he said, "not intellectual brilliance or parental social class," that led to their living to a ripe old age.

4. Make Enough Money

Does money buy happiness? It depends on the kind of happiness you are talking about. Once you are earning a living wage and have enough money to take care of food, shelter, clothing, and a little fun (an average of somewhere between $75,000 and $100,000 in today's dollars), more and more money does not buy you more and more Momentary Happiness. Note, of course, the word "average." The cost of living in different parts of a country and the number of mouths this salary has to feed affect what your income level must be for this plateau effect in Momentary Happiness to occur.

However, research shows that wealth can improve your Overall Happiness. For example, people who make $500,000 are likely to report higher Overall Happiness levels than do people who make $150,000. Why might this be? In some cases, people who make a lot of money aspired to wealth when they were younger, thus embracing money as one of their long-term goals. Achieving it produces the bump in Overall Happiness associated with the second item above—conquering difficult-to-achieve challenges.

Another reason money may buy more Overall Happiness is cultural. If you associate respect and social standing with wealth, then your Overall Happiness will rise as your income rises. In a 2011 article covering a sample from 123 countries, Ed Diener and his colleagues concluded that the higher Overall Happiness scores enjoyed by the wealthy result from higher levels of social respect rather than from having more material goods. As H. L. Mencken once put it, a rich man is someone who makes "$100 more than his wife's sister's husband."

Is Overall Happiness an important measure of the inner dimension of your success? That is a question only you can answer. The satisfaction of a lifetime of accomplishments is certainly something worth aspiring to. But so is a certain amount of Momentary Happiness each and every day. You have to decide where to set the balance for yourself.

Finally, as I hope to show you in the next and final section, there is one more happiness level—deeper than the other two—still ahead, and this one may be the most important one we have talked about so far.

THE THIRD PATH: WISDOM EXPERIENCES

Is there a form of happiness beyond both the tangerine's taste and the joys of close relationships? Many think so. But there is no adequate name for the kind of experience and no social agreement on exactly what it is. Over the years I have considered names such as Transcendent Happiness, Blessed Happiness, Ultimate Happiness, and Spiritual Happiness. But nothing using the word "happiness" really works.

As I mentioned at the beginning of the chapter, Aristotle called this quality in human life eudemonia—the spirit of goodness or the good that we seek for its own sake and not for the purpose of achieving any other good. I also identified the Hebrew word "simcha" (one of the many words in Hebrew that can be translated as "happiness") as a helpful concept. There are many definitions of simcha, ranging from simple joy and satisfaction to the feeling of spiritual exultation. As I said, I like best a broader definition provided by Rabbi Akiva Tatz: "The experience of the soul that comes when you are doing what you should be doing." I often experience this form of simcha while teaching, and I also think back on certain family holidays and meditation experiences with simcha-inspired feelings.

The same student who introduced me to the word "simcha" pointed out that it can be used as a verb and as a noun. She quoted from a book for Jewish teenagers that described simcha as the experience of "moving along your own road, your unique path to your unique destination . . . the path that leads to *yourself*." It is a path that is as likely to include tension, pain, and tears as it is happiness. But, she wrote, the tears of simcha are "good tears."

When you look back on your own life to your own pivotal experiences, how often did these experiences include either a mixture of both "positive" and "negative" emotions or a full surrender to profound feelings of grief, sorrow, sadness, or pain to break through to something significant? On a moment-for-moment basis, have "bad" times been at least as instructive to your survival, achievements, and satisfactions as the "good" ones? I have learned a lot about myself during my least "happy" times—times when I admitted I was lonely, confused, disappointed, or ashamed. If that is also true for you, then the word "happiness" (of both the Momentary and Overall types) may not fully define what you have in mind when you try to describe the inner dimension of success.

The leading psychologists who study happiness now agree that our culture's preoccupation with positive emotions as the primary measure of a good life may be leaving out this critical factor. In his book *Flourish: A Visionary New Understanding of Happiness and Well-Being*, my University of Pennsylvania colleague Marty Seligman argues that the cheerful moods of Momentary Happiness and the positive memories that provide the sources for Overall Happiness are "not entitled to a central place in any theory" of the meaningful life. The former are too trivial and the latter lack the social engagement and sense of purpose he sees as important.

Seligman suggests combining five elements to create a life worth living. These five are positive emotions, engagement, relationships, a sense of meaning that comes from serving a purpose larger than yourself, and accomplishments, both short-term and long-term. These five, when folded together, create something bigger than both Momentary and Overall Happiness—an ultimate good Seligman labels as "Well-being."

Another positive psychology leader, New York University's Jonathan Haidt , has offered a slightly different and, he admits, entirely subjective summary of what he considers the ultimate good. In his book *The Happiness Hypothesis: Finding Modern Truth in Ancient Wisdom*, he asks, "What can you do to have a good, happy, fulfilling, and meaningful life?" You will not find it, he answers, by searching for the positive emotions of Momentary Happiness or cultivating the happy memories of Overall Happiness. Instead, he recommends striving to get "the right relationships between yourself and others, between yourself and your work, and between yourself and something larger than yourself." From these three efforts, he concludes, "a sense of purpose and meaning will emerge" that constitutes the most genuine form of happiness available to people.

It seems, then, that there is a consensus developing within positive psychology that concepts such as eudemonia, simcha, flourishing, and well-being are worth consideration—along with happiness—as sources of inner success. What is lacking is an agreed term we can use to describe them. So here is one I would propose: "Wisdom Experiences." In the next two sections I will try to help you understand how Wisdom Experiences are different and why they deserve an important place on your list of inner success factors.

THE POSITIVE VALUE OF NEGATIVE EMOTIONS

The big differentiator of Wisdom Experiences from everything else to do with happiness is the inclusion of distinctly "unhappy" feelings. When it comes to gaining wisdom, negative emotions have a place of honor right next to positive ones.

In chapter 1, we talked about the importance of letting yourself be "dissatisfied" with the status quo to inspire action and change in your life. Hard times often force you to reflect on your larger goals. And it is from those reflections that ideas and insights for the future often come. Uncomfortable emotions such as fear and insecurity often warn you of real and impending dangers. In fact, research shows that mildly depressed and pessimistic people tend to see reality more clearly than optimists. People who set higher goals and fall short are often more dissatisfied with the result they achieve, but actually achieve much higher results than people who set lower goals and feel happy when they achieve them. And many creative artists seem to do their best work when they surrender to the full array of life's emotions, not just the happy ones.

The price of enlightenment seems to be suffering, not smiling.

Albert Einstein echoed these sentiments. "To make a goal of comfort or happiness has never appealed to me," he said. "A system of ethics built on this basis would be sufficient only for a herd of cattle."

The philosopher Immanuel Kant, who lived from 1724 to 1804, also questioned whether happiness was a legitimate goal for a good human life. He argued that people should focus on doing the right thing even if that comes at the price of our happiness. And one of the most famous (and difficult to understand) philosophers of the twentieth century, Ludwig Wittgenstein, once commented, "I don't know why we are here, but I'm pretty sure that it is not in order to enjoy ourselves."

In Aldous Huxley's 1932 novel, *Brave New World*, the hero (called "the Savage") confronts a society in which unhappiness is outlawed. The "brave new world" turns out to be one in which you would not want to live. Children go to sleep listening to the mantra "Everybody's happy now." Genetic engineering has raised the population's average Overall Happiness to a very high level. And a drug named "soma" (analogous to modern-day drugs that treat depression) takes care of any rough edges.

The price of universal happiness, however, is high. Beauty, truth, art, and science have yielded to comfort. So have individuality and self-determination.

"But I don't want comfort," the Savage says. "I want God, I want poetry, I want real danger, I want freedom, I want goodness. I want sin."

"In fact," says the Controller for Western Europe, Mustapha Mond, "you're claiming the right to be unhappy."

"All right, then," says the Savage. "I'm claiming the right to be unhappy."

The Controller then lists all the nightmares that the right to unhappiness includes, from growing old and impotent to experiencing fear, disease, mediocrity, and shame.

There is a long silence, and the Savage finally responds, "I claim them all."

The Savage's declaration is a response to a false dilemma—you do not face his stark, all-or-nothing choice between happiness and the rest of life. But Huxley's novel challenges you to consider where you rank happiness against other inner aspects of life, such as courage, honesty, independence, humility, and compassion. As you do so, consider the scientists and philosophers, noted above, who rejected happiness as a premier goal.

Finally, reflect on this: none of the world's great religions endorse "the pursuit of happiness" as the goal of our inner lives. Indeed, it is one of the few things they all agree on.

CAN THESE SAGES ALL BE WRONG?
....

Here is a quick round-the-world tour of major religions to show how little any concept of "happiness" plays in their visions of the meaningful, spiritual life. These thumbnail sketches cannot do justice to these great spiritual traditions, but I offer them to make my point about happiness.

Hinduism. The Hindu religion is a sprawling, ancient set of beliefs, practices, and gods that originated in India many thousands of years ago. At its core is the theory of reincarnation—that our souls are reborn over and over and that our rebirth in the next life is based on our actions in the current one. There are four different spiritual pathways to purify one's actions and ensure a better rebirth: a life devoted to worship and love of the divine (Bhakti Yoga), a life given to meditation (Raja Yoga), a life of study and wisdom (Jnana Yoga), and a life of duty and service (Karma Yoga). The overall goal for someone on any of these paths is *moksha*—or liberation from the human desires for such things as fame, fortune, pleasure, and happiness. An inner quality of wisdom characterizes those who have sincerely followed the spiritual path.

Buddhism. The Buddha lived about 500 B.C. He started on his spiritual path by practicing Hindu disciplines and eventually came to his own insights about the meaning of life. His teachings center on what he called the Four Noble Truths of human existence: (1) life is suffering; (2) suffering originates in human attachments, cravings, and desires; (3) there is a way to escape this endless cycle of suffering; and (4) the way out is to practice a rigorous life of meditation featuring sustained effort, concentration, and mindfulness. These practices lead to our minds being filled with virtuous thoughts and intentions. These, in turn, lead us to speak, act, and engage in livelihoods that make escape from the cycle of suffering possible. Buddha called these practices the "Eightfold Path." The goal of all this is "nirvana"— an end to the cycle of rebirths and the cessation of all desires, including the desire for happiness. One of the most famous living Buddhist teachers today is the Dalai Lama, and he has coauthored a book with the word "happiness" in the title: *The Art of Happiness: A Handbook for Living*. But the book is not

about the emotion of happiness at all—it is about the roots of
suffering, the balm of compassion, and meditation as the road
to wisdom.

Judaism. The Jewish faith was born over three thousand years ago
in the deserts of the Middle East and centers on the special
relationship and covenant between the Jewish people and their
one God. The most important Jewish prophet is Moses, and the
most important thing Moses did was receive God's laws for the
Jewish people on Mount Sinai. These laws included the Ten
Commandments, familiar to Christians, as well as the first five
books of the Jewish Bible (called the Torah). The Torah stands at
the center of the Jewish faith and provides the basis for how Jews
worship God, conduct themselves within their families, and
behave in the community. One of my favorite biblical books from
the Jewish faith is Ecclesiastes, which tells the story of a powerful
king who tried to find the meaning of life. His search took him
from the halls of political power and the houses of pleasure to a
life of service to others and a determined quest for wisdom. In
the end, he concluded that all human endeavors—even for
service and wisdom—spring from and end up in a kind of empty
foolishness he called "vanity." He says the best advice is simply to
"fear God and keep his commandments; that is the whole duty of
man." Judaism concerns itself with many values, but happiness
does not appear to be at the center of it. Instead, life has meaning
in man's search for a true relationship with God.

Christianity. Christianity is centered on the life and teachings of
Jesus of Nazareth, who was born to a Jewish family just over
two thousand years ago. Jesus presented himself to the Jewish
people as the Messiah, or Savior, promised in the Jewish religion.
Christians believe that Jesus was the Son of God and that it is
through a belief in his divinity that one can earn salvation and an
eternal life with God after death. Just as the Buddha incorporated
many Hindu ideas into Buddhism, Jesus melded many ideas from
Judaism into his teachings. As we will see in chapter 7, some
modern evangelical Christian ministers have gained substantial
followings by mixing religious rhetoric with promises that "God's
Power" can bring worldly fame, fortune, and happiness to believers. But I think it safe to say that Jesus himself, based on the
record provided in the Gospels, did not live a life that exemplified
those worldly values. He was poor; he spent his short time on

earth preaching about the Kingdom of God to come and healing the sick, blind, and lame. Even though he could have prevented it by recanting his message, he died a painful death from being nailed to a cross by Roman soldiers. His spiritual teachings honor humility, service, sacrifice, and suffering. Happiness comes only after death and only in union with God. When asked how we should live, he responded with two suggestions. First, love God with all your heart. Second, love your neighbor as yourself. He made no mention of happiness. But his teachings display profound wisdom.

Islam. The Islamic faith originates with the holy prophet Muhammad, who lived between A.D. 570 and 632. Like Christianity, it is based on a belief in the one God who first revealed himself to the Jews. Unlike Christianity, Islam regards Muhammad, not Jesus, as the last and final messenger of God to man. Muhammad's revelations are recorded in the Qur'an, the holy teachings of the faith. A Muslim is someone who adheres to the Islamic faith, the center of which is love of God and obedience to his commandments as set forth by Muhammad. Muslims believe that Five Pillars outline the right way to live. These pillars are reciting the Islamic prayer or creed, praying five times each day, giving alms, fasting at Ramadan, and making a holy pilgrimage to Mecca at least once during one's lifetime. The goal of a life well lived is resurrection and life everlasting. Far from happiness, the Islamic faith centers on prayer, alms, fasting, and the rigors of pilgrimage.

There is an irony when it comes to religion and happiness. Research suggests that belief in *any* religion raises your level of Overall Happiness quite a bit. Religious faith gives people a sense of purpose as well as a place to turn in times of suffering. But this effect comes not from seeking happiness but from devoting yourself to something beyond your personal well-being. As the philosopher John Stuart Mill noted in the quote that opened this chapter, "Those only are happy who have their minds fixed on some object other than their own happiness."

YOUR CONCLUSIONS ON HAPPINESS

Now it is time to make some decisions. First, with everything you now understand about the word "happiness," how would you define it? The Wise Angel had his view. What's yours? A good test of whether you really have a definition is boiling it down so it can fit on the lines below.

I define happiness as:

_____

_____

_____

_____

_____

Second, how does your definition of happiness fold into your thinking about success? Which kinds of happiness are important to your success and in what rough order of priority? To give this second question a bit of structure, I have provided you with three prompts to start you thinking.

| Momentary Happiness |

What priority does Momentary Happiness have in your definition of success?

Vital   Important   Relevant   None

Give a specific example of the kind of Momentary Happiness you want to preserve or enhance as part of your success in life.

_____

_____

_____

_____

_____

_____

What specific steps can you take right now to increase the Momentary Happiness in your life?

_____

_____

_____

_____

_____

_____

| Overall Happiness |

What priority does Overall Happiness have in your definition of success?

Vital   Important   Relevant   None

Give a specific example of the kind of Overall Happiness you want to preserve or enhance as part of your success in life.

_____

_____

_____

_____

_____

_____

What specific steps can you take right now to increase the Overall Happiness in your life?

_____

_____

_____

_____

_____

_____

_____

| Wisdom Experiences: Eudemonia, Flourishing, Simcha |

What priority do Wisdom Experiences have in your definition of success?

Vital   Important   Relevant   None

Give specific examples of the kinds of Wisdom Experiences you want to preserve or enhance as part of your success in life.

_____

_____

_____

_____

_____

_____

_____

What specific steps can you take right now to increase the Wisdom Experiences in your life?

_____

_____

_____

_____

_____

_____

_____

_____

CONCLUSION

In Samuel Beckett's play *Waiting for Godot,* two men find themselves in a no-man's-land where time is suspended and there is only a single disturbingly abstract purpose to existence: to wait for a person named Godot to arrive. At one point, the characters discuss the role of happiness in their lives.

> **Vladimir:** Say you are, even if it is not true.
>
> **Estragon:** What am I to say?
>
> **Vladimir:** Say, I am happy.
>
> **Estragon:** I am happy.
>
> **Vladimir:** So am I.
>
> **Estragon:** So am I.
>
> **Vladimir:** We are happy.
>
> **Estragon:** We are happy. (Silence.) What do we do now, now that we are happy?
>
> **Vladimir:** Wait for Godot.

Beckett seems to saying that happiness is fine in its place, but it does not solve the puzzle of what life is about. Similarly, this chapter has suggested that people who think that they have answered the question "What is success?" by saying "Happiness" have only begun their quest, not come to the end of it. As we have discovered in these pages, happiness means many things, and you must decide for yourself what forms of happiness you consider worth pursuing as part of your definition of a successful life. I hope I have challenged your assumptions about happiness in this chapter, but my goal was not to persuade you to my way of thinking; it was to spur you to come to your own conclusions.

With these thoughts in mind on the inner aspects of success, we are ready to begin looking at some of the drivers that push you toward achievement. We start in the next chapter with the three goals that modern culture holds out as most desirable: status, fame, and fortune.

Are you ready for some reality television? Turn the page.

Success Step #2

DEFINE HAPPINESS FOR YOURSELF

Happiness and success may not be the same thing. Remember:

Momentary Happiness comes from slowing down and paying attention to what is happening around you. Everything you need to be happy is simple.

Overall Happiness is not just about positive emotions. It is the result of achieving long-term goals that require effort and, sometimes, painful sacrifice.

Wisdom Experiences may be more important to inner success than any form of conventional happiness.

Society's Answer:
Seek Status, Fame, and Fortune

I always wanted to be somebody, but I guess I should have
been more specific.

—LILY TOMLIN

I've been poor and I've been rich. Rich is better!

—BEATRICE KAUFMAN

An entrepreneur named Carl Bolch Jr.—the owner
of one of the largest gasoline and convenience
store chains in the American South—once told my
students a story about the importance of pie-eating contests when it
comes to success. Soon after his business relocated from Alabama to
Georgia in the mid-1970s, he hired one of the top law firms in the state
capital of Atlanta to help him with his legal work. As time passed, he
came to rely on a particular partner as a trusted business adviser for
his firm. After a few more years, with his company prospering, Bolch
decided it was time to hire a full-time, in-house lawyer as the firm's
general counsel. He went to his friend and asked if there were any lawyers he might recommend for the job.

"How about me?" the lawyer said.

"Well, that would be great," Bolch replied. "But I will not be able
to pay you anything close to what you are making at the law firm."

"That's OK," the lawyer said. "I'll take the job. You decide what you want to pay me."

Bolch was curious and asked if there was something wrong with his friend's law firm work.

"No," the lawyer said. "There is nothing wrong. It is just a question of more pie."

"More pie?"

The lawyer explained. "Working the way I have all my life is like a pie-eating contest. I worked in high school to get into a great college. Then I worked in college to get into a great law school. Then I worked at law school to get a job at a top-flight law firm. Then I worked at the law firm to make partner. I've finally figured out that it is all just a big pie-eating contest. You win, and the prize is always . . . MORE PIE. Who wants that?"

Bolch hired him on the spot, and they have been working closely together ever since.

"Here is the funny part," Bolch concluded. "The first day he reported for work, he wore Bermuda shorts and a Hawaiian shirt. He often wears sandals instead of shoes. And he is a better lawyer than ever."

Carl Bolch's lawyer had learned a basic lesson about success. When everyone around you agrees on what success means, it is all too easy to join them. And if you allow others to define your goals for you, then there is a pretty good chance you will end up holding a prize you did not choose and do not want.

At that point, you will finally have to define success for yourself.

The previous chapter started this process by asking you to think more deeply about the inner experience of happiness. This one challenges you to examine two of the most important outside influences on your success beliefs: culture and family. Each of these can pose unique problems.

For example, like Carl Bolch's lawyer, you may get thrown off course by the need for social approval and status. If you embrace cultural ideals of success—especially when these are exaggerated by the mass media—you can literally become a success "addict." Success addicts are people who obsessively seek the rush of self-satisfaction that comes with being in the limelight. They measure their self-esteem entirely in the fame-and-fortune currencies that culture celebrates. Buddhists have a name for people who cannot get enough status, wealth, or power. They are called Hungry Ghosts—spirits in Buddhist mythology that have bodies the size of elephants and heads the size of pins. With such a small mouth trying to feed such a huge body, a Hungry Ghost can never get enough. His hunger never ends; his desires are never satisfied.

There are many kinds of Hungry Ghosts, and they can be found in almost every field. In science, these sad creatures fake lab results to secure publication in top journals. In business, they overstate earnings and trade on the stock market using illegal, inside information. And in the publishing world, Hungry Ghost celebrity authors plagiarize others' works to win spots on bestseller lists.

In addition, families sometimes complicate the journey to authentic success by laying a heavy burden of expectations on their children. The poet Rainer Maria Rilke once said that children often "dance to the unlived lives of their parents." In her book *Gifted Lives*, Joan Freeman writes about what happens to children when their parents express "love with strings attached." If you sensed that your parents' affections were conditional—that you could earn their love only by achieving the goals they mandated—you may have gotten scant practice conceiving and accomplishing your own, self-generated ambitions. And if you were unassertive as a child, you may have spent your energies striving to meet parental expectations that were more negotiable than you realized.

Later in life, this habit of striving to satisfy other people's aspirations can be hard to break. Decades into adult life, you may still be working to meet family expectations that no longer exist. Moreover, the longer it takes to break free of them, the more courage it may take to do so. As the stories in this and future chapters will show, people often start this journey to autonomy by seeking inspiration from their childhood interests. They reach back to the passions that developed spontaneously, before outside influences on what counted as "success" drowned out their inner voices.

Near the end of the chapter, I will give you a chance to begin moving beyond these social and family expectations. You will do the Lottery Exercise. The idea behind this self-assessment is simple. Assume you have won the lottery, and your social status is secure. You are already rich and famous. What will you do with your life now? If you have no clear answer to this question, you may be working too much for the rewards of parental or social approval and not hard enough on goals you genuinely value and have originated for yourself.

CULTURAL VALUES: WHY THE BUDDHA IS FAT
....

Where do your success beliefs come from? As I noted in chapter 1, French philosopher Jean-Jacques Rousseau taught us that individuals take their cues about what is "good or desirable" in life from what they think their culture judges to be good and desirable.

For example, *New York Times* reporter Edward Wong once wrote about a visit to the Bozai Gumbaz of Afghanistan, a rocky, barren place in the northeastern corner of the country. Western donors had attempted to establish a program there to teach literacy, but they had run into an insurmountable cultural barrier. No children came to the programs because they were too busy minding their families' herds. "The Kyrgyz [people] only care about sheep and yaks," Wong was told. "They say if we have sheep and yaks, we have success in life." The children were, in essence, tending their parents' retirement investments.

Had the donors thought more about it, perhaps they could have offered the families some additional sheep and yaks in return for allowing the children a chance to read—or sent some tutors out to the pastures where the children were. In any case, the lesson is clear: if you want to change behavior—including your own—you need to start by understanding the cultural success norms that drive people's decisions.

Many of the messages a culture sends about success are invisible. Have you ever wondered why so many images of Buddha depict him as fat? Historically, it makes no sense. Buddha was a trim, fit man from northern India who taught moderation and mindfulness. He was a vegetarian. He lived a strenuous life teaching disciples about his Four Noble Truths and the Eightfold Path to enlightenment. But go into a Chinese restaurant or gift shop virtually anywhere in the world, and you will see statues of fat, happy Buddhas.

Fat Buddha is a legacy of a period of Chinese history that equated weight with success. When Buddhism crossed from India to China several thousand years ago, there was a rotund, Santa Claus–like Chinese folk deity named Budai popular in local culture. Budai morphed into Fat Buddha and remains a success symbol that Chinese merchants all over the world place in their stores to attract good fortune.

Some contemporary cultures still embrace the ideal of fatness as a symbol of success and wealth. The fashion magazine *Marie Claire* reported on an example from Mauritania, "where big is beautiful and stretch marks are sexy." Mothers who want their young daughters to snag a wealthy husband send their girls to special facilities where they are "fed a diet of up to 16,000 calories a day—more than four times that of a male bodybuilder—to prepare them for marriage." The practice is left over from medieval times when, "to the ancient Moors, a fat wife (much like fat livestock) was a symbol of a man's wealth, proof that he had enough riches to feed her generously while others perished in the drought-prone terrain."

Meanwhile, back in America, success is thin and fat suggests failure. Consider the plight of Jennifer Livingston, a thirty-seven-year-old overweight television newscaster for WKBT in La Crosse, Wisconsin. One evening after her broadcast, the station received an e-mail from an angry viewer demanding that she be removed from her job because her weight made her an "unsuitable role model for young people, especially girls." In an on-air rebuttal that became a YouTube sensation, Livingston admitted her body was a source of shame to her: "You could call me fat and, yes, even obese on a doctor's chart. . . . [D]on't you think I know that?" But she defended her personal dignity and successfully retained her job. "You don't know me. You are not a friend or a part of my family . . . so you know nothing about me but what you see on the outside," she said. "And I am much, much more than a number on a scale." She called on her viewers—especially children—not to let the ignorance of others define their self-worth.

Success values within any given community are often invisible because they are so little debated. From your earliest years, day in and day out, you heard countless messages about what it means to be successful. Many of these were spoken at the kitchen table. In one home, the parents talked at dinner about "if you go to college . . . " In another home, they said "when you go to college . . . " In a third, it was "when you finish graduate school. . . ." In the first house, being admitted to college counted as a major success. In the second, it met existing expectations. In the third, it was just the first, necessary step on a much higher ladder.

Similarly, as you grew up you watched people around you striving to get into certain schools, dating certain kinds of people, buying certain products, and seeking certain kinds of jobs. The cultural props and staging behind television shows and films gave you even more clues about what you should be striving for. Parents, siblings, coaches, bosses, clergy, inspirational speakers, and even the lyrics to popular songs communicated powerful suggestions about success. All these cultural inputs have worked their way into your subconscious mind.

The invisible cues provided by your culture then set the benchmarks that, when you meet or exceed them, give you a sense of achievement. Those same benchmarks also inspire dismal, defeated feelings when you think you have fallen short. Occasionally, they assert themselves as vague sources of inner conflict. You wake up one day and realize that you have been in a pie-eating contest and the thought of winning more pie suddenly makes no sense.

The cumulative effect of all this is powerful—a form of cultural hypnosis. When you contemplate a new goal that pushes against the social conventions of your family and culture, your imagination may ignite with a short burst of energy. Then conventional norms reassert themselves, pulling you back to more comfortable, familiar aspirations.

Let's look at a few examples of how hard these forces can be to overcome and the rewards that await those who break free of them.

WAKING UP

In his memoir *Dreams from My Father*, President Barack Obama describes an experience in his early twenties when he became aware of his subconscious success beliefs. His first job after graduating from Columbia University was at a New York company called Business International, where he wrote and edited newsletters for American firms doing business overseas. "Sometimes," Obama writes in his book, "coming out of an interview with Japanese financiers or German bond traders, I would catch my reflection in the elevator doors—see myself in a suit and tie, a briefcase in my hand—and for a split second I would imagine myself as a captain of industry, barking out orders and closing the deal, before I remembered who it was that I wanted to be and felt pangs of guilt for my lack of resolve."

It took a year for the young Obama to realize that the only way to break free of the person he saw reflected in that elevator was to leave the business world. His supervisor, Lou Celi, tried to talk him out of quitting. "He just seemed not exactly clear about what he wanted to do," Celi told one of Obama's biographers, David Maraniss. "I told him he might be making a mistake, leaving a job when he did not have any plans except a vague notion that he maybe would do some public sector work."

The future president may not yet have known exactly what he wanted to do. But he had figured out one thing he did *not* want to do: fulfill the conventional New York business mogul success fantasy.

What I find interesting about this story, however, is not how far away from Wall Street the mature Barack Obama landed, but rather how close he ended up to fulfilling his youthful success fantasy. He rejected a future as a "captain of industry," but, after a period of introspection, he found his way into politics. And, as president, he has had to wear a suit and tie—"barking orders and closing the deal." What he was really seeing in that mirror as a young man was his unconscious desire to be a man of influence and importance, a big-league player within his culture. With that target set, he determined for himself the kind of influence he would wield—and on behalf of what interests. His fantasy came true, but the deals he ended up closing were treaties, trade agreements, and legislative bargains rather than mergers and acquisitions. Barrack Obama did not escape his culture's success values, but he did an excellent job of channeling them in a direction he set for himself.

If you want to know how hard it is to move beyond the success values endorsed by your family and culture, consider the case of Kurt Timken. Timken grew up in Ohio, where his father ran a Fortune 500 firm that makes steel and ball bearings. The company had been founded by Timken's great-great-grandfather, and he was groomed his entire life to take his turn at the helm. He attended an exclusive prep school (Phillips Academy Andover) and a top college (Pomona College near Los Angeles, California). He then worked at the firm for a few years before attending Harvard Business School.

He was set for life. Then he rejected it all to pursue his own unique vision of success. His journey shows how hard that can sometimes be.

"Everyone needs fuel for their engine," he told the writer Po Bronson. "Making seven figures on Wall Street is cheap wood, it burns too fast." Timken wanted something more substantial.

The crisis came after Harvard, when he and his wife, both working long hours for their respective employers (he for Rockwell International and she for Disney), lost sight of each other and their marriage. The resulting divorce was Timken's wake-up call. At thirty, he was doing everything he had been trained for and was rocketing along a fast track to leadership that would eventually have led him back to the firm that carried his family's name. But, he told Bronson, "I was still not hopping out of bed in the morning, excited to get to work."

So he quit.

That gave him the space to break through the expectations that had been defining his life. Reflecting back on an interest he had had since childhood, he decided to aim for becoming a police officer. The leap from an Ivy League business career to something as radically different as becoming a street cop makes President Obama's switch from business to politics look comparatively easy. Moreover, Timken learned that cultural forces create barriers even after you have overcome your own doubts about changing your life's direction.

Timken had done his homework and was sure that a police career was right for him, but the world of law enforcement was not so sure that he was right for it. Policing has a culture of its own—one that is handed down from father to son, from uncle to cousin, and from friend to friend. Timken was an outsider to that culture.

First, the FBI turned him down.

Then the Los Angeles Police Department turned him down.

Next, the Los Angeles County Sheriff's Department rejected his application.

Finally, Timken enrolled in the Rio Hondo College Police Academy, graduating near the top of his class. But he still could not find anyone who believed that someone with his background was serious about backing up a partner in a gun battle or leaping into action at midnight to intervene in a gang war.

What kept him going was a copy of a hundred-year-old letter he carried in his pocket. It was a note written at a time of crisis early in the Timken Company's history. "We'll hang in there like grim death," his great-grandfather had written. "We've got grit even if we don't have sense." Timken felt the same way. He knew his goal to become a policeman did not make a lot of sense. "But I had grit," he later said.

In the end, it took him two years to land his first police job in El Monte, California, just east of East Los Angeles. El Monte hired him only after he agreed to volunteer for a full year in a community relations unit that worked with gangs. He is now a full-fledged police professional, a senior detective in the thick of California's sometimes violent war against gangs and drugs. He is occasionally deputized for duty with the federal Drug Enforcement Administration and has received glowing profiles in the alumni publications of both Andover and Harvard Business School.

He loves his work, and Timken now tells anyone who will listen that what he does has "real purpose."

Bottom line: unless you abandon your society and live on a remote island, the values your family and culture instilled in you will play a defining role in how you measure your success. To define it for yourself—as both President Obama and Detective Kurt Timken did—you need to consider which of those values you endorse and which ones you reject.

Then you need to be prepared to work patiently, moving forward step by step as you battle the doubts that are sure to keep you up at night and the well-meaning advisers who will urge you back to the conventional path.

FAMILY: CULTURE'S MAGNIFYING GLASS
....

As Kurt Timken's story suggests, one of the rites of passage on the journey to define success is confronting family expectations. Even if you had a supportive family that nurtured your autonomy, you may still have some work to do as you break free of your natural desire to please the people who raised you. Meanwhile, children charged with living out the unfulfilled dreams of their parents often confront serious psychological barriers blocking the road to personal fulfillment.

The celebrity tennis star Andre Agassi was not born with a racket in his hands, but his emotionally explosive father, Mike Agassi, made him grip one almost as soon as he could make a fist. By the time he was seven, his father had him hitting 2,500 tennis balls over the net each day, 17,500 balls each week, and almost a million balls per year. "A child who hits one million balls each year will be unbeatable," his father said.

His father also yelled a lot. In his autobiography, *Open*, Agassi writes that his father "yells everything twice, sometimes three times, sometimes ten." He stood behind him on the court and yelled directly into his ear. "I rarely see him," writes Agassi, "[I] only hear him, day and night, yelling in my ear. More topspin! Hit harder! Hit *harder*. Not in the net! Damn it, Andre! *Never in the net!* . . . You're going to be number one in the world! You're going to make lots of money. *That's the plan, and that's the end of it."*

Agassi was the youngest of the four children in his family, and his father had driven each of them to become a tennis star. His sister Rita had rebelled and quit; his sister Tami had attained a relatively high level of skill and then stopped improving; his brother, Philly, had shown the talent to make it but lacked what his father called "the killer instinct." After Philly lost a match in a top youth tournament without arguing a bad line call by his opponent, Mike Agassi began accusing him of being a "born loser" and gave up on him. Andre was his father's last, best hope.

When the Agassi family went house hunting in Las Vegas, the real estate agent talked up the local schools, low crime rates, and great deals available on a mortgage. But his father was interested only in whether a tennis court would fit on the lot. He would "storm into the house, whip out his tape measure and count off thirty-six feet by seventy-eight feet." Then he would yell, "Doesn't fit! Come on! Let's go!"

When he was eleven, Agassi won a sportsmanship trophy at the national youth tournament for the player who exhibited the most grace on the court. After the ceremony was over, his father ripped the trophy from his hands, lifted it over his head, and smashed it on the cement. Neither of them said a word about this incident—during or after the episode. Agassi's mother, meanwhile, was even more afraid of her husband's temper than Andre. She never intervened.

Although he would go on to fulfill his father's hopes and be ranked number one in the world, he did it all with a sense of detachment from himself. "I play tennis for a living," he writes in his autobiography, "even though I hate tennis, hate it with a dark and secret passion, and always have." After he won his first Wimbledon championship, he learned that "winning change[d] nothing." For him, "A win doesn't feel as good as a loss feels bad, and the good feeling doesn't last as long as the bad. Not even close." As an adult, he says, he played because it was all he knew how to do.

In the end, Agassi was able to reclaim his life through his relationships with two women—his first wife, the actress Brooke Shields; and his second, fellow tennis star Steffi Graf. Brooke Shields pointed him toward the source of his troubles. Before he could have a genuine, lasting relationship with anyone, he would have to deal with his demons. Only he could do that. And he believed her. Steffi Graf, meanwhile, proved to be the one person in the world who could actually understand his strange world from the inside. Her father was almost as competitive as Mike Agassi (the two men nearly came to blows the first time they met). She was also the only female player at his level—someone who had won the same four Grand Slam tournaments as well as an Olympic Gold medal. They connected, and with that connection came commitments to her, their children, and eventually a nonprofit educational foundation to support abused children. At Agassi's experimental school in Las Vegas—a 26,000-square-foot complex for five hundred at-risk students—the school motto is etched on the front window: "BELIEVE."

Note carefully: Andre Agassi did not reject the success lessons of hard work, practice, and high standards of professional excellence when he rejected his father's psychologically abusive system for teaching him tennis. But he came to see his father very, very clearly as he began formulating his own independent life goals.

In one of the most remarkable passages in his autobiography, Agassi writes of accidentally running into his father just before the final professional tennis match of his career, the 2006 U.S. Open in New York. Agassi was suffering from severe back pain. He could not walk without limping. But he was determined to play in this last tournament. He hoped to leave the court with honor even if he could not leave it with a victory. In a way, he wanted to at last claim that sports-manship prize his father had smashed in his youth. As Agassi made his way toward the court, a man stepped out of the shadows and grabbed his arm. It was his father. By that time, Mike Agassi was a professional tennis scout who spent much of his time outside the United States. The two seldom saw one another.

"Quit," his father urged. He could not endure the sight of seeing his son play hurt. He wanted him to forfeit the match.

Agassi walked away.

"I'm sorry, pops," he said. "I can't quit. This can't end with me quitting."

Andre Agassi was, at last, living his own life. He owned his own professional standards and his own future.

Agassi's father had a uniquely abusive system for training his children to be tennis stars, but it is all too normal in its "hothouse" atmosphere for instilling success values. Orthodox religions, tight-knit ethnic communities, evangelical groups, "Model Minority" Asian family units, and upper-class economic elites living in country-club-dominated enclaves all know the power of family as a system for transmitting cultural beliefs related to success. In extreme cases, they remove themselves entirely from mainstream culture, educate their children at home or in their own schools, and create mini–economic systems to sustain their cultural isolation.

But in most loving families, parents understand that a time comes when children must break free. Indeed, some cultural and religious rituals establish this as a family's obligation. For example, Amish religious groups relax the rules of their ultraconservative lifestyle and require college-age young people to leave their farms for one or two years so the children can consider if they genuinely want to be baptized and live as adult members of the community. They call this period Rumspringa, a German term that means "running around." And, as I noted in the introduction, young people in Western societies frequently go through Odyssey Years between college and marriage as they set out to discover their own values and goals before returning to take their places in the social order.

Ultimately, you need not reject your family to discover who you are, what you want to do, and what people (or person) you want to do it with. But you need to establish your own, unique identity and freely choose the life goals you endorse. Some people take these steps sooner and some do it later. But can you really be successful if you never make a free, independent, and informed judgment about your family's vision of a successful life?

SUCCESS ADDICTS: HUNGRY GHOSTS
....

With this preliminary understanding of how culture and family shape your success beliefs, let's turn to the problem of what happens when people acquire an obsession with the symbols of conventional success. This can turn them into Hungry Ghosts. In the West (and, through the operation of the global market, in many developing countries), the "Big Two"—fame and fortune—dominate the mass media images about what success means. But anyone who relentlessly seeks status, recognition, or power to bolster his or her self-image as a "somebody" is at risk. Here are a few examples.

Hungry Ghosts for Fame

Not long ago, the social activist Greg Mortenson, bestselling author of *Three Cups of Tea: One Man's Mission to Promote Peace One School at a Time* and *Stones into Schools: Promoting Peace with Education in Afghanistan and Pakistan,* faced a personal crisis. The popular television show *60 Minutes* ran a story questioning whether he and his Central Asia Institute were telling the whole truth about their work bringing educational opportunities to young girls in Afghanistan. Before this story broke, I had heard Mortenson speak at a New York conference on new models for social change. Like many, I had felt the thrill of being in the presence of someone who was using his life to accomplish something truly meaningful.

In the *60 Minutes* segment, the author Jon Krakauer (*Into Thin Air*) alleged that Mortenson had fabricated parts of his life story, overstated the number of Afghan schools he had built, and siphoned off hundreds of thousands of charitable dollars to fund his globe-trotting lifestyle as a celebrated author. Krakauer's *Three Cups of Deceit: How Greg Mortenson, Humanitarian Hero, Lost His Way* praised Mortenson's good works and then systematically revealed his lies. The Central Asia Institute issued denials, but Mortenson later admitted that he had misrepresented facts in his books. Subsequent investigations confirmed that he had exaggerated a number of his accomplishments.

Mortenson's story is a cautionary tale for anyone interested in success. As Duke University's Dan Ariely has shown in his book *The (Honest) Truth About Dishonesty: How We Lie to Everyone—Especially Ourselves,* we are all tempted to deceive in certain circumstances, especially when the lies are small, when we have strong interests at stake, see others getting away with it, or happen to have an above-average talent for rationalization. Perhaps this last factor played a role in Mortenson's case, but I still found it hard to believe that someone like Mortenson, who was doing a substantial amount of good in the world, would throw it all away just to fool people into thinking he was doing a little bit more.

I underestimated the power that fame and fortune can have over even the most well-meaning people. Mortenson fell victim to a fate that afflicts many people who become preoccupied with their own success: the more attention he received, the more he craved. But it was never quite enough.

According to the biologist David Sloan Wilson, author of *Evolution for Everyone: How Darwin's Theory Can Change the Way We Think About Our Lives*, the mass media may be responsible for creating the increasing number of Hungry Ghosts we see in the world around us. The human appetite for attention, he has commented, could formerly be satisfied with the kind of prominence available in any small-scale community. But as the global media and their 24/7 celebrity culture have grown, so too has the hunger for celebrity. "The lust for fame has taken on [a] pathological form," he says.

Mortenson's case is especially distressing because he was doing something useful that his own actions sabotaged. The typical Hungry Ghost for Fame makes no pretense of doing good works, however. For example, I once encountered a man at a conference who was much closer to the usual mold—a Generation Y writer named Tucker Max. He is the bestselling author of a series of raunchy memoirs about his life with titles like *I Hope They Serve Beer in Hell* and *Assholes Finish First*.

To feed his Hungry Ghost appetite, Max found a niche writing about his experiences with sex and alcohol. His life's work was to get drunk and have as much sex as possible, or, alternatively, to become so drunk that sex was impossible. Then write about it. His books have sold over two million copies, mostly, Max said in a 2012 interview with *The New Yorker*, to "dudes who can't spell dude."

What caught my eye in this interview was that Tucker Max had reformed. Now thirty-six, he was seeing a psychoanalyst four times a week and switching to a diet of lentils and organic whey. His success formula had definitely soured, and sex with strange women had become a thing of the past. He told the reporter that "the thought of going to a strip club makes me want to vomit," and his to-do list now included Zen archery and South American dance lessons. He had started going to a Buddhist center near his home in Austin, Texas.

In short, he had entered a new phase of his life, having finally grasped the truth of the well-known happiness aphorism: "Happiness is measured not by the number of days you live, but rather by the number of days you remember." My doubts returned, however, when I read Max's answer to a question about his future plans. The reporter asked what the title of his next book might be, should he decide to write one chronicling his new, more sober lifestyle. He replied, "*Still Awesome, Just Different*." Perhaps, after all, Max was still a Hungry Ghost, albeit one that had acquired a new and more sustainable way to continue its endless search for celebrity.

Mortenson's and Max's stories are instructive, but fame can have even more tragic effects on people who overdose on it. One of the most popular forms of entertainment today is reality television, a genre in which unknown people appear as themselves before cameras that record their daily (and nightly) lives. Reality TV has taken over the game segment (*Survivor*), the variety show segment (*American Idol* and *The Voice*), the soap opera segment (*The Bachelor* and *The Bachelorette*), and the comedy segment (*Jersey Shore*). These shows may soon be gone and forgotten, but the genre of reality entertainment will be flourishing for many years to come. Why? Because the reality genre is inexpensive to produce and, like the lottery, gives ordinary people the chance to become certifiably famous.

The reality of reality TV, of course, is less than glamorous. Says Tom Beers, the executive producer of several such shows: "We sit down with everyone before we start and tell them that fame doesn't make them smarter or more attractive. They should enjoy the ride but realize it's going to end."

Nevertheless, many do not heed his advice. With talent agencies standing ready to book former reality TV stars for appearances at malls, 5K races, and local charity events, it is all too easy for these ordinary people to become Hungry Ghosts for Fame. And when the cameras stop rolling, a darker side emerges: the notable risk of suicide. "Reality TV can be very dangerous," one medical expert has commented. "The combination of the disappointment that you're not happy with your new life combined with the new shame [from being humiliated on a show] that is magnified by the public eye can literally make a lethal combination." A number of people associated with shows such as *Kitchen Nightmares*, *Hell's Kitchen*, *Teen Mom*, and *Supernanny* have either taken or tried to take their own lives.

The next time you are tempted by the idea that fame will bring you success, think about two questions. First, just how much acclaim would you need to be truly "famous"? The most famous people in any era are known to only a small percentage of living humans. The rock singer Bono is not a household name in the villages of central India. If fame is your goal, you may discover that you can never be famous enough. Consider the pain of withdrawal before you become addicted to a drug.

Second, nobody is famous forever. The website China.org.cn provides a list of the "Top Ten" emperors in the long history of China. Can you name any of them? They were absolute rulers over millions of people, but their names mean nothing unless you happen to be a student of Chinese history. For comparison, consider how long it will take the world to forget the names of the cast members on *Teen Mom*.

If you want to read more about Hungry Ghosts for Fame, open up the latest copy of the *Hollywood Reporter*. In the meantime, we are turning to *The Wall Street Journal*. That's where reporters cover the Hungry Ghosts for Fortune.

Hungry Ghosts for Fortune

If fame is fleeting, what about fortune? Everyone worries about money, and waking up without any can be a true emergency. But when we talk about the American Dream, we are talking about getting rich. The fantasy of untold wealth is a fixture in our culture—and is rapidly becoming the dream of choice in many emerging economies, notably those of Brazil, Russia, India, and China.

We looked closely at the relationship between money and happiness in chapter 2. On the one hand, we have a basic truth expressed by Beatrice Kaufman, wife of the playwright George S. Kaufman as reported in the *Washington Post* back in 1937. "I've been poor and I've been rich," she said. "Rich is better!" Studies of lottery winners show that, on average, most are more satisfied with their lives two years after winning than they were before.

On the other hand, one of New York's richest women, a reclusive widow named Huguette Clark, once summed up her experience living for eight decades in a forty-two-room Fifth Avenue apartment. "Wealth is a menace to happiness," she reported. Riches change the way people treat you—and not always for the better.

Other examples come from the ranks of lottery winners. Although, as I noted above, lottery winners are generally better off in their lives after they win, there are many notable exceptions to this rule. A man named William "Bud" Post won $16.2 million in the Pennsylvania lottery in 1988. Soon after he won, his brother tried to have him killed to collect the inheritance. Eventually, Post spent (or lost) all of his winnings. He was living off Social Security when he died in January 2006.

One thing about money is certain: wealth can be as addictive as fame. The novelist David Foster Wallace put it well in a speech he gave at Kenyon College: "If you worship money and things—if they are where you tap real meaning in life—then you will never have enough."

Many of the most striking cases of Hungry Ghosts for Fortune reside on Wall Street. For example, one of the largest Wall Street insider trading rings of all time unraveled with the conviction and sentencing of a Sri Lankan hedge fund manager named Raj Rajaratnam. Rajaratnam was worth well over $1 billion at the time he was trading on illegal stock tips.

Among his confidants during his insider trading spree was another multimillionaire, named Rajat Gupta, who was also convicted in the scandal. Gupta was the former head of the prestigious global consulting firm McKinsey & Company and was serving on the board of directors of the well-known investment bank Goldman Sachs at the time he and Rajaratnam kindled their relationship.

Several wiretapped conversations between these insiders reveal what was motivating them. It seems Gupta coveted a role at KKR, one of the world's largest private-equity firms. In an August 15, 2008, taped call, Rajaratnam told another conspirator: "[Gupta's] enamored with Kravis, and I think he wants to be in that circle. That's a billionaire's circle. . . . I think here he sees an opportunity to make $100 million over the next 5 or 10 years without doing a lot of work."

Neither Rajaratnam nor Gupta needed money. Instead, both were gripped by a desire to get into (or stay in) the "billionaire's circle." They became Hungry Ghosts for Fortune in order to gain (or retain) their coveted status as two of the world's wealthiest people, a quest for success that led them to federal prison.

Many people incorrectly cite the Bible as saying, "Money is the root of all evil." But money itself is not the problem. We all need and respect money. The actual quote from the First Epistle of Timothy in the New Testament reads: "The *love of* money is the root of many evils" (emphasis mine). We come to love money when we start using it to keep score.

Lesson: if you want to avoid becoming a Hungry Ghost for Fortune, don't use money to achieve social recognition. Use it to pay your bills.

ALTERNATIVES TO STATUS, FAME, AND FORTUNE: INFORMED RESPECT AND FINANCIAL SECURITY

If aspiring to status, fame, and fortune for their own sake can be risky, what goals might keep you on a better path—one that combines both the inner and the outer aspects of success we talked about in chapter 1? A student in my Success class named J. J. Fliegelman once contributed an especially insightful answer to this question. People fall into the fame-and-fortune trap, he said, because they get hooked on the wrong kind of respect—a form that philosopher Stephen Darwall has called "recognition respect." Recognition respect is that feeling that comes when people who do not know you nevertheless treat you as if you are something special. It is the cotton candy of social reinforcement. It gives you an immediate rush, but it has no staying power or substance. Darwall compared this with a deeper and more substantive type of approval I call "informed respect."

Consider two people who are equally (and fabulously) rich. The first is a wealthy heiress who inherited her money and lives a socialite life of shopping, posing for pictures at parties, and scanning the style sections of newspapers for mentions of herself. The second is a hard-charging entrepreneur who earned every penny of her wealth through innovation and effort. At an exclusive resort hotel, both of these people will be treated with equal "recognition respect" based on their high net worth status. For the heiress, however, this respect experience will be much more important because it is the only form of external respect she ever receives. She measures her self-worth in terms of this recognition. Even the slightest lapse by a resort staff member will offend her, and she will probably surround herself with people who are aware of her need for this status-driven form of deference.

The entrepreneur will also appreciate being recognized and treated well by the hotel staff. However, because her self-worth is not anchored in social recognition, she will value much more highly the "informed respect" she receives from people who know her talents and appreciate the excellence of her accomplishments. Informed respect is the healthier alternative to recognition respect. It is earned and thoughtful.

Fame and celebrity are exaggerated forms of recognition respect. When Greg Mortenson shifted his attention from his actual work as a social entrepreneur to cultivating celebrity status, he sacrificed the informed respect of the small community concerned with educating

Afghan girls and instead sought recognition respect from a mass audience. It was a poor trade.

Similarly, when Carl Bolch's lawyer spoke of winning only more and more "pie" in his life, he was expressing the realization that he had been chasing the status that came with recognition-based credentials rather than purposeful achievements. He started a new life when he left his prestigious law firm, took a pay cut, and joined an entrepreneurial team that was building a business.

In addition to helping you realize you may be chasing the wrong goals, understanding the difference between recognition and informed respect can deflect certain forms of unjustified criticism. For example, when Jennifer Livingston, the overweight television newscaster, was attacked for her appearance, she effectively defended herself by arguing that the attack was based on recognition-level perceptions rather than informed judgments of her ability or character. "You don't know me . . . so you know nothing about me but what you see on the outside," she said.

A highly successful college basketball coach, Mike Krzyzewski of Duke University, once made a wise comment about exactly this kind of criticism. He was asked by a *Wall Street Journal* reporter for his reaction to a talk-radio commentator who had second-guessed his coaching in a big game. "A lot of people have opinions," he replied, but "they don't have all the information that's necessary to form *valued* opinions. I would rather listen to people who I trust. I react to that, not to talk shows and articles."

If seeking respect is a worthy substitute for chasing fame, what might be the analogous alternative to the pursuit of riches? I believe financial security might be a good target. And if you happen to make more money than you need to secure a good life for you and your family, then you might try the following strategy as a way to foster a greater sense of success in your life: give some of your money away. One of the wealthiest men in American history, the steel mogul Andrew Carnegie, wrote early in his life that there is "no idol more debasing than the worship of money." Carnegie's energy, drive, and innovations in steel production earned him a great fortune in spite of his youthful distaste for money. But he redeemed his self-respect later in life by systematically giving away as much of his wealth as he could—building hundreds of libraries in cities and towns across America and supporting a host of causes. His book *The Gospel of Wealth*, in which he advocated his radical approach to corporate philanthropy, remains the inspiration for such people as Microsoft's Bill

Gates and Berkshire Hathaway's Warren Buffett. You probably do not have wealth on this scale, but you might be surprised at how much richer your life can become when you put some of your assets to work on behalf of causes you believe in.

THE LOTTERY EXERCISE: NOW WHAT?

As we conclude our look at culture's effect on your beliefs about success, I want to challenge you with the "vision" experiment I mentioned at the beginning of this chapter. I call it the Lottery Exercise.

Here is the test question. Assume you have won a $100 million lottery and, as a result, have achieved celebrity status. You have also taken all the prudent measures required to care for your immediate family and invest your money wisely. You are assured of having millions for the rest of your life.

You have acquired a secure status and are permanently rich and famous.

Now what? What will you do with your life?

Give the matter some thought. Then write your answer below. I will ask you to revisit this response after reading the next chapter, so consider this a first draft of your plan.

_____

_____

_____

_____

_____

_____

_____

_____

With your answer in mind, let's take a look at a real-life story about someone who faced just this situation and see how she handled it.

As part of my success research, I keep a file on lottery winners. I was once paging through the newspaper when this headline caught my eye: "The $112 Million Dollar Woman." It was a story about a single mother and former office worker named Cynthia Stafford who had just won a $112 million jackpot in the California lottery. It was a heartwarming story. She had been working at a low-paying job and raising her five nephews and nieces, all of whom she adopted in the wake of a car accident that killed her brother. She definitely needed money. And then, in one electrifying moment, Cynthia Stafford leaped from obscurity to fame and rose from rags to riches.

A remarkable twist topped off the story. "I knew I'd get here," Stafford told the reporter in her Los Angeles home. "It was just a matter of visualizing it." Hard-pressed to pay her bills, she had lulled herself to sleep at night by imagining that she was holding a winning lottery check with the number 112 on it "followed by lots of zeroes." She enhanced this image until she could see every detail in her mind's eye, down to the lime-green blouse she would be wearing when she won.

And, she said, everything had happened exactly as she envisioned it, even the blouse. "That part kept surprising me," she said. "I thought I'd lose weight by then and wouldn't still have that top." When she learned she had the winning ticket, "I sat in silence for a minute because it confirmed how powerful our minds can be. Then I started screaming and crying!" As for what might happen if she ran through all her money? "I would simply visualize it again and make it happen," she said.

Whatever you might think about Stafford's actual ability to manipulate the California lottery computer with her mind, we can say two things for sure about her status in the wake of her win.

First, she was certifiably rich.

Second, the media's widespread coverage of her visualization story made her instantly famous with a very specific audience. Millions of people found her tale proof positive that a widely touted success system advocated in Rhonda Byrne's 2006 mega-bestseller, *The Secret*, actually worked. Byrne and her fellow success gurus call their dream-it-achieve-it method the "Law of Attraction." The law states that you pull into your life whatever you focus your mind on. If you think people will love you, they will. If you think you will make a lot of money, you will. Cynthia Stafford's lottery win became exhibit A for the believers in the Law of Attraction.

Of course, both the media and believers in *The Secret* failed to note that millions of lottery ticket buyers had to lose for Stafford to win, including many who visualized winning just as hard as she did. But these facts did nothing to dampen anyone's enthusiasm.

With this story as background, the door was open for Cynthia Stafford to launch a global tour as a success celebrity. Recognition respect in unlimited quantities was available.

However, she chose a different path.

First, she made sure her family had financial security. She created educational trust funds for her five nephews and nieces.

Beyond that, she stopped trumpeting her visualization story. As she later told an interviewer for the *Huffington Post*, "I don't want to call winning Lotto a miracle, but what's happened for us is certainly a blessing."

Then, instead of becoming a false prophet for the Law of Attraction, she decided to invest in some of her lifelong interests. Her mother had taken her to plays and museums when she was a child. She appreciated how the arts had expanded her own perspectives on life and was distressed at how budget cuts were gutting arts education in the schools. She also realized that she was a "people person"—someone who enjoyed meeting and mingling with others. Finally, she knew she was a simple soul at heart. As she put it, "I'm pretty down to earth."

With these insights in mind, she forged a relationship with Dream-Works cofounder David Geffen by making a substantial contribution to a Los Angeles theater he founded—the Geffen Playhouse. She joined its board of directors. She began hosting Gifted Day at the Geffen events for students from L.A.'s toughest neighborhoods and schools, giving them a chance to go behind the scenes of live theater productions. She also invited residents of local senior centers to come so that young and old could mix at the theater.

In addition, she bought the film rights to Don DeLillo's novel *White Noise*, winner of the 1985 National Book Award, and is serving, along with her new husband—a well-known Los Angeles actor named Lanre Idewu—as executive producer for a film based on that book. She and Idewu are CEO and COO respectively of Queen Nefertari Productions. She describes herself on her website as an "entrepreneur, philanthropist, and talk show host" who focuses her efforts on programs for children with special needs and women's rights. She has toured several African countries in search of worthy projects and was selected by the Lifetime Network (a women's cable television channel) for a Remarkable Women award.

From all this, here is what I think her answer has been to the Lottery Exercise:

- First take care of those you love;
- then pick a few things you are genuinely passionate about and invest significant time and money in them;
- finally, see where your new relationships and opportunities lead you.

"I'm comfortable with myself," Stafford told *The Huffington Post.* "My life is pretty much the same [as before the lottery]. I just have more resources to do what I love to do."

Stafford, it seems, found her way. She refused to settle for the glitzy but ultimately unsatisfying path of the Hungry Ghost. She turned her back on recognition respect. Instead, she has taken actions to earn some genuine, informed respect from her Los Angeles community.

Would you do this well if you won the lottery?

CONCLUSION

Boarding a crowded New York subway, I once spotted an empty seat next to a homeless man. As I wedged myself into it, he had to shift his garbage bag a bit. After a few seconds, he mumbled, "You're supposed to say you're sorry." I wasn't sure he was speaking to me. He spoke again, more clearly this time, "When you make somebody move something, you're supposed to say you're sorry." I got it. "I'm sorry," I said very sincerely. We rode on in silence.

Moments like this help me remember that culture too often defines our standards for what it means to be successful. As poor as this man was, he had more freedom than the two disgraced would-be members of the billionaires' club we met in this chapter, Raj Rajaratnam and Rajat Gupta. And, although this homeless man will probably never enter the posh clubs where New York celebrities throw their parties, he is entitled to ask for something even more desirable than fame—the basic respect every human being deserves.

In this chapter, you got a chance to consider how many of your success beliefs derive from unconscious assumptions you have absorbed from your family and culture. Are you caught up in a race to collect professional credentials? What's the point of winning a credential-based pie-eating contest when the only prize for winning is more pie? People such as Kurt Timken, the police officer with a Harvard MBA, can point you in a new direction. Timken stepped away from the corporate fast track in favor of a life of public service. In the process, he earned the informed respect of a small community that can see the value of his day-to-day work. And Andre Agassi's story shows how even the most famous among us can be little more than slaves to a frustrated parent's dream. Both Timken and Agassi broke free by recognizing that they needed to define success for themselves.

Beyond the lure of professional status lies the domain of fame and fortune. This is the land where success addicts—Hungry Ghosts— roam the countryside with appetites for admiration and power that are impossible to satisfy. To start you thinking about your deeper, more authentic goals, I asked you to consider how you would live your life after winning a big lottery. Money provides a form of security and is the gateway to many options. The interesting question I challenged you to answer, however, was what you would do with these assets if you actually had them. Are there any action steps, no matter how small, you could take today that would put you on the path you outlined in your answer to the Lottery Exercise? Could you reach out to join a new organization, sign up to learn a new skill, or make a donation to a cause you believe in? If so, why not do it? That step could put you in contact with someone who could change your life.

With these insights in mind, you are ready for the next step. You have examined a number of the standard answers to the question "What is success?" These include happiness, professional status, fame, and fortune. Beyond these four responses lies one more that many people point to as a unique way to combine inner satisfaction with outer achievement: meaningful work.

There is a perfect job for you somewhere. In the next chapter, you will start looking for it.

Success Step #3

GAIN PERSPECTIVE ON YOUR FAMILY AND YOUR CULTURAL BELIEFS

Many people equate success with high professional status or with being rich and famous. But most have not thought very hard about these goals. They just accept them as given from their families and their culture. As you consider your own idea of success, keep these factors in mind:

1. You can never be successful if you spend your life living someone else's dreams. Have you established your own identity?

2. People who chase status, fame, or fortune for its own sake will never feel secure enough, famous enough, or rich enough. Avoid the sad fate of the Hungry Ghost.

3. When you get past all the cultural success symbols, two things stand out as worth achieving: financial security and the informed respect of people who know you well.

An Inspired Answer:
Find Meaningful Work

Life's too short for the wrong job.

—ADVERTISING SLOGAN FOR
A GERMAN ONLINE RECRUITMENT WEBSITE

R obert Chambers had been working for five years as the Internet sales manager at a Lebanon, New Hampshire, car dealership. To maintain his sanity, he had learned to look the other way when questionable business practices were taking place on the sales floor. But on this particular day he witnessed behavior he could not ignore.

A "woodchuck" (the sales staff's pet name for a customer from the rural New England countryside) had just come in and was being greeted by the floor salesman on duty. Chambers listened from his cubicle as the customer explained who he was and what he needed. The man lived in a backwoods area, and his job depended on a reliable set of wheels. From his tone, Chambers could tell this man believed in an old-style New England brand of straight dealing and expected the salesman to behave the same way. Chambers watched with increasing disgust as the dealership's carefully scripted sales process unfolded— the one designed to produce the highest possible profit for the company and payoff for the salesman, regardless of what might be best for the customer.

First, the salesman convinced the customer that a used car would be a better value for him than a new one. The dealer paid as little as $1,000 for trade-ins on older vehicles with seventy thousand to ninety thousand miles on them. It spent $500 for the service needed to pass the state inspection and gave the car or truck a high-gloss shine. It then slapped a $5,000 sticker price on the windshield and put the vehicle on the lot. That was a $3,500 profit on a $1,500 investment. New cars, by contrast, brought in profits of $2,000 or less on investments of $20,000 to $30,000.

Step two narrowed the customer's focus to a particular vehicle—the one the dealership had tagged for that week's extra $1,000 sales commission. Sometimes this "bounty" was just a game—a way to get the staff energized and competing as they all tried to outdo one another selling the same used car or truck. Sometimes it was a quick way to move a clunker off the lot.

This week it was a clunker.

Chambers watched as the customer climbed into the driver's seat on the nearby lot and backed out for a test drive. As Chambers would later comment, "The [car] business has refined their sales techniques over a hundred years to get you into a car, to get you to like it, and to get you to sign the paper and drive out of there in one day."

The final dip into this customer's pocket came when the salesman ushered the man into the business office. There, Chambers knew, he would be offered "attractive" financing—a loan that was structured to look like a good deal but was actually a high-interest-rate time bomb that could blow up, wrecking the customer's personal credit. In this case, as Chambers learned a few minutes later, the manager was able to sell not only the loan but also some expensive insurance. Altogether, the manager alone had added more than $1,500 of additional profits and commissions to an already lucrative sale.

The customer drove off in the vehicle. And, as soon as he had disappeared, the manager and the salesman emerged from the business office high-fiving each other.

Meanwhile, Chambers found himself experiencing an emotion he had not expected to feel that day—outrage. When you lose respect for your job, Chambers discovered, you gradually lose respect for yourself. Disillusionment gives way to irritation. Irritation builds to peaks of resentment, cynicism, and anger as you see patterns of sloppy or unethical behavior repeated day after day. Life, you suddenly remember, is too short for this kind of job.

Sometimes, as it did for Chambers that day, the anger can fuel a decision to take action. And when it does, your life can change.

"I watched this guy driving off in a car that was going to die within a year—and he had signed a loan for five years. How can you do this to people? I quit within a week," Chambers said.

Robert Chambers was not an especially religious or moral person. But his professional life prior to that day had taught him the difference between honest and dishonest work. His first job had been as an electronics technician in the U.S. Navy, working on aircraft carriers to maintain the operational readiness of warplanes. After that, he learned computer engineering and held a series of jobs, but his work never developed into a defined career. As the years passed, he was employed by a telephone company, a bank, a friend's computer business, a New Hampshire computer services firm, and a financial services software company in New York. Then a financial crisis hit Wall Street, and he found himself out of a job again. He moved back to New Hampshire with his wife and considered retirement. But there was not quite enough money for that. He found the car dealership job through a friend.

What Chambers saw that day upset him on two levels. The sheer injustice of it, of course, turned his stomach. But he also saw what his systems-engineer mind considered a "system failure." The process that poor and working-class people were using to buy an essential item for their lives—cars—was broken. The high-interest car loans they bought kept them in debt; they missed more days at work when their older cars broke down; and they paid more for car repairs and gas than people with newer, more fuel-efficient vehicles. The dealerships prospered; the poor stayed poor.

His anger and insight gave birth to an idea. He decided he would try to create a new system for people in rural New Hampshire to buy cars. He founded a nonprofit organization soon to be called More Than Wheels. It took Chambers a year of hard work to line up the banks, donors, and foundation support to get his group up and running. The centerpiece of his concept was simplicity itself: he coupled the new-car-buying process for qualified rural customers with a low-cost bank loan and personal financial counseling.

Since its founding, More Than Wheels has made tens of millions of dollars in car loans and, as part of the car-buying process, taught debt management and household budgeting to hundreds of rural residents in New England. Chambers's system has also been good for the banking business. His clients repay their loans. Meanwhile, More

Than Wheels has expanded beyond New Hampshire using a combination of modest fees built into the loans it places as well as corporate and foundation grants to sustain itself and grow.

It was not long before Chambers found himself invited to visit the White House to meet President Obama. There, with a group of fellow social entrepreneurs, he advised the president and his economic staff on innovative ways to help the struggling American middle class.

AN INNER DIMENSION TO SUCCESS: MEANINGFUL WORK

In chapter 2, on happiness, we met a man I called the Wise Angel. He was an older, working-class individual who showed up at a Wharton School seminar on whether higher incomes made people happier. When the time came for questions, he commented, "I am just a member of the public. . . . But you mention the word 'happiness' and I am confused. What has that to do with anything you were saying about income? As I see it, happiness is just three things: good health, meaningful work, and love. You have that, you are happy."

His comment set me thinking. I had an idea of what good health is, and I counted myself fortunate that love was (and is) part of my life. But the idea of "meaningful work" was new to me.

I have been researching this ever since, and I have designed this chapter to help you draw your own conclusions about what it may have to do with success.

In the sections below, I will first outline three distinct ways people think about their occupations—as jobs, careers, or meaningful work. We will pause for a moment to appreciate what even the most ordinary job or career can contribute to your life—provided you do not find yourself in the kind of toxic environment Robert Chambers faced at his car dealership. Then we will determine what the idea of meaningful work adds to that picture.

From there, you will get a chance to consider seven specific foundations on which to build a conception of work as more than just a job or a career. There are, of course, almost as many forms of meaningful work as there are people, but my research on the success literature suggests that some combination of these seven categories is a likely target to consider in your personal search for success. These seven foundations are captured by the acronym PERFECT.

- Personal growth and development
- Entrepreneurial independence
- Religious or spiritual identity
- Family
- Expressing yourself through ideas, invention, or the arts
- Community—serving a cause, helping people in need
- Talent-based striving for excellence

At the end of the chapter, I will ask you to reflect on the examples we have examined and draft your own, personal definition of meaningful work for this stage of your life. You can then consider what steps you might take to find more meaning in the work you already do or target new work that could provide you with a deeper sense of purpose than you are experiencing now.

Your concept of success may be about more than work. But doing work that matters to you is probably a step in the right direction.

WHAT HAVE YOU GOT—A JOB, A CAREER, OR A CALLING?

Let's start by analyzing the work you are already doing (or have been doing recently). Researchers led by Yale University professor Amy Wrzesniewski once surveyed 196 employees working for two organizations: the student health service at a large state university and the administrative staff at a small liberal arts college. The participants in the study cut across a wide spectrum of ages, responsibilities, and income levels. The goal was to discover how these employees thought about their work.

The study discovered that they had three distinctive ways of describing what they did and why they did it. Moreover, the sample divided almost exactly into thirds—with one-third adopting each of the three frames of reference. In the descriptions below, see which of these three labels best applies to the work you are doing now or have done in the recent past. Keep in mind that you are not limited to choosing only one—the survey respondents were free to select any and all labels as being "very much like me."

Jobs. Respondents in one group considered their work primarily as a paycheck-producing "job." They labored mainly to support their lives away from the office and focused on family, friends, leisure activities, and other interests. They had no special loyalty to their employer, did not see their jobs as stepping stones to promotions within their line of work, and saw little inherently interesting about what they did. The best parts of their weeks were always the parts when they were not at work. The older workers were eagerly looking forward to retirement.

Careers. A second way employees thought of their work was in "career" terms. They considered themselves as working in a defined area of practice, such as a profession (doctor, lawyer, accountant), skill domain (writing, management, computer specialist), or organizational hierarchy (union, hospital, university). And they saw work as a steady progression toward more responsibility, higher status, and better pay. Work had meaning for them primarily as holding out the promise of a "future self" they wanted to become within their area of practice. One sign of this focus was a difference between younger and older employees doing the same job. Younger people were more likely to see their work (as a nurse, for example) in career terms. Older people doing the same work were more likely to see it as a job. Perhaps, having either failed to realize their earlier career ambitions or having achieved them but found them wanting, these older employees thought more about their paychecks and retirement plans and less about the "future selves" that their work had once promised.

Callings. The third approach people brought to their work was a category the researchers labeled a "calling." These employees felt lucky to have their jobs because the work reflected something important about them or gave them the chance to express a unique, personal value. Some embraced the work because they believed in its social importance, while others did so because it gave them a chance to affirm their core identities—to be the kind of people they wanted to be. One factor in people's perception that they had a calling was the sense that their work provided high levels of professional satisfaction and self-esteem. People with callings thought nothing of working longer hours at no extra pay and were much less interested in retirement.

Having a calling is what I think the Wise Angel had in mind when he declared that "meaningful work" was a key dimension of happiness. I like his phrase better than Professor Wrzesniewski's idea of a "calling" —which has quasi-religious connotations that can be confusing. You do not need to sit on a mountaintop and hear a voice calling you to be a nurse or a computer programmer. Nor, as Robert Chambers's story illustrates, must you rediscover a lifelong, God-given passion that becomes the basis for your life's work. After all, the inspiration behind More Than Wheels came later in his life, during a bad day at a car dealership.

A final, interesting conclusion from the Wrzesniewski study had to do with the relationship between a person's long-term commitment to work in a career and his or her sense of meaning associated with it. The data showed that people who saw themselves in jobs almost never saw the work as meaningful, whereas those in careers more often did. In the academic settings where the study was done, many of these careerists were people in higher-status, higher-paid positions that required advanced degrees. But we will see below that careers of every kind and at every status level can provide powerful sources of personal meaning.

If you hear an inner voice speak or you discover a lifelong passion, go for it. In fact, we will look at how some people come to their vocations this way in chapter 5. As this chapter develops, however, you will find examples that illustrate many different pathways that can lead to the discovery of meaning in your work. Don't let the quest to find "one true purpose" in life become a barrier to embracing work that creates value and delivers personal satisfaction.

As I said in chapter 1, success is not a static, one-and-done process. It's dynamic. If you stay in motion, learn as you go, and remain open to the insights you gain on the journey, good things often follow.

DEEPLY FELT EXPERIENCES

Given that higher-status and career-oriented workers saw their occupations as more meaningful, Professor Wrzesniewski and her colleagues wondered if people in the lowest-status, lowest-pay positions covered in the study would tend to consider their employment merely as jobs. To investigate this, they separated out a sample of twenty-four people who served as administrative assistants and compared their survey answers. To their surprise, they found that the group split as follows: nine thought of their work as a "job," seven as a "career," and eight as a "calling" (i.e., meaningful work).

Although the numbers were small and the sample was taken from relatively low-stress academic institutions, the suggestion is clear: people in identical positions can view what they do as falling under any of the three work labels. Their attitudes, not the activities that filled their days, made the difference. Thus, contrary to what you might think, there is no list of jobs that are certifiably and objectively "meaningful" versus "menial."

That leads to an obvious question: what might make one administrative assistant see his or her work as meaningful while another views it as only a paycheck? Unfortunately, the study did not investigate this question. But the PERFECT model we will examine later provides one set of answers that derive from my own research. I also want to highlight the work of another success researcher who used a very different kind of methodology to shed light on this question.

For his book *What Should I Do with My Life?*, cultural commentator Po Bronson collected more than nine hundred stories of people searching for more meaning in their work. He recorded seventy in-depth interviews and used fifty-three of them as the foundations for book chapters. He talked to what he called Phi Beta Slackers (smart people content to follow conventional career paths offering them the least resistance), ministers, models, lawyers, social workers, writers, truck drivers, and entrepreneurs, among many others.

Here is what he discovered. First, he confirmed the Wrzesniewski study finding that different people view the same kind of work very differently. One minister may be burned out from pastoring a church and feel like an impostor. Another may profess that no work on earth could be more meaningful than serving God through service to a church congregation.

Second, he uncovered an interesting pattern in the stories of those who saw their work as most fulfilling. Many of them could point to specific motivating experiences as the sources of their meaningful work narrative. Bronson summed up his findings in the conclusion to his book this way: "I used to think that certain jobs were 'cool,' and more likely to inspire passion. Now I know that passion is rooted in deeply felt experiences, which can happen anywhere." His fifty-three stories also make clear that he could have added, "and at any time in your life."

For example, a top surgeon at a children's hospital may find her work meaningful because she dreamed of becoming a doctor when she was young—a deeply felt memory that still animates her work. Meanwhile, just down the hallway of that same hospital, a low-paid janitor cleans the same floors of the cancer ward day after day. To most, this is a boring, repetitive job. But to this particular janitor, the work is meaningful. He is cleaning some of the same spaces where his only child was treated for cancer as an infant, including the offices of the medical staff who had a hand in his child's cure.

The connection between work and purpose also helps unlock the mystery noted above: how can one person view his or her work as a job while another finds it meaningful? As one secretary interviewed about her work put it, "I chose this path. I like what I do. I really feel that it makes a difference to the firm and to my boss."

The meaning-at-work question, then, may not be "What is the work?" Rather, it may be "What are the memories, experiences, aspirations, values, or stories that connect you to what you do every day and give it purpose?"

One sign that deeply felt experiences are, in fact, important sources of meaningful work are the many symbols and ceremonies that different professions use to create a sense of shared identity and purpose. Professional rituals associated with rites of passage are conscious, deliberate attempts to create "memorable moments" that help people recall the meaning of what they are doing. Young medical students have "white coat ceremonies" in which an older, experienced doctor helps each one don his or her first white coat before entering the hospital-based, clinical phase of medical training. These ceremonies are often accompanied by recitations of a modern version of the ancient Hippocratic oath, a pledge to do no harm and use medical skills to serve patients and not a doctor's own interests. Nurses have a similar "pinning" ceremony for nursing school graduates to remind them of the professional identity they are assuming.

Even people with no special profession often carry a personally significant token to help them remember their aspirations. After our class discussion on meaningful work in the Success course one semester, a student named Charles came up and showed me the symbol he uses to remind himself of his larger, meaningful-work goals. Charles was the immigrant son of a working-class Jamaican family and had, through a series of minor miracles, ended up at an Ivy League university. Like some of his classmates, he was planning to take his first job after college at a prestigious New York consulting firm, but his ultimate goal was to find work helping people in developing countries gain economic prosperity.

He knew that New York's money-and-status culture would make it hard for him to keep these goals in mind, so he had devised a symbolic solution: a pendant he had committed to wearing around his neck until he was able to enter his targeted field. It was a small, hand-crafted item that a child had made for him when he was working on a development project in a poor, rural area in Central America two summers earlier. "I have decided to wear this every day to remember what I really want to do," he said. As I looked at his pendant, I wondered if so small a symbol was up to the big role that Charles was asking it to play. I hoped so.

As you think about your own future, therefore, consider what deeply felt experiences may serve as sources of inspiration to find meaningful work. Your family's immigrant background may inspire you, as it did Charles, to seek ways of improving economic conditions for people in the developing world. The loss of a friend to illness or accident may spur you to get involved in work related to curing the disease or fixing the safety failure that cut his or her life short. The role a special teacher played in your life story may motivate you to go into a similar line of work so you can inspire others in the same way.

SEVEN FOUNDATIONS FOR MEANINGFUL WORK

In the Success class, I introduce the concept of meaningful work by using this simple diagram of three interlocking circles:

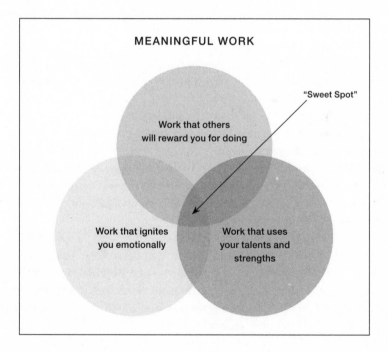

Reward-Driven Work. Start by looking at the top circle—work that others will reward you for doing. That includes everything from being a checkout person at a grocery store to helping land a spacecraft on

Mars. This circle represents a basic truth: no matter how mundane or interesting your work may be, it needs to create some amount of value that justifies some level of reward.

Indeed, many people thrive on work that occupies only this one circle. The career specialist Karen Burns wrote a provocative article for *U.S. News & World Report* titled "Why You Don't Need to Love Your Job." She made the important point that most people who merely like rather than love their work lead very fulfilled lives. They pay their bills, raise children, enjoy where they live, and contribute to their communities. In addition, assuming they do not have to endure the kind of toxic work environment Robert Chambers dealt with at his car dealership, their work gives them the following:

- *Status.* Work requires you to play a defined social role that carries an associated status. When someone asks "What do you do?," you have an honorable answer.
- *Self-Esteem.* This is closely related to status. Most jobs give you a chance to do the work well or badly. When you do it well, you can hold your head up.
- *Feelings of Self-Sufficiency.* A paying job allows you to stand on your own two feet—or contribute your part to your family's needs.
- *Social Affiliation.* Work requires you to interact with and relate to other people. Humans are social animals; interaction is a basic need.
- *Self-Knowledge.* Work may expose you to unexpected or novel problems. You learn something about yourself by observing how you respond to challenging events and people. Your life story adds some new episodes.

The best way to appreciate how profound these basic benefits are is to listen to the voices of the unemployed—people who have been shut out of the top circle. As a laid-off human resources manager put it, "Your whole life your job defines who you are. All of a sudden that's gone, and you don't know what to take pride in anymore." In the search for work with more meaning, therefore, don't forget the psychological benefits that even the most basic employment can provide.

Talent-Driven Work. Now move to the circle on the right: work that uses your talents and strengths. It makes sense to seek work that uses your talents, and chapter 5 will help you figure out exactly what those talents may be and how you might apply them to different professions.

But there are also some hidden risks in doing work only because you happen to be good at it. Take, for example, the "golden handcuff" problem. Many of the business-school students I teach are extremely talented in quantitative analysis. They often end up in the high-paying finance, consulting, or accounting industries that can use their analytic talents and strengths. As the years pass after graduation, however, I hear from many of my former students that these well-paid jobs have grown wearisome. They are doing work that pays them and that uses their talents, but they no longer like what they do. Then the problem emerges: the pay is so high and their lifestyle has grown so dependent on the pay that they cannot find a more satisfying alternative. They are handcuffed to their careers.

Thus, the intersection of the "reward" circle with the "talent" circle on the right can provide a measure of satisfaction. But it can also lead to a dead end if you let the rewards you receive block you from seeking greater satisfaction and meaning.

Work That Ignites You Emotionally. The circle on the left includes any work you are passionate about, paid or not. This circle includes hobbies and community activities as well as conventional employment. Many people who are bound to their jobs by pension, health care, or high-salary handcuffs seek satisfaction in life by doing "passion-related" work in a domain completely separate from their work for pay. To the extent that these extracurricular activities also use their talents, so much the better.

For example, I once encountered a story about a self-employed carpenter named Richard Ryder who lives not far from my home near Philadelphia. Ryder works as a builder, but his passion is his hobby: as a Civil War reenactor, he dresses in period clothes and military uniforms from the 1860–65 era in American history (in his case from the Union rather than the Confederate side) and periodically assembles with others at the great Civil War battlefields to relive these engagements.

I reference Ryder because he has found something to do in this hobby that also utilizes special skills and hence occupies the intersection of the bottom two circles in the figure. As a carpenter who is also a history buff and a skilled communicator, he assumes a unique "character" wherever he goes: a Union army funeral director. Having made a close study of the embalming and undertaking practices of the Civil War period, he uses his carpentry skills to build authentic wooden coffins (and has even purchased a few actual historical caskets) and now speaks about his specialized knowledge to local library and community groups. On the battlefields, he sets up an elaborate camp-style funeral parlor of the type the Union army had on the march, complete with his coffins and a full set of embalming tools. He tells everyone who will listen more than they need to know about the fine arts of handling dead bodies as practiced in the Civil War period. "The only rule my wife has," he commented to a reporter after one of his talks, "is I can't keep the coffins in the house."

Meaningful Work. The place where all three circles intersect—the "sweet spot" in the middle—is where many people find the most sustainable forms of meaningful work. The balance of the chapter will explore examples of people who landed in this area. As you read these stories, consider what it might take to find work that simultaneously pays you, uses your unique talents, and either springs from a deeply felt experience or generates strong feelings of emotional satisfaction.

Foundation #1: Personal Growth and Development

Jacqueline Khan worked for thirty years with the Detroit Board of Education. Her job: truant officer. She investigated why students did not show up at school, worked with them and their families, and tried to get the kids back into the system. It was socially useful work, but there was something missing. "I liked it," she said, "but I didn't think I could learn any more." She nevertheless stayed in the job until her retirement plan had fully vested. "I wanted to have a pension, and I wanted to have health care. . . . I waited until I knew that I would be secure financially."

But even as she played out her tenure at the school board, she was investing in what she would do with the rest of her life. She went to school at night and earned a two-year associate's degree in nursing. By the time of her official retirement, she had earned a full-fledged bachelor of science nursing diploma. Her goal was to become part of an intensive care team at a hospital—a goal she achieved when she landed a job in her early fifties in a Detroit hospital trauma unit. "In nursing," she explained, "you have to be up to the challenge all the time. You have to be strong." Interviewed in her midsixties, she still loved the work: "[I am] still evolving. . . . I want to have an opportunity to do something new and different every day . . . to be involved in something that keeps my mind active."

Jacqueline Kahn has been in helping professions throughout her life. But she finds her nursing work meaningful not only because she can serve others (a foundation we will take up below) but also because it gives her ways to measure her continuing growth and development as a person. Her "gray hairs," as she puts it, give her credibility with families in distress as well as with older patients who are all too often treated with disrespect.

Jacqueline Kahn found meaning in personal development as a senior worker. But this foundation for meaning can also be especially relevant to younger people just starting out in the workforce. As Holly Robinson noted in an essay for the *Huffington Post*, "Jobs are like college courses. Each one you take teaches you a set of new skills and offers a fresh perspective on life. They aren't meant to be permanent, most of them. They are only stepping stones." Stepping stones to what? To work that fulfills you on the basis of the additional foundations discussed below. As you learn more about yourself through the work you do, you can become more purposeful in selecting the work you do next.

Foundation #2: Entrepreneurial Independence

Mary Lee Herrington graduated from the University of Pennsylvania Law School near the top of her class and four years later was earning $250,000 a year at a respected London law firm. She was also putting in sixty-hour weeks and feeling the stress of deadline-driven, intense work she had little control over. She had gone to law school looking for a career: a professional degree, an identity as a "lawyer," and financial security. She had achieved all of these goals, but she now had a much more vivid, experiential sense of the trade-offs she had made to attain them.

The work was mentally challenging, but she saw herself as a highly paid cog in a very big machine—not an image that had much meaning for her. She turned one of the wheels, but she seldom had the satisfaction of seeing the end product of her labors. The legal documentation process for multibillion-dollar corporate deals requires contributions from a small army of professional accountants, lawyers, and analysts. For some, the puzzle of getting this complex work done perfectly under deadline pressure—combined with the world-class pay and prospects of even higher status and pay down the road—might have been enough to sustain career motivation. But when Mary Lee Herrington discovered chunks of her hair falling out from the stress, she knew it was time to make a change.

But to what?

She found herself looking back on law school and asking what it was she actually liked about it. To her surprise, she realized that it had nothing whatsoever to do with law books. What she enjoyed was organizing the gala events that marked the social calendar of student life. "It was really creative," she told a *New York Times* reporter. "It was fun; I loved all the details: the party favors, the programs."

So she quit, turned part of her apartment into an office, and started her own wedding-planning service called Forever & Ever Events. Her first customer was a friend of a friend, and she was thrilled when she banked the $2,000 fee the client agreed to pay.

She quickly discovered that starting your own business is not a way to work less. In fact, she sometimes put in seventeen-hour days as a wedding date approached. And between events, she often worked late into the night doing spreadsheets and writing copy for her website. But she was no longer a cog; she was the whole machine. Her stress was now the kind that people enjoy—like the stress of a good workout.

It was not long before she had a pipeline of referrals from satisfied customers, even as glowing comments from London's top wedding bloggers began popping up on her website. "I no longer walk with a slight depressed hunch," she told the *Times*. In addition, her friends noticed how much more animated she was. "Before, I never wanted to talk about work, other than to complain." Now—as often happens when work is a positive part of your personal story—her job became a favorite topic.

People find their way to a life of entrepreneurial independence from almost every imaginable background. I once met a restaurant owner and executive chef named Robert Chickering in Santa Fe, New Mexico. I was immediately struck by the way he hovered over his tables like a mother goose minding so many goslings. He was obviously a man in love with his work, and his restaurant (named Galisteo Bistro) was one of the best in the city. Over dessert, my wife and I engaged him in conversation and learned, to our surprise, that he had once been the principal bassist with the Minnesota Orchestra. He had played in the Santa Fe Opera orchestra over several summers, and he and his wife had fallen in love with the area. His parents had run a restaurant when he was growing up, he explained, so he had an intuitive grasp of the trade. Music had been meaningful to him earlier in life—in fact, he had defied his parents to pursue his passion for the upright double bass. But the charm had worn off. Tired of the travel, the lack of control over his own time, and the backdoor politics of a big-city symphony, he quit and now creates new signature dishes blending Italian cooking with the flavors of the southwestern United States. Chickering told us he considers his entrepreneurial life every bit as meaningful as his musical one had once been.

The philosopher Bertrand Russell has described the problem that Mary Lee Herrington solved once and Robert Chickering twice. In our career-obsessed, bureaucratic world, Russell wrote, people settle too readily for a life of achieving uninspired goals set by others. They repress their "creative impulse, out of which a free and vigorous life might have sprung." His advice was to become "the artificer of what [your] own nature feels to be good." The test of whether you have found such work is simple: you feel self-respect and pride. Meaningful work, Russell wrote, makes you "happy in [your] soul, in spite of all outward troubles and difficulties."

In his book *Outliers: The Story of Success*, Malcolm Gladwell echoed Russell's sentiment, defining meaningful work as "three things— autonomy, complexity, and a connection between effort and reward. " He went on, "It is not how much money we make that ultimately makes us happy between nine and five. It's whether our work fulfills us. . . . Work that fulfills those three criteria is meaningful." And Gladwell should know. That is exactly the work he has created for himself as an independent, bestselling writer and social commentator.

The Herrington, Chickering, and Gladwell examples teach an important lesson. Meaningful work can be as simple as "autonomous work." For many, it springs from a story about how they created lives of entrepreneurial independence.

Foundation #3. Religious or Spiritual Identity

In October 2010, the Mount Merapi volcano erupted in Indonesia, claiming dozens of victims in nearby villages. The local people revered the volcano and interpreted its eruptions as punishments for offending the gods who lived there. The news of this terrible event included, almost as a footnote, the report of a death on the mountainside. "A charred body was discovered in an attitude of prayer," the announcement said. It was the body of an eighty-three-year-old man named Mbah Maridjan, otherwise known to Indonesians as the "gatekeeper." In an interview a few months earlier, Maridjan had explained his work. Through the power of his prayers and supplications, "My job is to stop lava from flowing down."

In 2006, he had become something of a public figure in Jakarta, arguing that the government was abusing the local environment and should "stop making nature suffer through our destructive behavior." Later that very year, the volcano had threatened to erupt. People begged Maridjan to come down from the mountain and avoid the danger. But he stood fast, refusing to cease the chants and prayers that guarded the villages below. The threat passed, and Maridjan acquired the status of a modern-day saint. As the people saw it, he had saved their lives.

The 2010 eruption finally ended the gatekeeper's life. But there was no doubt in anyone's mind that his work had been meaningful. "We knew long ago that Mbah Maridjan would be taken by Merapi," said a spokesman for the government on the day his body was found. "Now that he's gone, we have to choose a new gatekeeper soon."

Earlier in this chapter, I set aside the word "calling" out of concern that it carried religious connotations for meaningful work that many people might find confusing. As we have seen, religious faith is not required for work to have meaning in hospitals or in entrepreneurial ventures. But let's be clear: vocations that embody commitment to religious or spiritual values can and do constitute meaningful work for millions of people. These include all who live as monks, nuns, priests, ministers, or rabbis, as well as an even larger number who work in social service and other support organizations motivated by religious faith. The underlying work can encompass everything from Maridjan's calling as the gatekeeper to saying prayers for the dead and healing the living.

Nor does religiously motivated work have to take place under the auspices of an organization, a church, or a temple. People who see their day-to-day labors in religious or spiritual terms can experience a deeper sense of meaning in their work. Pastor Rick Warren's best-selling book *The Purpose Driven Life* (which we will discuss again in chapter 9) identifies five distinct pathways by which faith can touch and change both work and family life: daily worship, living in community with people who share your faith, following God's laws in every aspect of your life, ministering to and helping people in need, and teaching your faith to others. The Episcopal Church's *Book of Common Prayer* says this in even simpler terms: "So guide us in the work we do," one prayer reads, "that we may do it not for the self alone, but for the common good."

Faith-based work may not be for everyone. But it is a royal road to meaning.

Foundation #4: Family

We saw in chapter 3 that overbearing parents can sometimes stunt their children's search for work autonomy. But the right kind of parent-child relationship can foster a deep sense of vocation-based meaning, promoting growth in parent and child alike. In fact, researchers have identified parenting itself as a form of meaningful work that satisfies all the criteria of work as a calling.

For example, a blogger once quoted Malcolm Gladwell's autonomy-based definition of meaningful work discussed in Foundation #2 above and asked for comments. A reader replied: "Here's how I define meaningful work: Any work that provides me the means to [support] my family." Millions would agree with him, and I could fill another book with examples of people who have quit or eased back on high-paying, high-stress jobs to give more attention to their spouses and/or children—especially after a health crisis or a divorce shocked them into realizing how pointless their work was without a family to give it meaning.

The family foundation for meaningful work runs both ways. Children given the freedom to choose their own path often find meaning in the work they select by striving to justify the confidence their families placed in them.

One of Florida's current senators, Marco Rubio, illustrates this point. He was born to Cuban parents who immigrated to the United States in the 1950s. After settling in Miami, Florida, his father found work as a bartender while his mother cleaned hotel rooms as a maid.

But they did not come to America so their children could follow in their footsteps and work in hotels. They came because they wanted their children to have a better life than was available in Cuba. An interviewer asked Rubio why he did not take a traditional service-sector job. "My parents," he replied, "drove it into us that a job is what you do to make a living; a career is when you get paid to do something you love. They had jobs so I could have a career."

Rubio found his calling in politics—a journey that started at a small college in Colorado, wove its way through Santa Fe Community College, and eventually brought him to the University of Florida and the University of Miami Law School. As a law student, he interned for a local congressman and worked as a volunteer on Republican campaigns. Once he caught the political bug, he discovered that Florida was the perfect place to offer his potent combination of youth, Cuban heritage, and conservative views. He quickly climbed the political ladder, emerging at the young age of thirty-five as the speaker of the Florida House of Representatives. Five years later, he was elected to the United States Senate, and he was soon being talked about as a potential presidential or vice presidential candidate.

His rapid rise to power suggests that Rubio has more than his share of ambition. But the story he tells about the meaning of his work is not a story of climbing a career ladder or even of believing in a set of conservative ideas. It is the story of a promise he made to his grandfather—whom he called "Papa"—when he was thirteen years old. Here is how he tells it in his book *An American Son*.

His graduation from law school in 1996 was a big day for everyone. Rubio had gotten further with his education than anyone else in the entire history of his family. His parents were proud. But Rubio needed to visit someone who could not be there before he could feel the full import of the event. He goes on:

> I visited Papa's grave the next day. I remembered holding his hand as he slipped away. I remembered him squeezing mine as I swore to him I would work hard and make something of myself. Twelve years after his death, I had finally made good on my promise. It was the first time I would experience a feeling I would experience again in the years to come: my parents and grandfather living vicariously through me. They had given me their dreams—dreams they had once had for themselves. And with my every accomplishment, I was giving their lives purpose and meaning. I proved they had lived and loved and made sacrifices that were not in vain. Their lives had mattered. I felt my grandfather's presence as I walked from his grave, and I feel it still.

The meaning of Marco Rubio's work is rooted in a "deeply felt experience"—a promise made to a dying grandfather. Its sustaining power comes from the almost mythic importance of family in his Latin culture. Together, they form an enduring story he can tell about the meaning of his work.

Foundation #5: Expressing Yourself Through Ideas, Invention, or the Arts

For those with creative talents, history suggests that work involving personal, original expression—whether through music, painting, words, designs, or inventions—can be deeply meaningful. The people who choose a life of self-expression are the creators of culture in each new generation. Some starve; some prosper; some die unknown; others are celebrated. But expressive work is meaningful only when the act of creation itself brings satisfaction to the creator. It loses this essential quality when the artist begins depending on the adulation of an audience to make him or her feel significant.

Dalia Moukarker, a young Palestinian flutist, has articulated the spirit of artistic work in a particularly eloquent way. She grew up in the West Bank village of Beit Jala, a few miles from Jerusalem. As a girl, she fell in love with playing the flute, and her bedroom wall was soon covered with posters of her hero, the Swiss flute soloist Emmanuel Pahud. Getting to music lessons in Jerusalem was complicated by the political boundaries between Palestine and Israel, and her four siblings did not always appreciate her practice in their small apartment. Still, she persisted and was eventually discovered when her performance stood out at a master class conducted by Pahud himself in the West Bank. The ensuing publicity—and an associated Web video—prompted a professor from Columbia University to send her a new flute. A foundation promoting Middle East peace through classical music then started sponsoring her lessons. Finally, she was chosen at the age of twenty to take one of only four seats for aspiring flutists at a top music conservatory in Germany.

Here is how Moukarker herself explains the meaning of her music: "Music for me is my voice. It help[s] me to speak. You [must] let it out," she said. "[A]nd then you . . . live." Her Israeli teacher, Raanan Eylon, put it this way: "There was an energy in her playing that I have heard as a teacher maybe five or six times in my 45 years of teaching. It was the energy of freedom."

Self-expressive work is not limited to traditional arts like music. It can encompass everything from drawing comics to creating new applications for computers. In our high-tech, innovation-driven era, an increasing number of people find meaning in work through original, digitally oriented design, invention, and innovation. For example, in the introduction to the book, I quoted from Seve Jobs's famous 2005 Stanford graduation speech. Jobs was one of the inventive geniuses of our era, and he clearly saw his product-design work at Apple as a form of self-expression that gave his life meaning.

Another example of someone who has created a meaningful high-tech life is Peter Thiel, founder of the online payment system PayPal and a part-time teacher at Stanford's Computer Science Department. Like Mary Lee Herrington, Thiel started off on a path to a legal career, graduating first from Stanford and then Stanford Law School. But he stumbled when he failed to snag a highly coveted prize for young lawyers: clerking for a Supreme Court justice. Stunned at having lost an academic competition for the first time in his life, he dropped out of law completely and went into business. There, his keen eye for high-potential business models such as PayPal and Facebook quickly made him a billionaire.

It's a great Silicon Valley story, but I do not offer it because Thiel switched from law to business and became wealthy investing in start-ups. I offer it because he has refused to let his fame and fortune prevent him from seeking meaning in his work. In the course he teaches at Stanford, he warns students against buying into the conventional academic race that drove him to perform well in school but ended up proving meaningless. Instead, he urges them to take a less structured, more creative path based on personal aptitudes and trial and error.

His new goal: to help impatient, creative teenagers completely bypass the conventional college-and-graduate-school system by annually backing twenty people under twenty years of age with grants of $50,000 per year for two years. The only stipulation: they need to have a world-class, outside-the-box idea and be impatient enough to get moving on it to drop out of college. He is trying to give them an early taste of what a lifetime spent on creative work can feel like.

Critics have lashed out at the Thiel Fellowships for encouraging students to skip college. For the twenty Thiel Fellows selected each year, however, there is little downside. If their ideas don't work out or they discover that this free-form style of career creativity is not their pathway to meaningful work, the prestige of having won this award will reopen the door of a college somewhere. If their project launches a company, they can join Steve Jobs, Mark Zuckerberg, and Bill Gates on the list of successful college dropouts.

Foundation #6: Community—Serving a Cause, Helping People in Need

A student in my Success course named Leah once wrote a short paper about her Zeide—the Yiddish name for "grandfather." He was about to celebrate his one-hundredth birthday when she wrote about him. She described him as an unusually kind, quiet man who was a beloved member of his Jewish community in Costa Rica. He enjoyed nothing more than being with his family and providing them with comfort, support, and wisdom.

In her paper, Leah wrote that her grandfather had been in a Nazi death camp in Poland in World War II. One day, she asked him how he had managed to survive the Holocaust. "I had friends," he replied.

"We took care of each other; we made sure everybody got to pray; we shared our food and kept each other safe. Whenever God puts you in a place where you can help others, you are not in such a bad place."

Work that serves a purpose bigger than yourself—whether it is helping people in your community or serving a cause you believe in—can be a source of deep meaning. And people often combine this source of satisfaction with some of the others we have discussed above. For example, Robert Chambers's More Than Wheels organization gave him a chance to help people and, at the same time, gain the satisfaction of starting up a new enterprise. Jacqueline Kahn's job in nursing allowed her to stay on her path to personal growth.

As an example of work that springs primarily from a spirit of service to a community and a cause, I want to offer a tribute to someone whom I got to know through my negotiation work at Wharton and who reminded me of the costs that can accompany a commitment to this foundation for meaningful work.

I met Heath Robinson on his first day of my weeklong Executive Negotiation Workshop in the summer of 2010. A friendly looking man in his early thirties, he sat in the back row behind a name card that read "U.S. Navy Development Group." He was looking a little nervous and out of place among the senior business and government leaders in the program. I wondered if he was going to fit in. Within twenty-four hours, I had a different thought: I had never taught anyone more remarkable. It was over dinner that night that he revealed his occupation. He was a team leader in one of the most elite units in today's American military, SEAL Team Six (officially known as the Naval Special Warfare Development Group). A year later, this group would become famous worldwide as the unit that carried out the successful operation in Pakistan against the al-Qaeda leader Osama bin Laden.

As the week progressed, Heath filled me in on the work world he occupied. It was one devoted to rigorous professional standards and ideals of self-sacrifice. Only two or three in ten volunteers who begin the regular six-month SEAL training course finish it successfully. Many fail during "Hell Week"—a five-and-a-half-day stretch during which trainees stay awake for seventy-two straight hours while pushing themselves to the limits of human endurance as they engage in both land-based and underwater exercises. SEAL Team Six, meanwhile, is the elite unit of around two hundred men drawn from the two thousand who make it into the SEALs. Less than half of those who try out for SEAL Team Six make it. Heath was the enlisted leader (he had never gone to college) for one of the unit's combat groups.

He was, above all, a man of action who had been decorated multiple times for combat valor.

Heath stood out in our group because of the quiet, self-contained "presence" he projected. When you talked with him, you immediately got a sense of being with someone who had nothing whatever to prove. He was just there: self-confident, modest, reserved, and alert. One night he would tell us a riveting tale about a midnight combat mission; the next day he was repeating something his wife had said to him on the phone about their infant daughter. It was apparent to me that he derived his meaning in life from several sources, but high on the list was his identity as a SEAL and the pride he took in his patriotic service.

A year later, in August 2011, I was working at home when I received a call from one of Heath's SEAL colleagues, Tom, who had participated in another one of our Wharton workshops. The day before, Tom explained, Heath and most of the men in his unit had been returning from a successful mission to rescue American soldiers pinned down by the Taliban in a remote part of Afghanistan. An enemy-launched rocket-propelled grenade had hit their helicopter, instantly killing everyone aboard as it crashed.

The feelings of loss and sadness I experienced that day gradually changed to gratitude as I considered the debt we owe to all those— from combat soldiers to firefighters, medics, police officers, and diplomats—who put themselves in harm's way to serve their communities. Their work can provide both them and us with a profound sense of meaning.

Foundation #7: Talent-Based Striving for Excellence

The ancient Greeks had an ideal of meaningful work that was summed up in the word "arete." Although arete is sometimes translated as "virtue," the better meaning is something like "work performed at the highest level of excellence and effectiveness." To the Greeks, a cobbler exhibited arete by producing faultless shoes. A warrior exhibited arete through steadfast bravery in the most dangerous conditions. Thus, for our final foundation of meaning in work, I offer you a chance to aspire to the highest standards of excellence in any field for which you have talents.

People arrive at the goal of arete in many ways.

One path starts with a passion and develops it into a lifelong commitment to excellence. For example, Fred Beckey is over ninety years old, but he sleeps on more couches in more friends' apartments than

most twentysomethings. "I love Fred," one of his admirers commented, "but I'll never let him know where I live." He has never married,
has never held a steady job, and spends most of his time outdoors.
His occupation? He climbs mountains. A *Wall Street Journal* columnist
covering extreme sports once dubbed him the most prolific "first as-
censionist" in mountain-climbing history. Beckey climbed his first
peak by himself at the age of thirteen and has never stopped. He has
published a number of books on climbing over the years, including
Fred Beckey's 100 Favorite North American Climbs. He now admits that
being the first person to climb a mountain is no big deal. "Looking
back," he told the reporter, "it's kind of meaningless. It's not really
that important if I made the first climb or the twentieth." But his interest in, expertise at, and passion for climbing are not meaningless—
they are his reason for being. The only thing that has changed for
him over the years is who he climbs with. People his age won't go with
him anymore. So he climbs with people decades younger than
himself—"kids" in their twenties and thirties. "They have more free
time and more energy," he says. "I can talk them into carrying the
rope sometimes."

Others start with a talent, commit to developing it, deepen it with
hard work, and finally arrive at a passionate commitment. Cal Newport, a computer science professor at Georgetown University, wrote
an essay for *The New York Times* about his career that illustrates this
strategy. When he was a college senior, Newport considered going
down three very different roads. He was interested in becoming a
professional writer and had already written one nonfiction book; he
was offered a good programming job at Microsoft in Seattle, Washington; and he was accepted into a computer science doctoral program at the Massachusetts Institute of Technology near Boston. He
chose the doctoral program not because computers were his passion
but because he had "a slight preference" for the East Coast as a place
to live. He knew "all about this Cult of Passion and its demands," he
said, "but I ignored it." What mattered to him was not which path he
chose, but what he did once he had started down it. He has grown to
love his academic career through both his mastery of it and his discovery of additional activities—such as teaching—that have brought
out more of his talents. His advice: "Passion is not something you follow. It is something that will follow you as you put in the hard work to
become valuable to the world."

Cicely Berry's story falls somewhere between Beckey's and Newport's. She started out as a student with an interest in poetry. That
interest developed into a professional talent for coaching vocal speech.

And that talent has fueled a passion for theater. As I write this, she has been the voice director of the Royal Shakespeare Company at Stratford-upon-Avon for over forty years. Her pupils are a who's who of modern stage and film, including Sean Connery, Judy Dench, Anthony Hopkins, and Jeremy Irons. The legendary actor Patrick Stewart (*Star Trek: The Next Generation* and leading stage parts too numerous to list) credits her with fundamentally grounding his technique by helping him to link language with character in his many Shakespearean roles. In her workshops, actors are likely to find themselves saying their lines while walking, running, rolling from side to side, sitting cross-legged and whispering, and tapping their toes with hands on hips. As a girl, she says, "I learned poetry and avoided everybody." Her interest in poetry gradually blossomed into an interest in the sounds of words, and she attended the Central School of Speech and Drama in London. In addition to her work at the Royal Shakespeare Company, she coaches British prime ministers as well as experimental theater groups. As for her future, she expresses the simple mantra of those who have found the spot where passion, rewards, and talents combine at work: "I'll do it until they tell me to stop," she says.

YOUR APPROACHES TO MEANINGFUL WORK

Now, it's your turn. Go back to chapter 3 and review your answer to the Lottery Exercise. Using your answer as a starting place, push yourself to think of new work activities from the "inside out"—beginning with what your heart tells you rather than with what your family or culture say you "should" be doing. Using the stories and examples you read in this chapter, can you move past the obvious goals of high professional status, fame, and fortune? What kind of work might you find uniquely satisfying at this stage of your life? Finally, remember the three overlapping circles with the "sweet spot" in the middle. That spot locates the place where your passions, talents, and ability to earn a living overlap.

•

As you think about what ignites you emotionally, consider the PERFECT categories we talked about above. Which two or three of these seven sources of meaning speak most directly to you? Make a list of some ideas that could combine several of these foundations for meaningful work.

Check off the PERFECT work motivations below that most inspire your own passions.

- ___ **P**ersonal growth and development
- ___ **E**ntrepreneurial independence
- ___ **R**eligious or spiritual identity
- ___ **F**amily
- ___ **E**xpressing yourself through ideas, invention, or the arts
- ___ **C**ommunity—serving a cause, helping people in need
- ___ **T**alent-based striving for excellence

Here's a final word of advice. The distance between a job or career and "meaningful work" is often shorter than you think. The leap can involve a rethinking or repurposing of what you are already doing rather than a complete break with it. For example, I once took an art gallery tour in the Chelsea section of New York City led by an enthusiastic, knowledgeable guide named Rafael Risemberg. In past lives, he had studied medicine at Cornell Medical School, dropping out when he finally admitted to himself that he hated being around sick people. Next, following an interest in art, he earned a doctorate in arts and education and won a position as a tenured professor at nearby Kean University in New Jersey. He had a career, but something essential was still missing. That gap began to fill in when he started the "New York Gallery Tours" in 2002 as a once-a-month hobby. The tours took off in 2007, and he did something many of his academic colleagues thought was foolish. He gave up university tenure to become a full-time entrepreneur.

He has been enjoying meaningful work ever since. "It has become the greatest intellectual and emotional passion I have ever known," he told me. "I literally leap out of bed each morning. My definition of meaningful work is waking up with a feeling of excitement about what each day will bring."

CONCLUSION

Malcolm Gladwell once wrote that "hard work is a prison sentence only if it does not have meaning. Once it does, it becomes the kind of thing that makes you grab your wife around the waist and dance a jig." Although Robert Chambers may not have danced a jig when he was asked to visit the White House, he showed us that there is more than one way to sell cars in New England. His old workplace was a prison; the new one he created inspires employees, educates customers, and even makes money for banks.

We have explored many pathways to meaningful work in this chapter, and I hope you have realized that some of them may be closer to where you are now than you might have thought. We examined the differences between work that people consider jobs, careers, and callings (though I prefer the term "meaningful work"). Meanwhile, Professor Amy Wrzesniewski's study suggested that a job one person may consider useful only for a paycheck can be deeply meaningful to the person sitting in the next cubicle.

Po Bronson offered the perspective that "deeply felt experiences" often serve as the sources of inspiration for meaningful work, while the Georgetown computer science professor Cal Newport suggested that the "Cult of Passion" is a distraction, arguing that meaning will often emerge from a commitment to hard work that allows you to deliver more and more value in what you do.

Finally, we explored the PERFECT model of meaningful work, and you got a chance to review examples of people finding meaning from work related to personal development, entrepreneurial independence, religious values, family, expressive arts and innovations, community service, and talent-based arete.

With this chapter, we conclude the first part of the book. You have now had a chance to think in some depth about what the word "success" means to you. We examined two key outside influences that can affect your definition when it comes to outer achievements—family and culture. In addition, we examined a number of inner success factors—feelings of Momentary Happiness, your sense of Overall Happiness, Wisdom Experiences, and the satisfactions that can come from meaningful work—as things you should also consider in defining success.

In the Success course we ask two big questions. You have now asked the first one: "What Is Success?" It is time to consider the Second Question: "How Will I Achieve It?"

Success Step #4

SEEK MEANINGFUL WORK

The world of work consists of jobs, careers, and work that has special, personal meaning beyond merely paychecks or status. When your work is meaningful, you can achieve success synergy: inner satisfactions and outer achievements can spring from the same source.

The search for meaningful work usually begins with your talents and deepens into something special. But sometimes it begins with a deeply felt experience that inspires you to put your talents to a special use.

As you begin your search, consider the sweet spot where talent, passion, and your ability to earn a living overlap as well as the seven PERFECT places where many people have found meaning in their work.

| PART TWO |

THE SECOND QUESTION

How Will I Achieve It?

The next five chapters explore how you will achieve success, however you define it. Most books in the vast "how to succeed" literature focus on this "how to" aspect of the subject, but they do so in a way that leaves out a very important person—you. For example, a common piece of advice from success gurus is "Set goals." This is good advice for many people. But it may not be good advice for you if you already set too many day-to-day goals and neglect the most important ones, such as good health, meaningful work, and personal relationships.

As you read on, therefore, look for ways you can customize your own personal success process. There is no one-size-fits-all system for gaining your heart's desire. The pages ahead will give you a chance to measure your unique capabilities, motivations, mental aptitudes, and social skills. Your job is to discover the talents and mindsets that can supply your most reliable sources of strength no matter what you choose to do.

Discover What You Can Do Better Than Most:
Capabilities

You have brains in your head.
You have feet in your shoes.
You can steer yourself
Any direction you choose.

—DR. SEUSS, *Oh, the Places You'll Go!*

You must bake with the flour you have.

—DANISH FOLK SAYING

When Julia Child, the world's first television food celebrity, was a student at Smith College, she majored in history and dreamed of becoming a writer. She was tall for a woman—six feet, two inches—and this made her a bit more self-conscious than most of her classmates. But she had a positive spirit, a ready laugh, and a sense of adventure. Plus, she could write better than most of her classmates. After graduation, she moved to New York and became a copywriter for the advertising department of a furniture dealer.

She soon realized, however, that she was not happy in her work. As she confided to her diary, "I am sadly an ordinary person . . . with talents I do not use." She had found a job writing, but she was dissatisfied with what she was being paid to write.

Fate intervened when World War II broke out. She was too tall to join the military, but after investigating her options, she signed up with the government's spy agency, the Office of Strategic Services, and moved to Washington, D.C. Once she was there, her intelligence and writing skills brought her to the attention of the top brass, and she soon became a researcher for the head of the agency, General William J. Donovan.

As an OSS employee, she also began to see herself differently. "I was a playgirl, looking for the light," she later commented. In 1944, she was posted to a top secret job in Ceylon (now called Sri Lanka) and learned a new skill: screening and cataloging thousands of highly classified communications from across Asia. It was there that she met the man who would become her partner for life, Paul Cushing Child. A lover not only of Julia but also of cooking, Paul introduced her to the world of fine food.

In 1948, now married to Paul and living with him in France, she had her moment of illumination—a dinner at a restaurant in Rouen consisting of oysters on the half shell, sole meunière, green salad, and a bottle of Pouilly-Fuissé. It was, she later said, "an opening up of the soul and spirit for me," and it provided the clear signal of excitement she needed to set her on the path of learning the art of French cooking for herself. She attended Le Cordon Bleu cooking school in Paris, which led to deeper study with some of France's top chefs.

Finally, she met two French women who were writing a cookbook and joined them to help make the book suitable for American audiences. That project combined virtually all of the skills she had learned up to that time, including her writing ability, her ability to organize large amounts of written data, and her newfound passion for French cooking. The resulting work, the 734-page *Mastering the Art of French Cooking*, published in 1961, went on to become one of the bestselling cookbooks of all time.

Then excitement struck one more time, and Julia Child had the discernment to sense it. Living in Cambridge, Massachusetts, in the early 1960s, she was asked to make a brief appearance on a public television show to demonstrate how to cook an omelet. She loved it. And viewers loved her back. They demanded to see more of the style and humor this unlikely looking expert brought into their homes and kitchens. She soon launched her own thirty-minute cooking show, *The French Chef*, and—now over fifty years old—learned something new about herself. She was a gifted performer who loved hamming it up for her audience. Her signature style involved pratfalls, whoops, shrieks, and picking up ingredients she had dropped onto the floor ("Remember you are alone in the kitchen, [so] who is going to see you?"). Julia Child's career shifted to embrace activities and a form of media that had not even existed when she was thinking of herself as "sadly an ordinary person."

One response to Julia Child's story is to consider a great deal of her success as the result of luck and circumstance. She happened to get a wartime job that led her to a loving husband. That husband had a passion for food. She had the leisure time to take cooking classes at a top culinary institute in France. Her new social network connected her to people who were looking for a collaborator on a cookbook. The cookbook was an unlikely bestseller. Finally, she was in the right place at the right time when a local television station needed someone to cook an omelet on the air and an accidental pratfall transformed her into a television personality. Julia Child, this version of her story would suggest, was a remarkably fortunate person.

I think that sells her short. Julia Child once summed up her success secret in a single sentence: "The more I cook, the more I like to cook." When you enjoy some activity, you tend to practice it. And when you practice hard at something, you keep getting better. Eventually, it is something you do better than most. Sometimes it becomes something you can do better than anyone else in the world.

Take Julia Child's sentence and fill it in for yourself to see what areas of excellence you are naturally drawn to—the things you do better than most that you also enjoy. These may end up forming some of the foundations for your success.

The more I _____, the more I like to _____.
The more I _____, the more I like to _____.

Before luck can work its magic, success starts with the thing you do better than most, whether that is writing, working with your hands, doing calculations in your head, making a tight and convincing argument, cooking, or creating designs. Most important, it usually resides in the unique *combination* of capabilities you bring to what you do. Tens of millions of people are passionate about cooking. An equal number are interested in and talented at writing. But how many cooks also write exceptionally well? Relatively few. And how many of those take the time to actually write a book about cooking? Fewer still. From there, with a little luck, an alert and helpful social network, and some persistence, you may be able to develop a sweet spot for your talents, turning them into a satisfying and rewarding way to spend some part of your life—just as Julia Child did.

CAPABILITIES: THEY ARE ALWAYS
CLOSER THAN YOU THINK
....

This chapter moves us from the question posed in part 1—"What is success?"—to the new question part 2 will address—"How will I achieve it?" In this and the chapters ahead we will look at your capabilities, motivations, sources of self-confidence, mind powers, and social influence skills.

We start with your capabilities.

One of the enduring themes in the literature of success is that the tools you need to make a more satisfying life are usually close at hand. As we will see in this chapter, your genes define the outlines of your basic capabilities, and success often comes from building on what you already know—and know how to do. Julia Child liked to ham it up at parties. That ability formed one of the foundations for her successful television career.

When I first met Eric Adler, the cofounder of the SEED Foundation, whom I profiled at the beginning of chapter 1, the last thing he wanted to talk about was the thing he knew the most about—working with high-school students. He had "been there and done that." Success had to be somewhere else.

Little did he realize that his true vocation was already within his grasp. Once he discovered how to apply his past experience in a new way, he became a nationally famous social entrepreneur who has pioneered a unique model to provide a high-powered high-school education to at-risk teenagers.

One of the most famous motivational speakers in America in the late 1800s and early 1900s was a lawyer turned Baptist minister named Russell Conwell. Conwell gave the same motivational speech somewhere between five thousand and six thousand times during his life and made enough money delivering it to launch a "workingman's" educational institution that remains an important part of Philadelphia to this day: Temple University.

Conwell's speech featured a fable that perfectly captures what so many of the successful people we have read about so far demonstrated: the future opens up when your past interests, experiences, and skills start resonating perfectly with an opportunity you find in the present. You may have heard Conwell's story before (it is a classic), but listen while I tell it again—based on a transcript of Conwell's speech.

ALI HAFED AND THE BUDDHIST PRIEST

When Reverend Conwell was a young man, he took an overland trip in the Middle East with a party of English travelers. The group hired an old Arab guide in Baghdad to lead their camels along the banks of the Tigris and the Euphrates rivers. This guide kept the party entertained with folktales and fables.

"Many of these stories I have forgotten," Conwell would tell his audiences, "and I am glad I have. But there is one I shall never forget."

Here is the story.

There was once a man named Ali Hafed, a prosperous farmer who lived near the Indus River in Persia. Hafed was a wealthy, happy man who owned a large farm with orchards, grain fields, and gardens.

One day, Ali Hafed was visited by a Buddhist priest, "one of the wise men of the East." Over the course of his stay, the priest told Ali Hafed how the world had been made, and at one point mentioned how diamonds had come into existence. The great wealth from even a few diamonds might be enough to place all of Ali Hafed's children on royal thrones, the priest said. Ali Hafed had no knowledge of diamonds, but he was seized with a great desire to get some. He begged the priest to tell him where these diamonds could be found.

"Well," said the priest, "if you find a river that runs through white sands and between high mountains, in those white sands you will always find diamonds."

Ali Hafed wondered if this could be true. "I don't believe there is any such river," he said.

"Oh yes, there are plenty of them. All you have to do is find them, and then you will have all the diamonds anyone could ever want."

So Ali Hafed sold his farm, left his family in the charge of a neighbor, and set off to search for the white sands, the high mountains, and the diamonds. He was years on the road. He traveled throughout the Middle East; he looked all across Europe. But search as he might, he found nothing. As years passed, he was reduced to rags and wretchedness. Eventually, in despair, he threw himself into the ocean off the coast of Spain and drowned, a broken man.

Meanwhile, back on Ali Hafed's farm, the new owner was watering his camel one day in the shallow water of the river just behind the main house, when he spied a "curious flash of light from the white sands of the stream." He pulled out a stone and saw that it reflected "all the hues of the rainbow." It was not long before he discovered that the river in Ali Hafed's backyard was littered with diamonds. One had only to reach into the stream to turn up ever larger and more beautiful stones. The farm went on to become one of the largest diamond mines the world had ever known.

After telling this story in his talk, Conwell would launch into a litany of examples of people who had found success—both literally and figuratively—in their own backyards. He adjusted the speech to suit each audience. In New York, Ali Hafed's backyard became the opportunities awaiting anyone willing to invest in New York. When he spoke to salespeople, Ali Hafed's backyard was a salesman's skill at listening to his customers to discover their needs. Everywhere he went, he emphasized that it was not the talents and opportunities people *lacked* that held them back—but rather the capabilities they *already possessed* that they were not using. Conwell would then conclude, "You must begin where you are and [with] what you are"—and start today, right now, this minute to find your own "acres of diamonds."

The Acres of Diamonds speech made Conwell rich and helped establish a great university. And, as Julia Child's story testifies, Conwell's basic insight remains as valid today as it was then. The *New York Times* writer David Brooks (author of *The Social Animal* and other books on contemporary culture) summed up the situation most people face these days. We have become, he wrote in his newspaper column, a society that rewards people who "maximize their talents" by discovering and exploiting "their own interests, lifestyles and capacities." To make progress in a world that encourages this freedom, he said, you must start with the aptitudes, skills, capabilities, and passions you already have. These become your bridges to what comes next. Sitting at home and complaining that life would be fine "if I only had . . . a better relationship, a different boss, a new job, money-making talent, an advanced degree, more lucky breaks," etc. gets you nowhere.

Identifying your unique combination of capabilities is not the final step in success. You will still face competition, frustration, failures, and false starts. But this is always the necessary first step. As the old Danish folk saying goes, each time you face a transition in life, "you must bake with the flour you have."

Unfortunately, finding your way forward by looking inside is as hard today as ever. First, as always, this is sensitive, personal work that requires patience, faith, and persistence. Your capabilities may be hidden in your own backyard, but they are still partially hidden—at least from you. Second, with the 24/7 distractions of social media, entertainment, news, and celebrity, it takes more self-discipline and honesty than ever before to assess yourself accurately.

In the pages below, I will give you some practical guidance and examples to get you started. I will start by showing you how to "notice" your unique capabilities. Then I will give you a chance to explore your backyard to see if you can find some diamonds of your own. These will take the form of your:

- interests and passions,
- aptitudes and skills,
- past experience, and
- personality strengths.

LOOKING FOR DIAMONDS:
THE ROLE OF DISCERNMENT

What exactly is involved in "looking" for diamonds? Is this something you do with your eyes or is there something else going on? In a society where many are seeking to maximize their talents, there are no shortages of expensive assessments, life coaches, and career-counseling systems to help you look. For some people, these may be just what are needed. But in the end, they all come back to your ability to be self-aware and honest with yourself about two things.

First, you must pay attention when you feel dissatisfied with the status quo. Without some measure of dissatisfaction, you lack the motivation to start your search. Julia Child faced this challenge early in her life. She realized she had reached the end of the line as a copywriter for a company in New York. She wanted something more—though she was not sure exactly what. That put her on the road to finding a new job, and she ended up working for a high-ranking official in the secret service.

Second, you must tune in to your inner voice—your intuition—and monitor the excitement you are feeling about your new directions. Sometimes, as happened to Julia Child while she was attending college, your longing for the culturally attractive goals of status, fame, or fortune can create false signals. She dreamed of being a professional novelist or writer. She got excited about her dream and headed for New York to live it. Once there, however, reality set in. She discovered that dreaming of "being" anything is usually a false signal. Writing advertising copy was not what she had had in mind when she imagined life as a "writer." She gave up on her dream of "being" something and seized the opportunity to "do" something when World War II came along.

As you put yourself in motion and start doing new things, be sensitive to your reactions. You are experimenting, and your inner sense
of excitement will direct you to the capabilities and interests you are
looking for. You will feel an initial rush, followed by a longer, slower
process of constructing your bridge to the future.

The Jesuits use a special word to describe this sort of process-based,
attentive self-awareness. They call it "discernment." Discernment is
one's willingness to listen for God's voice as you make important
choices regarding lifestyle, vocation, and relationships. But you don't
need to believe in God to cultivate your powers of discernment. You
just need to learn how to listen to your heart and start looking for the
four diamonds we will discuss below—the capabilities that are in your
own backyard and that will create your bridge to the future.

Diamond #1: Interests and Passions

No matter who you are or what stage of life you are in, you have natural interests and passions for particular activities, subjects, sports,
people, careers, purposes, shows, media, or even games. And these
are a very good place to start as you look inside. I am always interested when someone says, "Yes, I have a passion for ___, but what does
that matter? Everyone has a passion for ___." Isn't this just another
way of following Ali Hafed on his misguided, lifelong quest for success everywhere except his backyard? First of all, "everyone" does not
share your passion for Broadway, Hollywood, detective work, running, hockey, or gardening. You just happen to know many who do
and fewer who do not—out of the tiny percentage of mankind you
have interacted with in some way. Second, some people in your world
are filling their lives with work directly or indirectly related to the
very things that fascinate you.

Why not join them?

Your interests or passions sometimes go all the way back to your
childhood. Think about the hobbies and activities that occupied your
youth. Is there something there worth tapping back into? When my
wife's younger brother was a boy, he had a unique habit. He would
write to Fortune 500 companies requesting their annual reports and
read them cover to cover. His boyhood room was stacked high with
colorful business publications that would put most of us to sleep. But
they kept him up at night—and he has made his career in professional investing. He currently sits on the governing board of his graduate school alma mater, the Yale School of Management.

Or take the case of one of the greatest aviators of her era, Betty Skelton. When she was eight, she was famous in her neighborhood for her collection of brochures from airplane manufacturers. Her excitement about flying soon infected her parents, and all three of them (Betty was an only child) began to take flying lessons. Soon, her mother and father became so interested in aviation they opened their own flight school. Betty made her first solo flight at the age of twelve by sneaking out one day and taking off in one of the instructional planes by herself—a daredevil stunt that upset her parents, who refused to let her fly solo again until she was sixteen.

As an adult, Skelton became a champion aviator and stunt pilot at air shows. She flew alongside the top navy pilots of her day as the "Sweetheart of the Blue Angels" and set both altitude and speed records. In 1960, just after the Mercury space program got under way, a magazine sent her to take the fitness tests being given to the men trying out to be the nation's first astronauts. She passed them all—earning, from the original seven Mercury astronauts, the affectionate title of astronaut "No. 7½."

As a child, did you have an avid interest that ignited your imagination? Go back to that interest now and see what it might take to get involved in it as an adult. You will be amazed at how much you will find in common with the people you meet as you start to reintroduce yourself to this field of activity—whether it be old comics, bicycling, nature, or the history of a world war.

Perhaps your youthful passion was for a sport. A professional golfer named Bubba Watson won the top golf tournament in the United States—the Masters—in 2012. He was thirty-three, and this was only his fourth win on the pro tour, an unusually modest record of accomplishment for a Masters winner that far into his career. He won the hearts of both the crowd and the general public, however, when he made a "miracle shot" during a sudden-death play-off round after tying for the lead at the end of the regular tournament. His 160-yard wedge shot from a terrible lie in the rough off the fairway zipped under the limbs of some nearby trees before rising, hooking sharply to the right, and coming to rest fifteen feet from the pin.

Unlike many professional athletes, Watson was never coached. In fact, he never had a single golf lesson. He was, in other words, a "natural"—someone who learned the game for fun as a child and stayed in it for love as an adult.

As *The Wall Street Journal* put it in an article about him after his Masters win, it was "love at first sight" for Bubba, at the age of six, the moment his father gave him his first golf club. Watson ran outside and immediately started hitting whiffle balls around the yard. "At the time," reported Watson, "I didn't know it was practice; it was just something fun to do." As his youthful swing developed, he began drawing five-foot circles on the driveway and then seeing how many strokes it took him to hit his whiffle ball all the way around the house and back into the circle—first going clockwise by hooking the ball around each corner and then going counterclockwise using slices to bend the ball around the house. If the ball landed in a bush, he played it from the bush. These childhood yard games turned out to be perfect preparation for his miracle shot at the 2012 Masters.

Of course, many childhood passions are pipe dreams. It is no use spending your time fantasizing about becoming a world-class basketball player if you are five foot four and cannot run. But there are many careers related to the multiple levels on which basketball is played all over the world that do not require you to be tall. Your passion for a sport can help spur thoughts related to coaching, local news coverage, Internet blogging, or even organizing Make-A-Wish Foundation dreams for sick children to meet celebrity athletes.

Moreover, if you are actor Michael J. Fox (who measures five foot four), you may find that being shorter than average as a child can become a source of competitive advantage—if you think about it the right way. In his case, his shortness gave him the extra motivation he needed to outwork and outhustle his peers. That useful habit stayed with him as an adult.

"As a kid who was short," Fox has said, "I've always thought, 'If being short is my biggest problem, then life is a bowl of cherries.' I still feel that way now, no matter what I face." Currently living with Parkinson's disease and increasingly unable to control his body's erratic shaking, Fox scored an Emmy nomination for guest-starring on a television series as a lawyer who used his Parkinson's condition to manipulate the sympathies of a judge and jury. In the hands of someone who sees even his handicaps as capabilities, a debilitating disease can become a distinctive asset.

Start your diamond hunt by surveying your passions and interests. Do not leave anything off the list just because you think it is too "common." After all, cooking and eating are pretty common interests. So are flying and golf. Yet these activities became the foundations for some successful lives, as we have seen in this section.

Diamond #2: Aptitudes and Skills

The search for your capabilities also involves cataloging the things you do "a bit better than others"—your natural talents. Note well: I am talking not about the things you "wish" you could do better than others but rather about what you can actually do better. This facet of success starts with understanding the role your genes play in your abilities.

Over one hundred years of research confirm that talent begins with genetic heritage. Nancy Segal, a psychology professor and director of the Twin Studies Center at California State University, Fullerton, has spent her life researching and writing about the effects of genes on ability and personality. Her specialty is the study of identical twins who have been separated at birth and reared in different families. Her overall conclusions are summarized in *Born Together—Reared Apart: The Landmark Minnesota Twin Study* and are as definitive as any scientific finding from the physical sciences: genes are the single most important variable in the skills and aptitudes people show later in life. As Professor Segal once summed it up, "virtually all measured human characteristics show some degree of genetic influence."

Take mental ability. In 1979, a group of scholars at the University of Minnesota led by Thomas J. Bouchard began investigating fifty-six sets of adult identical twins who had been reared apart in adoptive homes that spanned the socioeconomic spectrum. The twins were located as adults and given over fifty hours of intensive psychological, physiological, and IQ tests. Comprehensive histories were taken related to their upbringings. This data was then compared with similar data collected from identical twins who had been reared together in the same households. If family environment contributes more than genes to later ability, one would expect to see bigger differences in IQ scores between the twins who had been reared by different families than between the twins who had been raised in the same households. The study published in the journal *Science* in 1990 showed there were no such differences. Identical twins ended up with the same IQ scores no matter who raised them.

The economist Bryan Caplan of George Mason University is the father of identical twins and has studied the social implications of twins studies as well as a related stream of "adoption" research that looks at whether adopted children turn out more like their adoptive or biological parents. Caplan's conclusion based on both research streams is laid out in his book *Selfish Reasons to Have More Kids: Why Being a Great Parent Is Less Work and More Fun Than You Think*. Although parents, himself included, tend to obsess over their kids' successes, he writes, the truth is that "the most influential gift that parents give their children is not money, connections, or help . . . but the right [DNA]." How you were raised may dictate your religious/political affiliations as well as the amount of affection you feel toward your parents, but your ultimate income level, educational attainment, and professional status will have a lot to do with the genes your parents passed on to you.

Given the importance of genes, the question becomes: what do your genes make possible for you and how can you build on that inherited foundation? I like to think of DNA as a set of *potential* capabilities. Your experiences in life—both in and out of your home—interact with your genes to bring out those capabilities so they can become skills and talents the outside world observes. The biologist Richard Dawkins illustrates the relationship between genes and abilities with an example of beavers and dam building. The genes of a beaver give it the capability for making dams. But it is the pressures of the beaver's environment that create its dam-building skills. Dawkins calls dam building an "extended phenotype," or expression, of the beavers' genes.

Because your skills and aptitudes have a genetic basis, they sometimes become obvious very early in your life. Research studies show that children as young as three endowed with mathematical ability can excel at tests which ask kids to estimate when "more" or "fewer" dots are displayed on a fast-changing screen. Scientists have a special name for this ability to guess at the answers to math problems without actually counting: "number sense." Better-than-average eye-hand coordination—such as that shown by six-year-old Bubba Watson when he gripped his first golf club—is another common example.

One of my Success students, Gina, recounted in class how, as a child, she had loved building models. She could sit for hours with Legos, Lincoln Logs, blocks, and Tinkertoys making whatever suited her fancy. As she grew older, she graduated to construction kits, SimCity computer games, and design programs. In college, she enjoyed most the classes that taught her how to create and test mathematical, analytic models.

It came as a bit of a surprise to me, therefore, when she entered class one day grinning broadly and reporting that she had landed her "dream job" working in finance on Wall Street. I feared that she had succumbed to the lure of fame and fortune and was joining the crowd to chase after the big money. Then she explained: she would be part of a high-powered team building mathematical models to analyze risks for emerging markets and new types of investments. As she spoke, I could see that, for her, the leap from Tinkertoys to complex financial models was merely a step on a single path. Her eyes lit up as she spoke of her new opportunity.

In your search for things you can do better than most, consider the pressures from your youthful environment that shaped and honed your skills. For example, recent research shows that there are distinct human genes for physical "endurance" versus physical "strength." People with the endurance gene are better long-distance runners; those with the strength gene are better sprinters. If you have the gene for sprinting and are asked by the coach of your middle-school track team to specialize in the hundred-yard dash event, your talent will accelerate faster than if you have the long-distance gene. Your "nature" would be expressing itself through the "nurture" of your new, intensive sprinting practice. And, everything being equal, you would have a good chance of becoming a relatively successful sprinter in high school and college. This same process can take place for anything having a strong genetic basis, from cognitive skills to social abilities.

Human intelligence makes the gene-environment interaction especially dynamic. Unlike a beaver, you can choose to expose yourself to new experiences and environmental pressures throughout your life. And when you find yourself able to make rapid progress in any new activity, the chances are that you have triggered a new genetic "expression." You will have discovered a genuine talent or aptitude.

As part of your survey to discover your natural aptitudes and skills, ask people who know you to suggest lists of what you do well with relatively little effort. Do you have a knack for fixing broken household appliances? Can you do math or word puzzles in your head? Everything counts. The next step is to think of the different ways those aptitudes can be used to create value for other people.

For example, Cape Cod native Liam Haveran grew up in the small town of Chatham, Massachusetts, and attended a technical high school, where he learned the plumber's trade. "It was great," he said. "It was what I wanted to do. It was nice being outside, meeting new people, [and] I enjoy working with my hands."

But a few years spent fixing sinks and toilets brought the realization that he needed to make a change. He liked the manual labor but not working in the small, dark crawl spaces that Cape Cod houses are famous for. "Those spidery, dust-filled spaces—that was what I hated about it," he said.

He befriended some local college students and, before long, he began taking classes at a local community college, working at his plumber's jobs by day and attending classes at night. As his schooling progressed, so did his thinking about what he might want to do. A fitness buff, he considered becoming a physical therapist or a chiropractor. That led to a wild idea: perhaps he could attend medical school. Before long, he was on a premed track. As a nontraditional student with a poor foundation in science and math, he found the schoolwork (combined with plumbing work) "daunting," he said. But he pressed on. "One of the characteristics I remember about Liam," his former high school guidance counselor commented, "is that perseverance."

His hard work paid off, and Haveran was finally admitted to the Philadelphia College of Osteopathic Medicine when he was thirty years old. Residencies followed, and Haveran quickly discovered that his love for working with his hands gave him a gift for surgery. Being a surgeon also gave him the satisfactions that come with having an immediate, positive effect on a patient's illness. "You could fix a problem with surgery," he said, which is not always the case with traditional, pill-based medicine.

He returned home to practice medicine, setting up his office not far from many of the Cape Cod homes he had formerly worked in as a plumber.

Liam Haveran has a talent for using his hands, a skill that formed the foundation for two separate but related careers: plumbing and surgery. What are some aptitudes you have that may form the foundation for new and interesting pathways into the future?

Diamond #3: Past Experience

All of the examples we have looked at so far share two central lessons. First, when it comes to capabilities, each stage of your life builds on the last. Successful people almost always find constructive ways to repurpose what they have already done to help launch themselves into their next stage. Your capabilities change and expand as you move from your first jobs in high school or college through later career moves, hobbies, and additional education and training.

Second, successful people are smart about reaching out to create the experiences they need to give them credibility for the leap. After her life-changing dinner in Rouen, Julia Child did not just go home and start reading French cookbooks. She enrolled in a top cooking school in France where she could learn from the best. Plumber turned surgeon Liam Haveran did not just stay at home dreaming of being a doctor. He started studying math to finish college and then applied to medical schools.

Both Child and Haveran followed this capabilities-based pathway toward the future:

Insight on Skills/Aptitudes ⟶ Idea for the Future ⟶ New Experience
⟶ Next Career Activity

New experiences—especially those associated with getting trained and credentialed by experts in a field—frequently open up areas of activity you have never explored. And it is in the combination of these activities with your prior experiences, skills, and aptitudes that you will often find fresh, potentially satisfying ways to spend time.

This is not an accident. The process of gaining new experiences usually exposes you to a social community of people deeply interested in a specialized area of knowledge or practice. That network then gives you both psychological reinforcement and access to new ideas and new ways of thinking about how to use your existing capabilities.

Finally, keep in mind that the process of gaining experience usually involves improvisation and trial and error. As we saw in the story about Julia Child, people often get new ideas about who they are and what they want to do as they expose themselves to a series of new experiences. You need to be ready to change direction as you figure out which aspects of a new activity actually suit you and which do not.

The Final Diamond: Your Personality Strengths

One of the most important capabilities you bring to any activity is your unique combination of personality-based strengths. For this part of your diamond hunt, I can help you directly by offering you a personality-strengths test I have developed and now use at Wharton. Over the years that I have taught the Success course, I have tried a variety of tests and profilers to help students understand the capabilities that arise from their personalities. I have assigned

- the Myers-Briggs Type Indicator (MBTI),
- the StrengthsFinder system developed by Donald O. Clifton and the Gallup Organization,
- the VIA Survey of Character Strengths created by Professors Martin Seligman and Christopher Peterson, available through the University of Pennsylvania's Positive Psychology Center, and
- various popular assessments based on the most rigorously researched model of personality—the Big Five typology of openness, conscientiousness, agreeableness, extroversion, and neuroticism pioneered by Paul T. Costa Jr., the chief scientist at the National Institutes of Health's Laboratory on Personality and Cognition, and his NIH colleague Robert R. McCrae.

Below, you will have a chance to take an assessment I devised that borrows and combines something from each of these sources and is targeted at four key aspects of your personality that I believe relate most directly to success: your attitudes about other people (Social Styles), your drive to achieve (Action-Orientations), your inclinations toward intellectual or creative activities (Mindsets), and your emotional response system (Emotional Temperaments).

Unlike some web-based personality profilers, this one has no mysterious, hidden algorithm behind it that magically tells you, after thirty minutes of answering questions, that you are an "achiever" or a "relater." There are just a series of words and labels I have carefully selected from the personality literature for your key personality traits. Your job is to decide which labels fit you most often.

The exercise requires two steps. First, take the assessment yourself. Next, supplement your perceptions about your own personality with feedback from people who know you well. After using this profiler in class, I require my students to seek comments on their strengths, weaknesses, personalities, and capabilities from the widest possible circle of people who know them—from parents and siblings to coworkers, bosses, clubs, housemates, and friends.

This dynamic process of gaining self-understanding from observing how other people see you is something the psychologist Charles Cooley called the "Looking-Glass Self" in his book *Human Nature and the Social Order.* We learn a lot when we see ourselves reflected in the looking glass of other people's perceptions. And you will be surprised to learn about the different versions of "you" other people reflect back to you based on the social role you play when you interact with them.

Of course, in the end, you—and only you—get the last word on defining yourself. As Shakespeare's mighty King Lear begins his slow descent into self-doubt, he asks his Fool, "Who is it that can tell me who I am?" His Fool replies that only Lear himself can answer that question.

THE SAME PERSONALITY ASSESSMENT

Below are sixteen short descriptions of personality traits that give you a chance to characterize yourself along four key dimensions of personal difference: **S**ocial Styles, **A**ction-Orientations, **M**indsets, and **E**motional Temperaments. The first letters of these four areas make the acronym SAME. They constitute the facets of your personality that I believe can help you most in defining your pathways to success. Mark the place on the continuum for each trait that seems most accurate for you most of the time. If you can easily switch between the two labels given, mark the spot halfway between the two.

Social Styles

1. "Introverts" are people who thrive on quietness and reflection and prefer social interaction with other people in smaller, more intimate groups. Socializing with large groups often depletes their personal energies. "Extroverts" are socially gregarious—people who enjoy large social gatherings and feel energized by socializing. Being alone for too long can sometimes make an extrovert uncomfortable and anxious.

Introvert				Extrovert
100	50	0	50	100
Highly Expressed	Moderate	No Preference	Moderate	Highly Expressed

2. "Agreeable" people are warmhearted. They strive to get along with everyone and to be liked by all. They prefer to follow. "Dominant" people have assertive, take-charge personalities. They prefer leading to following. They like being in command.

Agreeable				Dominant
100	50	0	50	100
Highly Expressed	Moderate	No Preference	Moderate	Highly Expressed

3. "Cooperative" people are quick to compromise in conflicts and negotiations. They prefer to measure themselves against internal rather than external benchmarks and like to measure success in terms of solving everyone's problems. A "competitor" enjoys winning the negotiation game, feels satisfaction when he or she hits external benchmarks that separate the "great" from the merely "good," and can turn even the most boring activity into a game of some sort to make it interesting.

Cooperator				Competitor
100	50	0	50	100
Highly Expressed	Moderate	No Preference	Moderate	Highly Expressed

4. "Adaptable" people can fit into almost any social setting. Like a good actor or actress, they can play many social roles with ease, depending on the demands of the situation. "Direct" people are blunt and greatly value authenticity. Less socially smooth than adaptable people, they pay more attention to problems and facts than to subtle social cues. With a direct person, "what you see is what you get."

Adaptable				Direct
100	50	0	50	100
Highly Expressed	Moderate	No Preference	Moderate	Highly Expressed

Action-Orientations

1. "Planners" are orderly people who like to make lists, stick to their agendas, and sometimes err in the direction of perfectionism. "Improvisors" are people who prefer to act based on intuition, instinct, and spontaneity. They are less organized than planners, but they think that's fine.

Planner				Improvisor
100	50	0	50	100
Highly Expressed	Moderate	No Preference	Moderate	Highly Expressed

2. "Strivers" are ambitious. They live for their work. They are passionate about getting ahead, getting things accomplished, staying busy, and working toward their long-range goals. They tend to measure success in terms of accomplishments. "Relaxed" people are less intense and industrious than strivers. They have jobs to make money so they can have time to enjoy themselves with friends and family, and take in the pleasures of life. A comfortable early retirement sounds good to people who are relaxed. They tend to measure success more in terms of overall quality of life rather than career accomplishments.

Striver				Relaxed
100	50	0	50	100
Highly Expressed	Moderate	No Preference	Moderate	Highly Expressed

3. "Deliberative" people take their time making up their minds between various alternatives, weighing all possibilities. They want to minimize regret and are more likely to second-guess themselves. "Decisive" people like to make decisions quickly based on the information at hand. They are biased toward taking action to see what happens, learning, and then making another move.

Deliberative				Decisive
100	50	0	50	100
Highly Expressed	Moderate	No Preference	Moderate	Highly Expressed

4. "Risk Takers" seek out novelty and thrills. They like roller-coaster rides—the steeper, the better. They would be more inclined to start a company with their own money, try their hand at professional poker, or think about becoming a stunt pilot. "Cautious" people like to play it safe, prefer the tried-and-true, and avoid needless risk. They dislike gambling and consider it foolhardy to seek out dangers simply to experience a thrill.

Risk Taker				Cautious
100	50	0	50	100
Highly Expressed	Moderate	No Preference	Moderate	Highly Expressed

Mindsets

1. "Intellectuals" like to play with and explore abstract ideas. They enjoy learning for the sake of learning and seek to understand current situations in terms of their histories. "Practical" people value ideas mainly in terms of how they will work. They do not enjoy abstract thinking or academic study unless they see the connection to concrete problems that need solutions.

Intellectual				Practical
100	50	0	50	100
Highly Expressed	Moderate	No Preference	Moderate	Highly Expressed

2. "Analytical" people look for objective data and proof to make sense of the situations they face. They are systematic thinkers who prefer clear lines. "Creative" people are open-minded, subjective, and more often live in the worlds of their imaginations. They prefer to scribble all over the page, or even tear the page into pieces and make something original with it.

Analytical				Creative
100	50	0	50	100
Highly Expressed	Moderate	No Preference	Moderate	Highly Expressed

3. "Traditionalists" are conservative when it comes to change. They like the way things are and seek to preserve the values and tested practices of the past before endorsing some uncertain plan for the future. "Revolutionaries" prefer to challenge the status quo. They value change, are quick to notice the flaws and unfairness in how things are working, and have idealistic visions of how to create a better world.

Traditionalist				Revolutionary
100	50	0	50	100
Highly Expressed	Moderate	No Preference	Moderate	Highly Expressed

4. "Knowledge Specialists" see the world through the lens of a few "defining ideas" (such as religion, politics, or science) and prefer to know a great deal about a few subjects. "Knowledge Generalists" are integrators of information and traditions. They read widely and constantly seek out a variety of experiences to enrich their overall judgment and understanding—but seldom think they have "got it all figured out." Philosopher Isaiah Berlin once wrote an essay called "The Hedgehog and the Fox" in which he described these two mindsets. "Hedgehogs" are the specialists. "Foxes" are the generalists.

Knowledge Specialist				Knowledge Generalist
100	50	0	50	100
Highly Expressed	Moderate	No Preference	Moderate	Highly Expressed

Emotional Temperaments

1. "Passionate" people experience their emotions intensely and consider them central to their experience of life. When they fall in love, their love is all-consuming. When they hate, their hatred burns like fire. "Even-Tempered" people are more into their heads than their hearts. They experience themselves more as thinking than feeling—even though they are aware of their emotions as being an aspect of their personality. They, too, fall in love. But they have to "figure it out," whereas a passionate person immediately knows what has happened.

Passionate				Even-Tempered
100	50	0	50	100
Highly Expressed	Moderate	No Preference	Moderate	Highly Expressed

2. "Optimists" place a positive emotional spin on most events. They see the cup as half full and are able to quickly recover from setbacks to find the silver lining in whatever happened. "Realists" take life as they find it: happy, sad, heroic, and tragic. Although realists are not pessimistic all the time, they are pessimistic much more often than is an optimist. Where the optimist sees the silver lining in every cloud, the realist sees the clouds—and plans for the rain to follow.

Optimist				Realist
100	50	0	50	100
Highly Expressed	Moderate	No Preference	Moderate	Highly Expressed

3. "Emotionally Expressive" people show their feelings and are easy for other people to read. When they are happy, others know it. When they are sad, they cannot hide it. They tend to be emotionally demonstrative and volatile. "Emotionally Restrained" people appear cool and collected on the outside, and do not indulge in emotional displays. They are harder for others to read and tend to rely more on rationality and logic in communicating. They have great poker faces.

Emotionally Expressive				Emotionally Restrained
100	50	0	50	100
Highly Expressed	Moderate	No Preference	Moderate	Highly Expressed

4. "Easily Stressed" people dislike the anxiety that often comes with pressure, deadlines, and emergencies. They look for guidance from others to get through the storm. "Calm-Under-Pressure" people thrive on crisis or deadline pressure. When the emergency is on, these people slow down, stay composed, and remain focused. Indeed, they sometimes need the stress of deadlines to stay motivated and alert.

Easily Stressed				Calm Under Pressure
100	50	0	50	100
Highly Expressed	Moderate	No Preference	Moderate	Highly Expressed

ANALYZING YOUR SAME RESULTS

This final section will help you analyze your results from the SAME exercise so you can use this information as part of your work on success. First, I will ask you to identify, from the items above, the shorter list of your "key personality traits." These are the ones where your mark was closest to the 100 level for being "highly expressed" rather than nearer to the 0 position at the midpoint. Feel free to include any traits that you marked between the 75 and 100 levels.

Your Key Personality Traits

Record your key personality traits—and only those traits—in the spaces below. The marks you had nearer to the middle of each scale represent functional, adaptive aspects of your personality that easily change to suit the situation or people you face. These are strengths, of course, but they are not the kind of *distinctive* strengths that might give you hints as to the direction you should take for a future career or an important next step in your life. What you are looking for are the strongest elements of your personality—the aspects that are "you" at your most authentic, stable, and differentiated. The part of you others would be most likely to notice or seek out for specialized activities.

Your Key Personality Traits

Social	Action	Mindset	Emotional
_____	_____	_____	_____
_____	_____	_____	_____
_____	_____	_____	_____
_____	_____	_____	_____

Once you have made your lists, see if any patterns emerge from the items you wrote down above. For example, if your profile shows key personality traits for extroverted, dominant, competitor, risk taker, and decisive, you obviously have a very strong social personality and you need to be in control of most situations. You would be a poor fit in a soft-spoken, team-based, relationship-oriented environment (say, being the head of human resources for a company or managing a child-care center) but would probably make a great boss on the trading floor of a major hedge fund. Moreover, these strong social traits would probably fit especially well with a practical mindset and a calm-under-pressure emotional response to crises. With this package of personality-based strengths, you would tend to handle emergencies relatively well.

By contrast, suppose you had only one key personality trait from each of the four categories: extrovert, relaxed, creative, and optimist. This might be a workable combination for someone doing creative work for an advertising agency. The three traits of extrovert, creative, and optimist would play well into the social, intellectual, and emotional demands of dealing with clients and selling in a creative market. The relaxed trait would describe someone who likes to work on their own schedule, enjoys leisure, and probably experiences "bursts" of industriousness rather than someone who relishes working on a rigid schedule.

When you are engaged in an activity that feels especially suited to you (i.e., it "fits" your key personality traits), very little friction is being generated between your capabilities and whatever you are doing. You may experience what positive psychologists call "flow"—a sense of absorption in your activity that causes you to lose track of time and perform whatever you are doing at your highest level of skill. But when you feel consistent dissatisfaction, the chances are good either that you are not using some of these key personality traits in the best way—or that you are being asked to display traits that do not come easily to you.

Here are some examples of key personality traits that may be well suited to particular jobs—although it is difficult to say for certain what traits would work without knowing both the industry and the company culture where the job is located. Use these examples to speculate on the kind of work activities, careers, or functions that might suit your personality especially well.

....

Sample Career/Personality Combinations

....

Accountant: introvert, planner, deliberative, analytical

Actor: improviser, adaptable, passionate, emotionally expressive

College professor: introvert, intellectual, analytical, knowledge specialist

Consultant: extrovert, planner, practical, analytical

Entrepreneur: competitor, risk taker, practical, optimist

Litigation attorney: competitor, decisive, realist, calm-under-pressure

Military Special Forces Operator: introvert, improvisor, decisive, calm-under-pressure

Politician: extrovert, agreeable, striver, deliberative

Sales: extrovert, agreeable, cooperator, optimist

A special case can be made that there is one occupation—parent—for which any combination of key personality traits is appropriate. The best parents combine their authentic selves with genuine love and concern for their children.

THE FINAL STEP: FEEDBACK
FROM YOUR SOCIAL NETWORK
....

With the information you have gathered above, it is time to go out to those in your social network and ask them for input. One simple way to do this is to copy the SAME assessment above and e-mail it to your friends, family, and colleagues. Ask them to suggest what they think would be your "top four" key personality traits. Ask them, if possible, to give some examples of your behavior that form the foundations for their perceptions. Then see how those perceptions overlap with each other and with your own self-assessment ratings. Where you have questions, follow up and ask to speak with the members of your social network who are the "outliers" or who make comments you would like to explore further.

CONCLUSION

Where should you begin as you start your search for the capabilities that will bring you success? In the nineteenth century, Temple University founder Russell Conwell suggested that your own backyard is a good place to look. So do the success writers of our own era. In Paulo Coelho's bestselling, modern success book *The Alchemist,* a young shepherd boy named Santiago suffers from Ali Hafed's illusion that great wealth is the secret to success. He sets off from his home in Spain to search for gold that is fabled to be hidden in the pyramids of Egypt. Luckily, unlike Hafed, Santiago does not die along the way. Instead, after many adventures and a series of encounters with wise teachers, he learns the essential lesson. The secret to success lies within himself—in his own "Personal Legend" (described by Coelho as the path "God has chosen" for each person that produces in him or her a sense of genuine "enthusiasm"). With that wisdom, Santiago is able to learn that the fortune he seeks is buried beneath the tree back in Spain where his journey began. He returns, digs up the treasure, and lives happily ever after with his true love, Fatima, a girl he met on his journey. The book has sold over twenty million copies.

This chapter has given you a chance to look inside yourself, to survey your interests, aptitudes, experience, and key personality traits. When you supplement these with the right credentials and the willingness to work steadily toward your goals, you have the foundations for excellence in almost any domain.

Virtually all of the examples we looked at—from celebrity chef Julia Child to plumber turned surgeon Liam Haveran—demonstrated the power of discovering your genuine capabilities and then putting them to higher and better uses. Often, as happened with Julia Child, an inspirational moment ignites a new interest or passion—and you suddenly find that your skills, experience, and personality flow together to carve out a new path in life. No matter what, you need to listen to your heart and keep searching for better ways to use your personality strengths.

With your capabilities in mind, we are ready to take the next step toward success—summoning the motivational energies that you need to keep those skills and aptitudes in motion.

What sets you on fire?

Success Step #5

LOOK INSIDE TO FIND YOUR UNIQUE COMBINATION OF CAPABILITIES

Don't go looking for diamonds in remote places when you already have them in your own backyard. Your diamonds include your

interests and passions,

aptitudes and skills,

past experiences, and

personality strengths.

Your success will spring not from a single, world-class talent but from your unique combination of these capabilities.

Set Yourself on Fire:
Motivation

Success is not the result of spontaneous combustion. You must first set yourself on fire.

— FRED SHERO, PROFESSIONAL ICE HOCKEY COACH

When the Princeton mathematician Andrew Wiles was ten years old, he started to solve the most puzzling problem in mathematical history, Fermat's Last Theorem (conceived in 1637). He did not get out pen and paper or begin writing proofs. Instead, after reading about the puzzle at his local public library, he felt the first stirrings of what would become a lifelong passion.

"It looked so simple, and yet all the great mathematicians in history couldn't solve it. . . . I knew from that moment that I would never let it go. I had to solve it," he said. Two decades later, as a mathematics professor at Princeton University, he learned that recent developments in math theory had made work on the theorem a "respectable" academic project. "I was electrified . . . the course of my life was changing," he said.

Beginning in 1986, he set aside all of his other research efforts to focus exclusively on making his childhood dream come true. He started by planning exactly how to proceed. First, he decided to work in complete secrecy in order to avoid the public attention and distractions that followed anyone known to be working on this world-famous puzzle. He also wanted to make sure that he would get credit for the solution, should he find it. Academic life, like sports and business, is a competitive enterprise, and Wiles, according to science and mathematics writer Simon Singh, had the "craving for glory" that often characterizes people who strive to be the best in their fields. Had Wiles revealed his progress at each stage of his work, someone might have stepped in at the last minute and beat him to the final proof. The only person who knew he was working on the Fermat problem was his wife—he kept even his closest colleagues at Princeton in the dark.

Second, to throw people off the scent, he decided to publish the small advances in math theory he expected to make along the way. This would also allow him to keep his scholarly reputation intact while he immersed himself in the Fermat problem.

Remarkably, Wiles never once used a computer. As eight long and frustrating years passed, his desk became a mass of "scribbles and doodles." This was his way, he later said, of letting his subconscious mind play with the complex problem. But his motivation was unrelenting: "I would wake up with [Fermat] first thing in the morning; I would be thinking about it all day; and I would be thinking about it when I went to sleep."

In the second year of his quest, disaster nearly struck. He woke up to headlines that a Japanese mathematician had solved the Fermat puzzle. Wiles held his breadth while the scholarly community picked apart the details of the proof—then exhaled when the proof failed. The hunt was still on.

In year five, Wiles caught a lucky break. During a chance encounter with John Coates, his friend and former Ph.D. supervisor, at an academic conference, he heard about some new work on a special set of equations that opened a bridge to the answer. Finally, in year seven, with hundreds of pages of proof to back it up, Wiles announced his discovery at a dramatic public lecture—only to spend yet another year addressing various technical concerns raised by his scholarly colleagues. In 1994—year eight of his journey—it became official: his colleagues agreed that Wiles had solved Fermat's Last Theorem, and he won a permanent place for himself in the math hall of fame. *People* magazine named him, along with Princess Diana and Oprah Winfrey, as one of 1993's most "intriguing" people of the year.

What motivates someone to devote his life to abstract, high-level math theory—and stay with it for years of concentrated, lonely work? Wiles explained his drive in a way that will resonate with anyone who loves solving puzzles or problems of any kind—from the daily crossword to curing cancer. It is, he said, like exploring a mysterious, unlit mansion with many rooms: "One enters the first room of the mansion, and it's dark. Completely dark." Gradually, after bumping into various objects, "you learn where each piece of furniture is." Finally, Wiles says, you find the light switch and at last you can see exactly where you are and where everything is. "Then you move into the next room" and repeat the process. The moments of insight and illumination come suddenly; the work to achieve them is slow, methodical, and painstaking; and the experience of finally discovering the solution is deeply satisfying.

The inner fires that kept Wiles focused were a perfect combination of intense curiosity, professional pride, and competitive drive. Wiles worked hard because he enjoyed his occupation. He worked in secret because he wanted to win a place in math history.

TWO KINDS OF MOTIVATION: INNER SATISFACTION AND OUTER REWARDS

Given your chosen success target, this chapter continues your work to answer the question "How will I achieve it?" In the preceding chapter you began the search for your inner "diamonds"—your interests, passions, skills, and personality strengths that allow you to do some things better than most. This chapter will help you explore the unique motivations that enable you to put those capabilities to work.

Wiles's story illustrates a key point about motivating yourself to succeed: you often need two kinds of energy. First, there is the slow-burning fuel of innate, satisfaction-based motivation such as Wiles's need to figure out the answers to complex puzzles. Second, there is the hotter, more urgent energy of competition for resources, rewards, and recognition. The first kind of motivation aims you in a direction and gives you a reliable, steady, renewable supply of energy to keep moving. The second turbocharges your performance, adds adrenaline, and powers you up when you need a motivational surge.

Many modern self-help writers disparage reward-based motivations. Pointing to Abraham Maslow's ideal of self-actualization, they suggest that satisfaction-based, do-what-you-love energy is all you need to succeed. The titles of popular books from this genre say it all: *Live the Life You Love* and *Do What You Love, the Money Will Follow.* But I strongly disagree with this either-or way of thinking.

Perhaps because I come from a practical background in law and business, I appreciate the power that competition brings to everything from sports and business to science and space exploration.

Satisfaction-based motivation is critically important to sustaining any interest or activity for a long period of time. But without reward-based drives, you may lack the intensity needed to do your best work. In fact, my colleague Angela Duckworth, the University of Pennsylvania psychologist, has shown that the promise of external rewards can even raise an IQ score. Simply by offering children a payment for doing well on an IQ test, she raised their scores by fifteen points. As the story of Andrew Wiles demonstrates and every major athletic or academic competition confirms, the highest levels of performance result from a combination of *both* satisfaction and reward-based motivations.

Consider the following example of effectively harnessing the combined powers of interest-based and competitive energy to advance innovation. A few years ago, an IBM computer named "Watson" made history by beating an all-star lineup of former champions from the quiz show *Jeopardy!* in a head-to-head contest between humans and computing power. The man who led the team that created Watson was David Ferrucci.

Ferrucci recruited a unique group of twenty-five volunteers—all talented computer scientists who would normally be working on their own private projects—to rally to the challenge of creating an artificial intelligence system that could defeat the smartest *Jeopardy!* players in the world. The team then operated out of a "war room" he created for the project and parked their egos at the door as Ferrucci melded them into a group that focused on competing as a team instead of competing as individuals.

At first, Watson gave irrelevant responses to the *Jeopardy!* prompts. It had been years since most of the team members had worked on the problem of programming computers to respond to spoken language, and it took time, effort, and patience for them to grapple with this issue. "We had to keep the team's collective intelligence from being overcome with egos or dragged down by desperation," Ferrucci commented. But the team was soon infected with Ferrucci's enthusiasm and gradually came to share his urgent desire to win what would be a nationally televised contest.

The competitive energy that charged the group helped them win. But their steadier, more satisfaction-based motivations inspired Ferrucci and some members of his team to continue their work. With their *Jeopardy!* victory behind them, they are adapting what they created to help humans and computers work more closely together in a number of important fields—notably health care. The Watson project innovations are likely to create significant value for generations to come.

FIND YOUR MOTIVATIONAL BALANCE
....

Researchers have been debating the origins and characteristics of human motivation for decades. Most now agree that motivations originate with brain chemistry. The natural release of dopamine in the reward centers of the brain, as well as the supplies and balance of neurochemicals such as endorphins, oxytocin, adrenaline, and serotonin, come together to create pleasant and unpleasant mental states. From their earliest childhood, humans seek experiences that produce pleasant mental states and seek to minimize those that cause pain, shame, or frustration.

Evolution has programmed in a relatively short list of human needs associated with these neurochemical rewards. Although different scholars give different answers as to which needs are the most "basic," the following list of six is a useful place to start.

To greater and lesser degrees, most people are naturally motivated to:

- satisfy primal needs for food, shelter, clothing, and reproduction;
- experience sensory pleasure;
- achieve social acceptance by satisfying the need for affiliation, group membership, and a sense of belonging;
- feel capable of autonomous action (i.e., to feel competent);
- gain status, power, money, or control of resources that are associated with holding a respected place in society; and
- discover and defend beliefs that provide a sense of meaning and order amid the uncertainties of life.

We will see later on that your SAME personality profiler from the preceding chapter can help you identify the needs that motivate you most. This can be useful because studies show that the greater the chemical reward to your brain, the greater the effort you may expend to obtain it. There is a phenomenon in psychology known as the "Crespi effect," named after the scholar who first demonstrated it in the 1940s. Professor L. P. Crespi showed that a rat running a maze will double its speed if it thinks there is double the reward waiting for it at the end of the tunnel.

The study of motivation spans more than one hundred years of psychological research—and researchers are still debating the relative importance of the satisfaction-based versus reward-based motives. On one side are the traditionalists who think that external rewards dominate. In the first half of the twentieth century, behavioral scientists believed that people, like puppies, learned to do things through conditioning—by being rewarded for doing them or punished for not doing them. Mainstream economics, which emerged about the same time, has a similar picture of human behavior. Do you want to sell more soap? Offer a discount. If you want children to learn their multiplication tables, offer a gold star on their homework.

This simple, clear picture of motivation was complicated by lab findings that rats and monkeys explore new areas of their environments, help each other in distress, and (in the case of monkeys) appear to enjoy solving simple puzzles—all without any traditional reward-based or penalty-based motivation. Indeed, sometimes animals will ignore available rewards to pursue these satisfaction-based activities.

This insight led to an explosion of research on so-called intrinsic motivation (my term for this is "satisfaction-based motivation") that added a welcome depth to our understanding of what makes people tick. To the basic motivations to eat, drink, reproduce, seek pleasure, and fight for status, scientists added the desire to affiliate with social groups and the need to experience ourselves as independent, competent agents in our own life experience. In his excellent book on satisfaction-based motivation, *Drive: The Surprising Truth About What Motivates Us*, Daniel Pink describes these as the innate desires for "freedom, challenge, and purpose."

This new research also explored the tensions and trade-offs that sometimes arise between the search for inner satisfactions and the quest for outer rewards. It turns out that the quest for rewards can sometimes crowd out—and even spoil—the inner satisfaction of an activity. For example, if you are an amateur artist who enjoys painting, some of that joy may fade if you start producing mass-market landscapes solely for the money. Your painting could become a repetitive chore instead of a labor of love.

If you let reward-based motivation take over completely, burnout will not be far behind. In his book *Modern Madness: The Emotional Fallout of Success*, the Washington, D.C., psychotherapist Douglas LaBier chronicled a litany of inner failures in the lives of outwardly successful executives. As they charged toward ever more unrealistic goals, they put their family relationships at risk and started looking the other way when their work involved conflicts with basic moral values. The results? Depression, withdrawal, and self-sabotaging behaviors such as extramarital affairs and abuse of alcohol or drugs. When no amount of money can compensate you for the stress and misery you are experiencing, you may also start to cut corners by turning in sloppy work, cheating to hit targets, and overstating expense accounts. Worse still, you have no energy left to seek genuine satisfactions outside work—with family, friends, hobbies, leisure activities, sports, or other interests.

If all you are getting from your hard-but-unsatisfying work is the opportunity to do more of it, it is time to make a change.

SATISFACTION-BASED MOTIVATION: THE ROLE OF PERSONALITY

The literature on satisfaction-based motivation tends to treat all the satisfactions on Daniel Pink's list—freedom, challenge, and purpose—as equally motivating to all people. But that is not how it works. A Wharton colleague of mine, Adam Grant, has documented the fact that different personality types require different motivational boosts to do the same work. He conducted a series of studies in call centers and other work settings and found that some people were motivated mainly by the challenge of getting the work done right, while others required a motivational boost from a reminder of the purpose behind the work. In his study he introduced all the call-center employees to some of the people whom their work directly benefited. The employees who had conscientious, industrious personalities found the purpose-based information interesting—but it had no effect on their productivity. Those who were less innately conscientious, however, worked harder after they better understood the purpose of their work.

If you think about it carefully, you will realize that there is a pattern to the activities from which you get the most innate satisfaction. Highly extroverted people get more satisfaction when they spend their days on challenges that require interacting with others. In fact, they can actually *replenish* their motivational energies this way. Highly intellectual people get more satisfaction from the challenges of engaging with abstract ideas. As you seek a good motivational balance, therefore, an important source of information comes from the SAME personality profiler you took in chapter 5. When your personality suits both your work and your social environment, you get a motivational "free ride." You are programmed to gain satisfaction from the situation you are in, which means you can sustain the effort longer with less risk of burnout. This fit between personality and activity is also relevant to your search for meaningful work—the subject of chapter 4.

Look back at the key personality traits you discovered in chapter 5 using the SAME (Social/Action-Oriented/Mindset/Emotional Temperament) framework. The trick is to find activities that dovetail with your personality and then do more of them. For example, action-oriented risk takers who seek lives of adrenaline-pumping excitement—such as the Navy SEALs I have worked with in my negotiation workshops—are energized by and attracted to danger. The SEAL motto is "The only easy day was yesterday." SEALs are most motivated when they are on the most perilous assignments. As one of their officers once told me, "The only motivation problems I have with my men is when they are stateside between deployments. They don't like being on the sidelines of the action. I have to keep them busy to keep them happy."

To help illustrate this point, I have provided four case studies below—one for each of the SAME categories: Social, Action-Oriented, Mindset, and Emotional Temperment. As you will see, it is easier to sustain motivation when your personality fits your activity. You can then turbocharge yourself with rewards-based motivation when the situation calls for extra effort. As you read these examples, ask yourself what kinds of activities you find energy producing rather than energy depleting. Then look for opportunities to engage in more energy-enhancing work in your day-to-day life.

Social: You Are Motivated to Help

To keep a promise he made to his parents, James Herr worked on his family's Pennsylvania chicken farm until he was twenty-one years old. But the lonely days left him longing for more. "He wanted to do something that would get him out and be around people," his son later said. In 1946, with his fiancée Miriam, he paid $1,750 for a fledgling potato-chip company and was soon making the chips by day and selling them door-to-door in the evenings. Decades later, their one-man-one-woman operation had blossomed into Herr Foods, employing over one thousand people and boasting annual sales of $100 million based on the popularity of Herr's Potato Chips.

Most of James Herr's success derived from his love of being around other people. He was a gifted salesman, and it was said he knew the first names not only of his biggest customers, but also of every person in his food-processing plant. And he used his gift for remembering names to inspire his employees, motivating them to take as much care as he did with the production details of turning out a high-quality, premium product. He was also deeply involved as a leader in his Mennonite church.

He was known in his community as much for his Christian faith and generosity as for his skill in business. And he kept most of his many philanthropic acts secret so that nobody would think he was using his charitable works to promote himself or his company.

He was offered the chance to cash in by selling his company many times, but he never did. Instead, he used his business to promote his values. His motto was simple: "Always try to be a blessing to people." He died at eighty-seven in his wife's arms—on the day of their sixty-fifth wedding anniversary.

James Herr was an extrovert; he loved mixing and mingling with strangers and friends alike. But even introverts need to be around people some of the time, and can replenish their motivational energies with the right kinds of social interaction. And most of us are renewed when we reach out to help others in need.

Ask yourself: for whom is your life a blessing?

Action-Oriented: You Are Motivated to Take Risks

Laura Dekker is a Dutch woman who gets bored quickly unless her life includes challenges and risks. As an introvert, she also values and enjoys spending time with herself. She has found a unique way to combine these motivations through the sport of competitive sailing.

At the age of sixteen, she completed a one-year project to sail her thirty-eight-foot, two-masted sailboat named *Guppy* on a record-breaking journey around the world. She stopped at various ports along the way so she could do homework for her Internet-based high school and connect with her parents and supporters. But all her actual sailing was done solo, allowing her to become the youngest person on record to circumnavigate the globe alone. The final leg of her journey was a nonstop voyage of 5,600 nautical miles across the Atlantic from Cape Town, South Africa, to Saint Martin in the Caribbean.

Born on a sailboat while her parents were docked in New Zealand during a seven-year, round-the-world cruise, Dekker spent the first years of her childhood on water. After the family returned home to the Netherlands, she made her first solo sailing trip at age six on her *Optimist* (a dinghy) crossing the lake where she lived. She started planning her round-the-world voyage when she was thirteen.

Her sailing exploits began causing a stir when, as a young teenager, she sailed solo from Holland to England. English authorities insisted that her father come to sail her home. When she formally announced her plan to sail around the world, Dutch officials inter-

vened, obtaining a court order to prevent her from leaving and arguing that she was too young for such a challenging journey.

She persevered and, with her parents' help, ultimately got the
court order lifted. On January 20, 2011, she set sail from Saint Martin,
and she returned to it on January 21, 2012, after circling the globe.
The Guinness World Records organization announced that it would
not be noting Dekker's achievement, having stopped recognizing records for youthful sailing accomplishments back in 2009 so as not to
encourage reckless attempts that might place children in harm's way.
But she was glad she set the record—even if it would not be recorded
by Guinness. Dekker's final blog entry for her journey also showed her
key traits: a strong Mindset orientation that matched up well with her
Action-based personality. She wrote that the journey had given her a
unique opportunity "to learn much about myself, to learn about the
world, and to fulfill my lifelong dream."

Mindset: You Are Motivated to Understand

According to the old saying, "Curiosity killed the cat—but satisfaction brought him back." The human impulse to "understand" is one
of our basic drives that can bring great satisfaction when met. As
Michael Shermer argues in his book *The Believing Brain: From Ghosts
and Gods to Politics and Conspiracies—How We Construct Beliefs and Reinforce Them as Truths*, people are "pattern seeking" animals. We gain a
sense of reassurance from insights that explain how the world works,
thus reducing the uncertainties of life and contributing to our sense
of stability in a chaotic universe.

As a twenty-one-year-old student at Cambridge, Stephen Hawking
was diagnosed with Lou Gehrig's disease—a neurodegenerative condition of the brain and spinal cord that ultimately causes a person to
lose complete control over his or her body. It is usually fatal within
two to three years. As his disease progressed, Hawking's ability to
function became more and more limited. When he was twenty-eight,
he was completely paralyzed and confined to a wheelchair. Beginning at the age of forty-three, he needed round-the-clock care. Eventually, he could communicate only by using eye movements to pick
out letters and spell words that were conveyed via computer and a
customized voice synthesizer. These days, he communicates via a tiny
infrared sensor that picks up pulses of movement from his cheek and
selects words displayed on a computer screen. It can take ten minutes
for Hawking to complete one sentence.

Faced with these obstacles, Hawking has continued to contribute stunning achievements that have changed astrophysics, revolutionizing our modern understanding of concepts such as black holes and the big bang theory of how the universe began. *A Brief History of Time*, his 1988 book, sold over ten million copies, and he has been honored with just about every prize his academic discipline can offer. Topping it all off, he (or his synthesized voice) has appeared as a guest on both *Star Trek* and *The Simpsons*—two of his favorite television shows.

Although Hawking's remarkable story displays many forms of motivation at work, his monumental drive to understand the hidden patterns in the world around us is what makes his life distinctive. "My goal is simple," Hawking explains. "It is a complete understanding of the universe, why it is as it is and why it exists at all." He combines a remarkably clear-eyed realism about the human condition with a soaring vision of what humans are capable of.

Emotional Temperment: You Are Motivated to Express Feelings

Emotionally expressive people need outlets for their feelings. For many, a passionate life connected in some way to art is a perfect way to channel their expressive motivations. One of the most famous intellectual circles of the early twentieth century was known as the Bloomsbury Group, a loose confederation of English artists and intellectuals who lived in London and included the novelist Virginia Woolf and the economist John Maynard Keynes. This group spawned one of the most famous love affairs of modern times between two women, the writers Vita Sackville-West and Violet Keppel.

Their passionate, socially unconventional relationship formed the background for no less than three books written at the time, including Virginia Woolf's *Orlando: A Biography*, and many more in the decades since. As one essayist described their relationship, "Violet loved Vita . . . so above and beyond what society allowed that she was deemed crazy, as are most women who are obsessively, wildly in love." In a letter to her beloved Vita, Violet wrote: "Heaven preserve us from all the sleek and dowdy virtues, such as punctuality, conscientiousness, fidelity and smugness." Violet Keppel's vivid, self-conscious inner life became the basis for her art, her poetry, and her many other writings. She set the pattern for a literary, bohemian lifestyle.

For someone with an emotional personality, self-expression is not work. It is a necessity. You do not need to summon special effort to be self-expressive in either your intimate relationships or some form of art.

As you look into your own personality, what motivations seem to come most naturally to you? Are you inspired by wide-ranging social interactions, gritty achievements, sustained attention to intellectual pursuits, or emotionally expressive activities? Are you putting these motivations to their most productive use? By matching your personality-based motivations with your most important activities, you increase your chances for success.

STAYING MOTIVATED: SIX RENEWAL RITUALS

No matter what your sourses of motivation, you need ways to renew it as you move through a day that poses different challenges and calls on different levels of effort. When I teach the Success course, I ask students to list all the private motivational rituals and techniques they use to keep themselves in motion and maintain their motivational balance. I am always amazed at the variety of strategies they report—from things as simple as taking hot showers or long walks to elaborate recordings of their own voices to use as alarm clocks and multistep rituals that help them get motivated to take high-stakes exams.

What are some of the ways you renew your motivational energies? Here are six techniques that can make the difference between success and failure. Test these in your life and see if they can help you stay energized to achieve your goals.

1. Make Yourself Accountable: Bring Your Posse

Social accountability can generate a lot of motivation. If you have trouble staying motivated yourself, set up a support group to reinforce everyone's energies. A woman named Deborah Bial has created a successful program that sends bright but underachieving inner-city kids to college. She now has six hundred students from eight cities attending forty different colleges. And they are thriving—90 percent graduate, half make the dean's list, and 25 percent earn academic honors.

Her organization is called the Posse Foundation and her insight is a powerful "shape the path" idea. She noticed that these teenagers tend to orient their lives around a peer group (i.e., their "posse"). So she created a program in which specially screened low-income students from the same city—all smart but with SAT scores and high-school records that would not get them admitted to top colleges—are admitted to the same school *as a group*. She then provides them with a set of social bonding experiences in high school that continue after they enroll in college. The posse holds its members accountable, motivating everyone in the group to do homework and take pride in their group identity. Said one former Posse Foundation scholar from Brandeis University who is now following a business career, "The buzz around school [was] that Posse kids are cool and smart." By providing a supportive peer group for these teenagers, Bial has tapped into a powerful set of reward-based and esteem-based incentives that are helping her students succeed.

This posse principle is the secret behind the success of almost all team sports, and a great coach is usually good at reminding his or her players that there is no "I" in the word "team." One of my favorite stories about sports motivation comes from a professional team that plays in my hometown of Philadelphia. In 1974, the Philadelphia Flyers—our National Hockey League franchise—was one game away from winning its first Stanley Cup championship (the World Series of professional hockey) in team history. Game six was the final home game of the series for Philadelphia and the team's best chance to claim the championship trophy. If Philadelphia lost, the final matchup would be in Boston before the fanatical, screaming fans of the opponents, the Boston Bruins.

Many coaches might have summoned a passionate, fire-and-brimstone speech to motivate their team in a situation like this. But that was not the way of Fred Shero, the Flyers' quiet, introverted coach. Nicknamed "the Fog" for his tendency to get lost in his own thoughts in the middle of practices, he liked to write offbeat motivational sayings on the locker room blackboard before games. One of his favorites was: "When you have bacon and eggs for breakfast, the chicken makes a contribution, but the pig makes a commitment."

On the night of the Stanley Cup championship game, as the players filed into the locker room, they all looked at the blackboard to see what Coach Shero wanted them to think about. Here is what he had scrawled there: "Win Today, and We Walk Together Forever."

The team went out on the ice and gave it everything they had, scoring a thrilling 1–0 victory and setting off one of the largest citywide celebrations in Philadelphia sports history. Over two million people lined the downtown streets the next day to cheer at their beloved team's parade. At a Flyers game I attended recently, a special booth was set up where several of the players from that 1974 team—nearly forty years after their Stanley Cup victory—

were autographing Flyers logo gear for eager fans. They were still "walking together."

The genius of Fred Shero's "Win Today, and We Walk Together Forever" message is the way it appealed to three of the six basic human needs listed at the beginning of this chapter. At the most obvious level, a "win today" would give the players a coveted *social status*: Stanley Cup champions. At the same time, by winning as a team, they would "walk together"—an appeal to the *social affiliation* and respect they would feel for each other. The word "forever" heightened the motivation one more level into something especially *meaningful*—their lives would change as that one day's work became a permanent part of their city's history.

2. Connect with Role Models: Find People Who Inspire You

Another very common way to maintain your motivation is to seek out and connect with inspiring role models. A variant on this is to collect motivational slogans, tapes, books, or speeches made by people who are effective at communicating the messages you need to hear. The success industry is especially well equipped to supply these because, in large measure, that is its basic business model. Indeed, motivational speakers make their living delivering the same basic message in as many ways as possible.

As part of my success research, I once drove down to South Philadelphia's giant indoor sports arena to an all-day Get Motivated! Seminar. The sponsors had been running full-page ads in the local papers to drum up an audience. For only five dollars, you could hear from an all-star lineup of inspiring role models that included Charlie Manuel (the coach of the Philadelphia Phillies, which had recently won baseball's World Series), ex–New York City mayor Rudy Giuliani of 9/11 fame, and retired five-star general and former secretary of state Colin Powell.

But the big draw for me was the chance to hear an eighty-two-year-old motivational speaker named Zig Ziglar, whose website identifies him as a "National Treasure." It isn't every day that you get a chance to watch an old pro like the Alabama-born Ziglar work his crowd magic in person. He would be retiring soon and I wanted to hear him. Unlike the other speakers, Zig (his real name is Hilary Hinton Ziglar) had not accomplished anything like winning a sports championship or saving the nation from its enemies. But he was a rock star in the world of sales training.

Zig started his professional speaking career in the 1970s with a Christian message before he transitioned to sales motivation and success. Although he sells a lot of books and tapes (the usual business for motivational speakers), I admired him because he never seemed to take himself too seriously and never pretended, as some success gurus do, to have coached luminaries such as the pope or Nelson Mandela. I had listened to some of Zig's tapes, and he sounded just like the guy who owns the Chevy dealership in my rural Virginia hometown. I can only describe it this way: his voice made me want to buy something from him—anything.

When I got to the arena, the parking lots were filling up and the food-cart vendors selling big pretzels and hot dogs were out in force. Inside, it looked like a Ringling Brothers circus had come to town—only it was a "success circus." Groups were selling motivational CDs, how-to-succeed books, self-hypnosis tapes, and all kinds of success gear. There were Get Motivated! tote bags and books, inspirational refrigerator magnets, and colorful wall posters declaring "Believe in Yourself and All Things Are Possible." Finally, the music cranked up and we all took our seats. Soon people were clapping, boogying, and shouting out responses to messages flashing up on the arena scoreboard.

Then we settled down to listen to the speakers. We heard the humble and soft-spoken Charlie Manuel remind us that teamwork is the way to win championships; the harder-edged Rudy Giuliani spoke about the need for "relentless preparation" to be ready for the unexpected. Colin Powell, introduced with great patriotic fanfare, spoke about what leadership really means.

Then came the man I had been waiting for, "National Treasure" Zig Ziglar.

He did not disappoint. His years melted away as he bounded onto the platform at the center of the arena and launched into his talk. He paced from one side of the stage to the other, now going down on a knee, now throwing his arms in the air, then lowering his voice to tell an inside joke about his over sixty years of marriage to his wife, Jean ("the Redhead"), now stabbing the air with his finger as he urged us to live every day of our lives with intensity and intention—just as he had done every day of his life. He had probably given this speech thousands of times, but he delivered every word as if he had just thought of it.

Early on, he hit a practical note, reminding us that success means taking care of business. There is no shame in having a little money.

"Money isn't the most important thing in life, but it's reasonably close to oxygen on the gotta-have-it scale."

His smooth accent gave his voice a folksy ring as he shifted gears and pleaded with us to banish the word "failure" from our vocabularies.

"You haven't really lost if you learn from a defeat!"

He wrapped it all up at the end by giving us one of his signature lines—the secret to his long and successful life in a single sentence.

"You can have anything in life you want, if you'll just help enough other people get what they want!"

He left the stage to thunderous applause.

Later that day, I marveled at the power some people have to inspire others. When you are feeling a little lost or perhaps at the end of your usefulness in a particular job, there is nothing like exposure to someone who has done something truly worthwhile to get you back in motion. And hearing some good solid advice—delivered with energy—can also help. Zig told us all exactly how to get ahead: give people something they want and they'll reward you for it, don't let failure get you down, and keep your eye on the money.

3. Create a Motivational Ritual: Make It a Habit

I am sure you have a few motivational rituals to help prepare you for peak performance moments or power you through activities that would otherwise be boring or repetitive. For example, few things do a better job of stirring up emotional energy than music. Stop in at any exercise club, and you are sure to find most people powering themselves through workouts plugged into their favorite motivational-song list. Sports teams often use shared musical rituals to get pumped before games. A group of exercise psychologists studying music as a motivator recorded the following report from one high-school football player:

> I guess the biggest thing here before the games, we listen to a Phil Collins song, *I Can Feel It in the Air Tonight,* and we turn off all the lights and even though it's a slow song, it has that one part where it breaks down, and at that time everybody starts screaming and banging on the lockers and then we go get on the buses and go to the game.

The human mind is wired to respond to associations. When you smell chocolate cookies, your mouth starts to salivate, even if you are not especially hungry. The same thing is true for motivation. Although music is one of the most powerful associational engines of them all, virtually any motivational routine can activate your energies.

Want to get motivated to cook a great dinner? Create a ritual of neatly laying out all the items you will need before you get started. Want to motivate yourself to do well on a test? I once had a student who dressed in her best, most stylish interview outfit every time she took an important exam. Her pretest ritual of dressing for success helped her focus. Although her classmates teased her for taking her work so seriously, she had the last laugh at graduation—where she took honors. She also landed a job she wanted after school based on her academic performance.

Once you start your motivational ritual, it is a lot easier to get any hard-to-start activity under way, from a sports contest to cooking.

4. Compete with Yourself: Make Up a Prize

Employers pay us for our work and, if we are lucky, praise us for our accomplishments. But the competitions that motivate you need not originate from sources outside yourself. Many people talk themselves into being energized by creating inner competitions, prizes, penalties, and challenges for what they are doing. Entrepreneur Mary Kay Ash (founder of Mary Kay Cosmetics) once put it this way: "Competition can be a very strong motivation. But I have learned that it becomes most powerful when you compete with yourself."

One way to do this is to create your own reward-penalty plan for exercise, dieting, studying, or completing work assignments. The award-winning novelist Joyce Carol Oates—author of over fifty novels, numerous short-story collections, and eight volumes of poetry—once told a reporter about a motivational trick she uses to keep herself productive. She happens to love, almost to the point of obsession, cleaning and straightening her house. "I go into a very happy state of mind when I am vacuuming," she said. So she uses that as bait to keep herself on track with a writing project. As she notes, "The cleaning is something I use as a reward if I get some work done."

5. Prove Someone Wrong: Show Them What You've Got

Have you ever felt the sting of someone saying, "You'll never make it—you might as well give up?" You don't actually need someone to say that to use it as motivation. Just turn on a technique my students and I call "I'll show them!" Although I think this motivational boost has its limitations—built as it is on measuring yourself against others' expectations—entire careers have been built on it.

The humor writer George Plimpton authored a series of award-winning books about his amateur exploits playing on a professional football team (*Paper Lion*), pitching in a Major League Baseball game (*Out of My League*), and performing at Harlem's Apollo Theater (the short story "I Played the Apollo"). Reflecting on his motivation, he later wrote that his life's work was a form of payback to high-school teachers who thought he would fail. He was driven "to show my mentors at Exeter that I had somehow managed to intrude onto the highest plateaus of their various disciplines." Similarly, a high-ranking nonprofit executive interviewed in *The New York Times* admitted that she was still running on the energy provided by a professor who had once refused to give her a summer internship decades earlier. "I have been trying to prove that guy wrong my whole adult life," she reported.

6. Channel Your Strongest Emotions: Turn Up the Heat

The most powerful, hardest-to-control energies come from your basic instincts and drives. These include protecting yourself and your family from harm; obtaining food, shelter, and clothing; ensuring financial security; finding sexual gratification; and, psychologically, maintaining your sense of individual dignity. You can tell when any of these are threatened because you will feel very strong and urgent emotions, usually anxiety, fear, and/or anger. Your human survival instincts are hardwired to your brain's strongest emotional response systems, and it is virtually impossible to resist being motivated by them when they are fully engaged. Your heartbeat and breathing speed up, muscles tense, adrenaline pumps, and attention narrows.

Here is the interesting thing about survival motivation: successful people are often able to channel it. As Fred Shero said in the quote that opened this chapter, "Success is not the result of spontaneous combustion. You must first set yourself on fire." These drives, properly invoked, are the fuel that lights the brightest of those fires. Anyone who has played competitive sports, worked on a deadline, negotiated a high-stakes deal, or performed onstage knows that a level of "creative stress" based on strong emotional energy can be crucial for success.

For example, I was once talking with a friend about his work as an attorney. He is an Ivy League–educated lawyer who had just brought a company back from the brink of bankruptcy by successfully negotiating legal settlements worth hundreds of millions of dollars.

His technique? He tapped into his primitive survival motivations. "I persuaded the opposing lawyers that I was dangerous and even a little crazy," he said. "I wanted them to think of the negotiation as something happening in a back alley in the middle of the night, and I was a mad, snarling dog about to attack them. That's what it takes sometimes if you are trying to settle bet-the-firm litigation."

My friend is actually one of the nicest and most intelligent men I know, though I doubt if the lawyers he negotiates against see that. He powers himself up to succeed in his rough-and-tumble litigation environment by bringing to his negotiations the same energy he would tap if he were protecting his family from muggers.

Practicing high-stakes law is not for everyone. But it works for him. When you can tap into physical survival motives, you can find reliable and powerful—although temporary—sources of motivational energy. A word of warning, however. If you overrely on this source of motivation, you may make yourself a heart-attack candidate. You are engaging extremely high stress levels.

CONCLUSION

Motivation is the energy that gets you up every day and keeps powering you toward your goals as you encounter obstacles large and small. It is what puts your capabilities to work.

A final note: underlying everything we talked about in this chapter is one inevitable fact that we did not discuss but that affects all our motivations—the limited time we have on this earth to achieve our life's work. About halfway through the Success course, I write the number 32,850 on the blackboard before the students get to class and then challenge them to figure out what the number means sometime before the class is over. See if you can figure it out right now. Any ideas?

If nobody guesses, I tell them at the end of class: it is the number of days you get to live if you are fortunate enough to be alive for ninety years. Every day that goes by, one digit ticks off that total.

I do not dwell on the fact that our days are numbered because it can be depressing to some people. Who needs to be reminded of death? But if you see this fact clearly, it changes everything—making life itself the most inspiring motivation of all. For example, a memorable part of Steve Jobs's famous 2005 Stanford graduation speech, which I quoted

near the end of the introduction, was his description of how he motivated himself through awareness of his own death.

As he put it:

> When I was 17, I read a quote that went something like: "If you
> live each day as if it was your last, some day you'll most certainly
> be right." It made an impression on me, and since then, for the
> past 33 years, I have looked in the mirror every morning and
> asked myself: "If today were the last day of my life, would I want to
> do what I am about to do today?" And whenever the answer has
> been "no" for too many days in a row, I know I need to change
> something. Remembering that I'll be dead soon is the most
> important tool I've ever encountered to help me make the big
> choices in life. Because almost everything—all external expecta-
> tions, all pride, all fear of embarrassment or failure—these things
> just fall away in the face of death, leaving only what is truly
> important. . . . You are already naked. There is no reason not to
> follow your heart.

If there is any reason to, as the hockey coach Fred Shero put it, "set
yourself on fire" with motivation, this is it. With only one life to live,
why not live it with purpose and energy? Why not make it memorable? What have you got to lose?

You are now ready to embark on the next stage of your journey—
one that will take you from your inventory of capabilities and motivations to an even deeper place. One of the most important assets needed
to succeed is resilience—the ability to pick yourself up when you fall.

The next chapter will help you discover the sources of your self-
confidence.

Success Step #6

ENERGIZE YOURSELF BY COMBINING SATISFACTION-BASED AND REWARD-BASED MOTIVATIONS

There are two kinds of motivational energy: the fast-burning power of
rewards and incentives and the slower-burning fuel of intrinsic satisfaction. Success comes from combining these two sources of energy and
using them the right way.

(continued on next page)

(continued from previous page)

If you rely solely on rewards, you will quickly burn out. If you rely solely on intrinsic satisfaction, you may lack intensity when it is needed. To create energy, match your work to your SAME personality strengths.

No one can stay motivated all the time. Recharge yourself. Here are the ways we discussed:

Make yourself accountable.

Connect with role models.

Create motivational rituals.

Compete with yourself.

Prove someone wrong.

Channel your strongest emotions.

Learn to Fail:
Self-Confidence

It is not always the people who start out the smartest who end up the smartest.

—ALFRED BINET, INVENTOR OF THE IQ TEST

In 2011, when professional golfer Rory McIlroy was twenty-one years old, he blew a four-stroke final-round lead in the most prestigious golf tournament in the world, the Masters. He ended up tied for fifteenth place. It was an epic collapse. He shot the worst round of golf in the history of the tournament for someone leading after three rounds. Here is what he said minutes after the tournament ended: "Hopefully, it will build a little bit of character in me."

Two months later, he won the U.S. Open with the lowest seventy-two-hole score in tournament history. After his win, he reflected on how his failure at the Masters had contributed to his U.S. Open success. "[The Masters] was a very valuable experience for me," he said. "I knew what I needed to do today to win."

Contrast McIlroy's attitude with a story that one of my students, Linda, told our Success class. She confessed that she had formerly suffered from a condition called "self-handicapping" that almost ruined her college career. This syndrome illustrates what can happen to someone who has talent but who seeks, above all, to avoid failure.

Linda faced a crisis during her first semester in college. She had been able to get good grades throughout high school by coasting on her natural ability. Moreover, throughout her youth, she had been lavishly praised by both her parents and her teachers as being unusually "smart." Her self-esteem gradually came to depend on this image of herself. The high grades she earned with minimal effort were proof positive that her parents and teachers were correct. Her admission to a top university put the matter beyond any reasonable doubt.

When she hit her freshman year at Wharton, however, she found herself getting Cs and Ds. Her first-semester grades struck at the core of her self-esteem, and she secretly feared that she might not be so smart after all. This idea literally terrified her.

Had Linda had the confidence to learn from failure, as Rory McIlroy did between the 2011 Masters and U.S. Open golf tournaments, her first-semester college disaster would have inspired her to redouble her efforts, learn new study habits, and throw herself into the challenge of earning better grades against the new competition she faced. Instead, her academic performance fell even further. But, perversely, she earned these lower grades in ways that protected her self-image as being "smart."

Instead of studying more, she studied less. Indeed, she often accepted invitations to parties or movies on the nights before big tests. That way, when she received a poor grade, she had a ready explanation: "I didn't really try."

She was also prone to severe headaches—usually right before an exam or when a paper deadline loomed. Again, this gave her an excuse: "I had a headache, so I couldn't do the work." Her alarmed parents insisted that she see an academic counselor—who quickly referred her to a psychologist. Her therapist eventually showed her that her subconscious mind, full of self-doubt and fearing the worst, was undermining her entire college career.

Linda ultimately got over her crisis by becoming more acutely aware of (and skeptical of) the glib rationalizations that marked her self-handicapping cycle. "I didn't really try" stopped working as an explanation for her substandard performance. By speaking regularly with her counselor, joining a support group, and establishing new study habits, she overcame her fear of failure and started focusing on step-by-step improvements.

She earned good grades sometimes and poor grades at other times. The competition in college, after all, was much stiffer than anything she had encountered before. But the rewards of learning to fail were worth it: she began to enjoy school and was proud of what she was learning and achieving. By the time I met her, she was back at the top of her academic game—performing well in all her classes and relishing the chance to win in Wharton's hypercompetitive environment.

Perhaps most important, she had gained an experience that would last a lifetime: like Rory McIlroy, she had taken on and overcome an epic collapse involving an activity she was supposed to be good at. This victory gave her a new kind of self-esteem—something based on the direct experience of surviving a difficult "rite of passage" rather than other people's opinions about a personal trait she had no control over.

If you, like Linda, find yourself shying away from chances to put yourself to the test, you may need some practice at learning to fail. As her story shows, the fear of failure can be hard to deal with, but a new attitude about it can literally change your life.

In the following pages, you will get to define more precisely exactly what self-confidence is and why the *right kind* of confidence is so central to achievement. As we will see, confidence operates on two levels.

What I call "Level One Confidence" relates to your basic and deepest sense of self—the belief in your own autonomy, moral character, and ability to take action in the world. These beliefs often form when you are young, but as Linda's story shows, they can be forged at any stage of life through successfully overcoming a challenging obstacle life throws in front of you. Level One Confidence can also be instilled through respect shown to you by people whom you yourself respect—based on their genuine accomplishments and character. Finally, this basic form of confidence sometimes develops through sincere faith in powers beyond your own (if you are a person inclined toward such faith). Indeed, when people speak of being "born again" through direct religious experiences, they are, in some sense, reporting a renewal of their Level One Confidence to take on whatever life may bring, good or bad.

The best kind of Level One Confidence, in my view, combines a secure belief in yourself with an equally firm commitment to high standards of personal character. There is something sad about a person who turns his or her belief that "I can do it" into an arrogant insistence that "I am the greatest."

The second type of self-confidence—Level Two—applies to specific skills and activities you undertake, such as Linda's drive to acquire new study habits to improve her academic performance. The Stanford psychologist Carol Dweck has led the way in exploring the nature of effective Level Two Confidence. Her research confirms an insight America's Founding Fathers would approve of: hard work, trial and error, and a willingness to learn from failure are the surest pathways to mastering any new interest or occupation. Professor Dweck has demonstrated that Level Two Confidence—built on the belief that you can "get smarter and better" when you set your mind to it—can literally transform your actual capabilities, including problem-solving ability, academic performance, and work outcomes.

LEVEL ONE CONFIDENCE:
BELIEVING IN YOUR TRUE SELF

The psychologist William James once said, "There is but one cause of human failure. And that is man's lack of faith in his true self." By "true self" James meant the consistent, deeper sense of self (modern scholars prefer the term "consciousness") that remains consistent throughout your day-to-day experience—the inner core that you are aware of when you fall asleep and that you experience again as soon as you wake up the next day. Although you may behave differently in different situations, you carry your "true self" with you from one situation to the next, and you consult it to discover your genuine feelings about the most important questions in life.

Getting to know this "true self" is one of the most important parts of living a successful life. The Temple of Apollo in the ancient Greek holy place of Delphi was the home of a famous oracle whom the Greeks consulted on all important occasions. Two simple words were written over the main doorway to this temple: "Know Thyself." The ancients knew that to properly interpret what the oracle might say you first had to understand your own biases, ambitions, and character.

Let's look at an example of someone who took some basic Level One Confidence in his true self and built two completely different careers on its foundation. The story concerns a man named Bill Richmond.

Richmond never went to college, but he gained something even more valuable than a diploma during World War II: rock-solid confidence in himself. Now ninety years old and living in Calabasas, California, he likes to talk about the distinctive success philosophy he learned during the war and applied for the rest of his life.

Born in 1922, Bill Richmond was nineteen when the Japanese attacked Pearl Harbor, catapulting the United States into World War II. He enlisted in the Marine Corps and signed up to be a pilot. He had never flown before, but he thought it might be worth a try. After only six hours of training, he flew a single-engine Piper Cub airplane solo and landed it safely. That initial success led to flight school, where he spent a year learning how to fly fighter planes. He graduated to become a frontline Marine combat aviator.

In 1946, he was mustered out of the Marines with both his life and some hard-earned Level One Confidence. If he was good enough to become a Marine Corps fighter pilot with no prior flying experience, he reasoned, he was probably good enough to handle most things life might throw at him. He summarized his Marine Corps experience in a simple phrase that would guide him for the rest of his life: "Do it, then learn how."

He did not have any inspired ideas about what to do after the war. But as he thought back on the activities he had enjoyed as a kid, he remembered that he had been a decent drummer in his middle-school band in Rockford, Illinois. He also loved jazz. So it was off to California—to try his hand at becoming a professional drummer.

"I could keep pretty good time and could look like I knew what I was doing," he told *The New York Times'* columnist Jane Brody. "In a few months I actually got a job in a downtown bar." He eventually joined a big band but quickly realized he would never make it as a true professional until he took the second step of his success system: "learn how." He enrolled in a music college to learn drumming for real, and before long he was playing in top bands backing up singers such as Ella Fitzgerald and Frank Sinatra. It was a rewarding, interesting career, and he followed it for fifteen years.

Fate then intervened to test his "Do it, then learn how" system a second time. He was nearly forty when, as part of his big-band work, he met comedian Jerry Lewis and joined his road show. Lewis noticed that Richmond had an infectious sense of humor, and it was not long before he was asking Richmond to write comedy routines for him. Eventually, Lewis requested that he join the writer Mel Brooks in crafting the screenplay for a 1961 Jerry Lewis movie called *The Ladies Man*. Brooks dropped out of the project early on, leaving Richmond to finish the movie on his own. *The Ladies Man* did very well at the box office, so it was time for Richmond to quit playing drums and take a formal screenwriting class. He went on to make another six films with Jerry Lewis, cowriting such classic comedy hits as *The Nutty Professor* and *The Errand Boy*. After that, he enjoyed a distinguished thirty-year career as a comedy writer for both movies and television, sharing in three Emmy Awards for his television work on *The Carol Burnett Show* in the 1970s.

He finally retired in 1995 at the age of seventy-three, and has been living an active life ever since—still confident that he can do whatever he sets his mind to. "The important thing," Richmond told Jane

Brody, is to be alert for surprises, because life often delivers things that are even better than you envisioned: "[B]e ready for an opening—serendipity—all the time."

Underlying Richmond's success is a deeper truth about life that applies to us all: no risk, no reward. And one level deeper than that is a truth about your willingness to take risks: it all starts with a secure foundation of Level One Confidence.

Modern experimental psychologists agree that discovering (or re-discovering) the true self is crucial to psychological health. Studies have shown that people prompted to think about the nature of this deeper self tend to experience more meaning in their lives. And one of the most life-changing experiences anyone can have is to be loved and accepted unconditionally as the person you really are rather than as someone you have pretended to be or a person someone else needs you to be. Having the sense that your true self is accepted by another person, warts and all, is a major moment in anyone's life.

When it comes to success, there are two key aspects of your true self that come into play. First, you need the basic sense of I-can-do-it agency that Bill Richmond displayed. This is the belief that, within what you perceive to be your physical and mental limits, you have what it takes to master whatever you might choose to do.

The other key element of the true self is your sense of self-worth or self-respect—the belief that you are, although not perfect, a basically good person who tries his or her best to do the right thing. You see yourself, in other words, as a person of integrity—even if others might disagree with you.

The philosopher and mystic George Gurdjieff once defined success as the "resourceful attainment of one's set aim in the cognizance of a clear conscience." Bill Richmond's war experiences no doubt tested his character, and his buoyant spirit after the war suggests that, what-ever moral challenges he faced in combat, he gave himself a passing grade.

When either of these true-self beliefs falters, you are at risk of fail-ure in William James's sense. Either you lose your confidence that "you can do it" and back away from challenges, or you lose faith in your own character, honesty, or courage and begin questioning the purpose of your life.

Russell Wasendorf Sr., the multimillionaire founder of a major bro-kerage firm and the best-known businessman in his hometown of Ce-dar Rapids, Iowa, was caught embezzling hundreds of millions of dollars of his customers' funds. He wrote a confession that read, in part, "I have committed fraud. For this I feel constant and intense guilt. . . . I had no access to additional capital [to make up for a cash shortage] and I was forced into a difficult decision: Should I go out of business or cheat? I guess my ego was too big to admit failure. So I cheated."

His I-can-do-it financial competence helped him evade being caught for many years. But he could not outrun his conscience. These words I quoted above appeared in a note he wrote just before he attempted suicide. He is now in prison.

How can you acquire (or how have you acquired) this basic Level One Confidence in your true self? Let's look at three different pathways that can lead to the kind of self-assurance James was talking about and that formed the foundation for Bill Richmond's colorful life story.

Pathway #1: Someone You Respect Believes That "You Can Do It"

A close friend once told me a story about a "foundation moment" in the construction of her basic sense of self-confidence. It happened when she was eight years old.

She was the third of four children in her family. All the siblings were very close in age and competed with one another for attention and recognition. My friend often struggled to stand out in the family "pecking order." As she put it, "I wasn't the oldest son or the oldest daughter, and I wasn't the youngest child. I was stuck in the middle." Unable to compete in a conventional way, she fell in love with reading and set to work on becoming the best-read member of the household. In the third grade alone, she read 342 books of every shape and size. "I wrote short book reports on them all in big loopy handwriting on lined yellow pads, and I won the school reading prize," she said. "Not long after that, my mother took me aside and told me something that I never forgot. She told me I was the smartest one in the family and that I could do whatever I wanted when I grew up."

Those words, my friend added, gave her both an identity—the "smart one"—and a goal: to live up to her mother's expectation that she would be a success. Both of these played their own quiet roles in her life as she went through school and college. Of course, she quickly realized that there were plenty of people much smarter than she was in the world and, more important, that being smart was just one ability among many that might go into being successful. But her mother's assurance that "you can do whatever you want" provided a foundation for her Level One Confidence that has lasted for many years.

As we will see in the next section, telling someone she is smart does not make it so. And a comment like this can backfire if a child hears "You are smart" as either a license to stop working hard or a conferred status that must never be tested lest it turn out to be untrue. But in my friend's case, it became the basis for believing in herself and spurred her to work even harder to "make it so."

As this story shows, your mind, especially when you are young, is open to all kinds of suggestions about your character and ability. Few suggestions are more powerful and longer lasting than a perfectly timed, authoritative, positive message from someone you respect that "you can do it." It is almost as if they have flipped on a light switch. When others express confidence in you, you start to believe in yourself.

The power of suggestion is well documented by scientists in several disciplines. For example, when a doctor confidently tells a patient that a medical treatment will relieve suffering, it often does—even when the medicine is a mere sugar pill. Before the arrival of modern scientific medicine, this "placebo effect" was responsible for most of the relief offered by doctors. The ancient Greek physician Galen once noted, "He cures most in whom most are confident."

Even today, as the Columbia University scientist Tor Wager has commented, "Your expectations can have profound impacts on your brain and on your health." Roughly 30 percent of the effectiveness of most medicines and medical procedures is said to come from the power of positive suggestion. In pain management, the percentage is even higher. Moreover, the effectiveness of a placebo treatment rises as the credibility of the fake medication goes up. People gain more pain relief from a pretend injection of "morphine" than from a fake aspirin. Studies have shown that when accompanied by clearly worded, positive suggestions:

- fake knee surgery helps treat real knee injuries;
- fake wart treatments result in warts disappearing in as many as 50 percent of subjects (compared with only 11 percent when no treatment at all is given);
- as many as 20 percent of people in clinical trials for drugs to treat both Parkinson's disease and migraine headaches show significant improvement after taking placebo medicines;
- people reminded that it is "flu season" report more flu symptoms; and
- people rubbed with fake poison ivy break out in real poison ivy rashes.

Researchers now think that the brain actually changes in response to these suggestions, triggering the release of dopamine and other chemicals that mimic the effect of the suggested remedy or illness. Of course, some people are more suggestible than others—just as some people are more susceptible to hypnosis than others. And scientists are only now beginning to take the study of the placebo effect seriously enough to harness it systematically. But there is no doubt that the brain can help heal the body (within the limits of physical laws) if a plausible treatment is presented in a positive light.

The expectation mechanism that triggers the placebo effect (and the "nocebo effect" when the suggestion is a negative one) can be just as powerful when it comes to successful achievement. This was shown more than one hundred years ago in an accidental experiment that took place when the U.S. government was conducting the national census in 1890. The inventor of a new punch-card system for the national census told a group of new typists he was training that he expected a well-trained operator could turn out about 550 punch cards in a day. After two weeks of practice, the new typists were punching an average of roughly that number, with a few hardworking punch-card operators typing as many as 700 cards a day.

Meanwhile, a second group of new typists was being trained by people who had no idea of the inventor's 550-card estimate. They simply told their new typists to punch as many cards as they could. The average daily production from this second group after two weeks of training was 2,100 cards each day. Unhindered by limiting expectations, this second group worked to the boundaries of their actual abilities instead of the limits of someone else's estimate of them.

In the famous 1966 "Pygmalion in the classroom" study by the Harvard psychologist Robert Rosenthal and his colleague Lenore Jacobson, experimenters told teachers in eighteen different classrooms that some special students in each class were "gifted" and that a test had shown these students were very likely to exhibit "unusual intellectual gains" during the school year. In fact, these students had been randomly selected and had no special gifts at all compared with their classmates.

Eight months later, these "gifted" students (20 percent of the students within each classroom) tested significantly higher than the rest of their classmates in terms of academic performance, with many showing dramatic, thirty-point gains on an IQ test. The teachers' expectations that these students would to do better had translated into significantly higher academic outcomes.

The phenomenon of transferred expectations, also called a "self-fulfilling prophecy," occurs for a combination of two reasons. The person holding the expectation treats the other person differently, giving him or her more challenging work to do. This leads to more learning. At the same time, the person receiving the suggestion accepts it as an accurate assessment of his or her ability, and that in turn increases the level of effort the person gives.

The lesson here is plain: you should understand the power of being in a high-performing/high-expectation social environment versus a low-performing/low-expectation one. Your social setting can strongly affect what you believe is possible—and that will affect your confidence, the effort you expend, and the results you achieve.

Recapping, other people are often the sources of your ideas about your true self. Both medical researchers and psychologists who have studied the power of suggestion have shown that displays of confidence by people you respect can induce measurable differences in the way you behave. In the case of the placebo effect, the benefit comes from involuntary, brain-chemical responses to suggestion. In the performance context, higher expectations can prompt you to exert more energy and effort.

The final "click" in this virtuous circle comes when you observe your own behavior in the light of the faith that others have placed in you and conclude that you are, in fact, the person they expected you to be. This assures you that their faith was justified and gives you the self-confidence to take on new and more difficult challenges.

Now it is your turn. Think back in your life and make a few notes below of people who gave you the benefit of their supportive voices. They could be those who encouraged you to believe "I can do it" in the general way my friend's mother did or in a more specific area of your life such as academics, music, sports, or work. These voices may belong to parents, relatives, coaches, teachers, counselors, or peers—anyone who has contributed meaningfully to your deeper "I can do it" sense.

People Who Delivered a You-Can-Do-It Message | Their Role in Your Life

1. _____

2. _____

3. _____

4. _____

5. _____

6. Use additional space to keep your list going.

Pathway #2: A Rite of Passage

People often establish the foundation for their Level One Confidence by passing through a significant personal challenge and emerging with the sense that they have proved themselves. Bill Richmond acquired a foundation for his Level One Confidence as a Marine Corps combat aviator during World War II after he saw that he was able to survive every challenge both the Marines and the enemy put to him. If he was good enough for the Marine Corps, he could always tell himself, he probably had what it took for civilian life.

Many people report that the rigors of military training and service—even for only a few years—played a key role in giving them Level One Confidence. But the military is only one of many possible rite-of-passage experiences. Research studies show that intense personal turmoil at any age in life—ranging from losing a parent or experiencing a serious health crisis to being laid off from work—can serve as a rite of passage. People who navigate through such periods successfully report that they experience a firmer sense of self marked by a reduced fear of death, fewer attachments to material goods, a stronger feeling of connection with others, and a new, more grounded sense of self-acceptance. Psychologists even have a name for such hardships: suffering-induced transformational experiences (SITEs).

Hopefully, you have not had to suffer through an extreme life trauma as your Level One Confidence rite of passage. If not, you have still had to overcome challenges and conflicts to get to where you are today. And these—whether encountered within a relatively safe structure provided by your family and trusted mentors or from unwelcome life events—have formed the foundation for your current sense that "I can do it." To move your life forward, it often pays to retrieve and reflect on these victories of the past.

As I see it, all experiences that force you out of your comfort zone and tap your inner resources can contribute to the Level One Confidence I am talking about. Depending on your age, gender, or stage of life, experiences such as the following can provide the building blocks for a positive belief in your true self:

- overcoming a significant failure in high school or college
- surviving the breakup of an important romantic relationship
- completing a challenging wilderness trek or training exercise that required self-reliance and ingenuity
- coming to terms with your sexual identity
- mastering a rigorous academic program in college or graduate school
- giving birth to a child
- coming through a career crisis and establishing yourself once again as a competent worker
- exercising self-discipline to regain your health after a serious illness
- surviving a psychological or emotional breakdown or crisis
- coping with the death of a loved one
- successfully transitioning from college to workplace, career to career, or career to retirement

Such trials, when you understand them in rite-of-passage terms, can lead to the internal conviction that, although you might not want to go through these testing experiences again, you are a stronger and more capable person for having done so in the past.

What pivotal experiences have helped shape your current sense that "I can do it"?

In the spaces below, list some of the events that have served as tests of your competence, character, or both.

1. _____

2. _____

3. _____

4. _____

5. _____

6. Use additional space to keep your list going.

Pathway #3: The Power of Faith

For some people, faith in themselves is grounded, at least in part, in a faith in spiritual powers greater than their own. Sometimes this faith provides the same positive healing power as the placebo effect we discussed above.

For example, my wife and I once visited New Mexico, where we made a pilgrimage to a famous chapel in Chimayo. A small room next to the sanctuary overflowed with the crutches and medical devices of those who had been cured by the "holy dirt" available only in a small room at the back of this church. Hundreds of thousands of people make the pilgrimage to visit the chapel every year—many in hopes that their faith will bring them relief from some form of suffering.

Less dramatically—but no less often—people discover (or rediscover) their true self by identifying with the uncompromising goodness and power of a religious leader, a saint, or a guiding doctrine. One of the bestselling success books of all time is *The Power of Positive Thinking* by the Reverend Norman Vincent Peale, who served as the minister at New York City's Marble Collegiate Church on Fifth Avenue for fifty-two years. Here is how Peale begins chapter 1: "Believe in yourself! Have faith in your abilities! Without a humble but reasonable confidence in your own powers, you cannot be successful or happy."

He then goes on to tell the story of a forty-year-old man who approached him at a business convention. The man was about to pitch the biggest business deal of his life but was feeling very discouraged about it. He lacked a secure Level One Confidence in himself.

"Why is it," the man asked Peale, "that all my life I have been tormented by inferiority feelings, by lack of confidence, by self-doubt?"

Peale suggested that the man take two steps. First, he needed to look deeply into his life to discover the sources of his disbelief in himself. This, Peale said, would require counseling by a professional and might take some time. Peale explained that there are various causes for persistent feelings of inferiority, and many go back to negative, deflating messages received in childhood.

But Peale's second suggestion was something the man could do right then and there. Peale wrote out a Bible verse from Saint Paul's Letter to the Philippians 4:13—"I can do all things through Christ who strengthens me."

Reverend Peale told his new friend to repeat this phrase to himself as he walked home that night, say it three times as he prepared for sleep, repeat it again three times after he woke up, and say it three final times on the way to his crucial meeting. "Do this with an attitude of faith," Peale said, "and you will receive sufficient strength and ability to deal with the problem." The psychological counseling he needed would help in the long run, Peale assured him, but "the formula which I am now going to give you can be a large factor in the eventual cure."

The man followed his advice and later reported that the Bible verse had worked "wonders," giving him the confidence to make his deal. Peale tells many similar stories in his book, but his advice comes down to this: "The greatest secret for eliminating the inferiority complex is to fill your mind to overflowing with faith. Develop a tremendous faith in God and that will give you a humble yet profoundly realistic faith in yourself."

In my study of success, few things have impressed me as much as the power of beliefs beyond human understanding to anchor people's Level One Confidence. The beliefs themselves range from conventional religious traditions such as the one Reverend Peale embraced to the quasi-magical powers espoused by the many success books that advocate faith-based visualization as the road to fame, fortune, and happiness.

Success belief systems based on religious, quasi-religious, and mystical mental powers have cropped up so often in history that scholars who study how-to-succeed movements have a name for them: mind power schools. One of the most famous quotations in the popular literature on success comes from Napoleon Hill, author of *Think and Grow Rich*, a bestselling mind power book from the 1930s. "Whatever the mind of man can conceive and believe," Hill wrote, "it can achieve." Hill based his formulation on the testimony of the most successful businessmen and inventors of his generation—people such as Andrew Carnegie, Thomas Edison, and Henry Ford, all of whom conceived, believed, and achieved things the average person thought impossible. Many modern entrepreneurs swear by Napoleon Hill's book—and this quote in particular. They say his words inspired them to summon the Level One Confidence they needed to believe in their own crazy ideas—and accomplish what they had previously thought could not be done.

I have now realized that, when it comes to Level One Confidence, what a person believes is less important than the faith and commitment he or she brings to the belief. It is no accident that every human society in recorded history has had a religion that addressed itself to powers beyond human comprehension at its core. And most of them have also provided essential guidance on the moral aspect of Level One Confidence: becoming a good person who lives by a worthy code of conduct.

What all these examples suggest to me is this: in an otherwise uncertain and difficult world, a belief in powers greater than your own creates a firm foundation for a faith in your own true self. Shakespeare's Hamlet put it this way: "There are more things in heaven and earth, Horatio, than are dreamt of in your philosophy."

The important thing is having a basic I-can-do-it belief. I leave you to consider whether it comes from a parent, a mentor, a rite of passage, your faith—or all of these put together.

LEVEL TWO CONFIDENCE:
THE SUCCESS MINDSET
....

Bill Richmond's confidence that he could take on almost any challenge was built on his World War II rite of passage, which gave rise to his strong Level One Confidence that "I can do it." But he built two successful careers on another kind of belief in himself—the belief that he could get substantially better at whatever he undertook by practicing, learning, and growing. This is what I call Level Two Confidence. This level provides you with resilience and the willingness to engage in trial and error that helps you acquire higher and higher degrees of skill.

The topic of self-confidence has attracted a great deal of attention from leading experimental psychologists, with the inevitable explosion of specialized vocabularies. For example, Stanford's Albert Bandura calls this trait "self-efficacy," while Notre Dame's Timothy Judge focuses on a concept he calls positive "core self-evaluations."

Professor Carol Dweck has coined the terms "fixed" versus "growth" mindsets to describe what she says are two contrasting beliefs people have about their own abilities. As she sees it, people with a fixed mindset think humans were born with a certain amount of unchanging intelligence or talent. They tend to coast on their natural ability and seek out only those activities that will allow them to demonstrate it—without putting it to a test that might result in failure.

Those with a growth mindset believe they can enhance their inborn intelligence and ability through their own efforts. People who embrace the belief that "effort pays" tend to accept and even seek out criticism; they look for ways to push their limits and grow. These are the people who the psychologist Alfred Binet—inventor in 1905 of the first IQ test—was talking about when he said in this chapter's opening quote, "It is not always the people who start out the smartest who end up the smartest."

Although Level Two Confidence theories differ in ways that are academically important, they all share four practical characteristics. Below, I summarize and illustrate these four so you can benchmark yourself against them—and see if there is room for you to improve how you think about your own Level Two Confidence potential to grow and develop.

1. People with Level Two Confidence Exhibit the Desire to Learn

Experiments demonstrate that people with strong Level Two Confidence have a keen thirst to learn more about whatever areas they are specializing in. In one study, children praised for their effort at solving IQ test puzzles were much more eager to take advantage of a chance to learn more about how to improve their scores than were students who were told that their test scores showed they were smart. Bill Richmond's habit of discovering areas for which he had an aptitude—flying, drumming, and screenwriting—and then immediately going to school to learn from experts suggests he had high levels of this mindset. People who think that success and failure mainly depend on fixed levels of natural ability, by contrast, often learn just enough to demonstrate some level of ability, earn praise, and then stop developing. They like to repeat the same performance over and over, and show less passion for taking their talent to the next level.

Do you routinely embrace chances to open up new areas of knowledge as well as learn more about the areas you already know well? That is the hallmark of someone with the kind of Level Two Confidence that allows people to get smarter.

2. People with Level Two Confidence Are Willing to Put Themselves to the Test

Psychologists who study Level Two Confidence have found that growth-oriented people actively take on challenges so they can improve their ability through practice, even if this means failing sometimes. Everyone gets nervous before a challenging test of their talent, but people with Level Two Confidence do not let this nervousness get in the way. They want to benchmark themselves.

Those who lack Level Two Confidence prefer to avoid risking their self-image as someone who is talented or smart. In the same experiment noted above, the students who were told their IQ test scores showed they were smart tended to lose interest and enjoyment as the experiment continued and the test questions got harder. Indeed, when given the chance, 40 percent of these students lied about their lower scores to protect their self-esteem. Those praised for their effort had no such problems. They said that they enjoyed the harder questions even more than the easier ones, and they reported their scores accurately when given the chance to misrepresent them.

Needless to say, a habit of shying away from challenges can have serious, long-term consequences on your overall success in life.

3. People with Level Two Confidence Focus on Effort as Much as Results

The story of Linda, the self-handicapping student you met at the beginning of this chapter, shows that people with limited amounts of Level Two Confidence are sometimes the victims of having been praised too much when they were younger for some fixed or innate ability. And as noted above, repeated experiments have demonstrated the value of praising effort rather than innate talent. If you are praised by others in the right way, this can lead you to *praise yourself* based on your genuine effort when you accomplish something significant and discount comments about the role of your natural ability. You should ignore any result—good or bad—that comes after you put in only a halfhearted effort. And you should be proud of any result that follows hard work—even when the result is not what you had hoped.

Indeed, one test of whether you have truly gained this aspect of Level Two Confidence is how you respond when, after your best effort, you still fall short of what you were hoping to achieve. Do you feel cheated—that you have been treated unfairly because you tried so hard but still came in behind the winner? That is a sign that you are still looking at success in terms of the outcome rather than your input. A person cultivating the right kind of Level Two Confidence will look instead at whether he or she can put more effort in next time—or learn to focus efforts in more productive ways that will improve the outcome.

K. Anders Ericcson, the leading academic researcher on acquiring professional expertise, summed up well the role of effort in Level Two Confidence in his book *The Road to Excellence: Acquisition of Expert Performance in Arts and Sciences, Sports and Games.* To get better at almost anything, he suggests, you need the patience to engage in extended periods of what he called "deliberate practice." This means taking well-defined, appropriately difficult aspects of your art, practicing them, getting informed feedback, and seeking opportunities for "repetition and corrections of errors." Ericcson's most famous finding, trumpeted by Malcolm Gladwell in *Outliers: The Story of Success*, is that world-class performers require ten thousand hours of deliberate practice to attain their expertise. But the lesson I take away from his work is less daunting: by learning to focus on effortful practice as much as results, you will get better at whatever you set your mind to.

4. People with Level Two Confidence Have Learned to Fail

Rory McIlroy, whose story began this chapter, exhibited one of the classic characteristics of people with a growth mindset. He took one of the greatest failures in a professional golf tournament—his fourth-round collapse in the 2011 Masters—and used it to learn what he needed to change for a victory in the U.S. Open a few months later. "[The Masters] was a very valuable experience for me," he said. "I knew what I needed to do today to win."

In her research, Professor Dweck has found that students with Level Two Confidence enjoy doing harder problems, even when they fail to solve them. They use their failure to help them figure out what they need to do better next time.

People who focus on learning, taking risks, and improving their effort will naturally be more resilient—they will bounce back more quickly and constructively from failure because they will tend to interpret it as a chance to learn rather than as a permanent blow to their sense of self. People who see every test outcome as a measure of their natural talent tend to interpret failure as a judgment on their self-worth. They become quickly discouraged and withdraw to some other activity in which they can reliably win.

This is the final concrete way you can cultivate the "right kind" of Level Two Confidence to help you succeed: interpret failure the right way. When you think you have failed at something, avoid generalizing from that single instance into a global sense that "I am a failure; I always screw things up." Instead, focus on exactly what happened that caused you to fail in this particular circumstance—you were up against tough competition, overlooked some hidden factor that turned out to be important, lost focus, or were careless. Then recall something else you have recently done well—helping a friend, learning a new computer application, or cooking a good meal. Finally, look back on your disappointment and find one specific thing you can learn from it that will enable you to do better next time.

RENEWING YOUR CONFIDENCE IN
THE FACE OF FAILURE
....

Confidence is something you "have," but it is also a bit like motivation. It ebbs and flows. Your confidence can be threatened on an almost daily basis by unexpected setbacks and insecurities. Artists and writers often report that, no matter how much experience they have, their confidence can plummet to almost zero when they sit down to start a new creative project. The fear of failure can be unnerving. Thus, most people need to rekindle their faith in themselves on a regular basis—at both Level One and Level Two.

People use an infinite variety of rituals to refresh their confidence, but I offer a few examples below to help you reflect on your own practices—and perhaps give you some new ideas. We look at ways people renew basic Level One Confidence first and then move on to some specific techniques for enhancing Level Two Confidence beliefs.

Renewing Level One Confidence in Yourself

At the most basic level, your self-confidence springs from two sources: your sense of competence and your belief in yourself as a "good person." Anything you can do to renew these two aspects of your belief system will strengthen your sense of purpose. Unlike the motivational boosts we encountered in chapter 6, working on your confidence is more than just bumping up your available physical and emotional energy. Renewals of confidence often involve both reflective thinking and new ideas for the future. Confidence springs from your overall attitude. Its characteristic state of mind is hopefulness. Here are some ideas for maintaining your belief in your true self.

Remind Yourself of the Big Picture. The novelist Maya Angelou once wrote of the stress she feels each time she sits down to write: "When I decide to write anything, I get caught up in my insecurity despite the prior accolades. I think, uh, uh, now they will know I am a charlatan."

She gets past her doubts by using a private ritual taught to her by a former teacher called "writing down my blessings." She pulls out a new yellow pad and "as I approach the clean page, I think of how blessed I am." She fills the page with her sincere gratitude to God for allowing her to see, to read, and to be with those she loves. Pretty soon, as she puts it, "the agent of madness [is] routed" and she can write again.

My mother—who, like Bill Richmond, was in the generation that fought World War II and spent that war wondering if her Marine Corps husband would make it home—kept a copy of Anne Morrow Lindbergh's inspirational book *The Gift from the Sea* next to her bed to remind herself daily of the ups and downs of life and renew her sense of confidence in her ability to cope with the days ahead. Anne Morrow was Charles Lindbergh's wife and the mother of a child who was kidnapped and murdered. She suffered more than her share of sorrow. She wrote this book to help others renew their faith in the future. As she put it, "The problem is . . . how to remain whole in the midst of the distractions of life; how to remain balanced, no matter what centrifugal forces tend to pull one off center; how to remain strong, no matter what shocks come."

Many keep a Bible close at hand to regain their balance. Any favorite book that restores your sense of perspective and hope can provide the basic renewal of faith in yourself that we all occasionally need to keep going.

Join Others in Renewing Your Faith. People attend regular religious services in part to reconnect with a primary source of their Level One Confidence—the power beyond themselves that they rely on in good times and bad. As I said earlier, I think exactly what you believe is less important than that you affirm whatever your beliefs are in ways you find appropriate. In fact, I find it personally inspiring to go to religious services of faiths that are new to me simply to feel the energy of people connecting to their basic beliefs.

For example, I once attended a remarkable church service led by the charismatic preachers Joel and Victoria Osteen at the sports arena where the Philadelphia 76ers basketball team and the Flyers hockey club have their home games. There were over thirty-five thousand people at this service, all holding their Bibles over their heads and chanting verses in cadences led by Pastor Osteen. The Osteen ministry is distinctive in its commitment to positive thinking, mind power, and the power of prayer to bring good things into people's lives. It explicitly weds faith in God to self-confidence and achievement.

Here is what those thirty-five thousand people stood and chanted at the beginning of this worship service:

This is my Bible: I am what it says I am; I have what it says I have; I can do what it says I can do. Today, I will be taught the Word of God. I'll boldly confess. My mind is alert; my heart is receptive; I will never be the same. I am about to receive the incorruptible, indestructible, ever-living Seed of the Word of God. I'll never be the same—never, never, never! I'll never be the same, in Jesus' Name.

It is easy to be cynical about "prosperity gospel" preachers, and some live lavish lifestyles that suggest they believe quite a bit more in building their bank accounts than in God. But I think the people who attend worship services of almost any kind deserve respect for seeking to renew their faith. It is an important aspect of community and spiritual life.

Keep Your Relationships in Good Repair. In his *Autobiography*, Benjamin Franklin talks about a habit he formed early in life of keeping his relationships with others in good repair—especially when he was afraid he had treated them unfairly, offended them, or acted dishonestly. Being a printer, he called these his "errata." In the Success class, I give students a chance to imitate Franklin's habit by looking back on their lives and asking either of two questions:

1. Is there anyone I have wronged that I should apologize to?
2. Is there anyone who has been generous to me that I should reach out to thank?

I then ask them to seek out these people and make things right.

Students report that this exercise is one of the most valuable experiences in the class, and has resulted in the renewal of ties between feuding siblings, heartwarming reunions with beloved teachers, and moments of honest self-assessment about nagging issues of conscience that had been troubling them on and off for years.

When you act like the person you think you should be at your best, you actually become that person—and this can renew your basic belief in your own character.

Try it for yourself. Pick one of the two questions above and seek someone out who deserves more of your attention.

Renewing Your Level Two Confidence

Rituals associated with bolstering Level Two Confidence tend to be tied to specific personal or professional activities. Here are some examples of what people do to keep their "I can do it" confidence up before special challenges. The connections between renewing Level Two Confidence and the motivational boosts we discussed in the previous chapter are somewhat closer.

Use Visualization to Rehearse. Neuroscientists report that visualizing a body movement activates exactly the same areas of the brain as does the actual movement—thus enabling golfers and tennis players to practice their swings with their eyes closed and without moving a muscle. In addition, visualizing yourself doing something in the future serves as a "rehearsal" for that activity, reducing some of the stress you may be feeling and giving you a chance to imagine how you might overcome certain obstacles that could arise. Both of these are beneficial to confidence.

The Olympic swimmer Michael Phelps, winner of eight gold medals in the 2008 Olympics, commented after his record-breaking feats, "Before the trials, I was doing a lot of relaxation exercises and visualization. And I think that that helped me to get a feel of what it was gonna be like when I got there. I knew that I had done everything that I could to get ready for that meet, both physically and mentally."

As you face a new challenge, try closing your eyes and imagining yourself going through the motions of whatever activity it involves. See if it relaxes you a bit to see yourself already doing it and succeeding.

Enact a Pre-Performance Ritual. Tobias Meyer is the auctioneer at Sotheby's auction house who ran the sale where Edvard Munch's 1895 iconic painting *The Scream* was sold for $119.9 million—the most money ever paid for a single work up to that time in art-auction history. His job requires complete attention and focus for a relatively short amount of time. "I am hired at that moment to make the [art] work as expensive as possible," he told a reporter shortly after the sale closed.

To get ready for this peak performance moment, Meyer goes through a very precise, confidence-enhancing ritual before every auction he runs. On auction day, he gets up at 7:00 A.M. and eats a specific breakfast of yogurt with honey and fruit. At 9:15, he attends a presale meeting and then jogs for thirty minutes on a treadmill at his gym. Next comes a lunch of chicken soup followed by a one-hour nap. He always wears the same set of gold-and-lapis-lazuli cuff links, a gift from his mother when he was fourteen years old. And, since 2004, he has used the same gavel he held when he set another art-world record by selling Picasso's *Boy with a Pipe* for $104.2 million. Thirty minutes before the sale begins, he drinks a four-shot latte. He then takes the freight elevator to the sales room.

He is ready.

Do you have a routine you go through that puts you in a confident frame of mind for new challenges? Try creating one.

Give Yourself Small Wins. In one of the best articles on Olympic training I have ever read, Daniel Chambliss tracked the techniques used by USA Swimming to get its athletes ready to compete in the Olympic games. One of the common threads in this training was to focus on a series of "small wins" in training rather than on the larger goal of winning a medal. As Chambliss summarized it, the swimmers "found their challenges in small things: working on a better start this week, polishing up their backstroke technique next week, planning how to pace their swim." As a result, they got the satisfaction of "very definable, minor achievements," which in turn gave them the confidence to attempt more small wins each and every day.

Achievement scholars define a small win as a "concrete, complete, implemented outcome of moderate importance . . . [a] controllable opportunity that produces visible results." Don't write a book; write a page. Don't climb a mountain; take a step on the path that goes up toward the summit. Don't hit a home run; make contact with the ball. Is there any way you can set up the big challenge by succeeding at something small that gets the ball rolling? You will build momentum—and Level Two Confidence.

Recite a Mantra. Bill Richmond used his "Do it, then learn how" mantra to remind himself that he had succeeded in the past and would probably do so again in the future. Others use prayers, Bible verses, success slogans, or poems. In the television show *Friday Night Lights*, a fictional Texas high-school football team chants a success mantra before every game: *"Clear Eyes! Full Hearts! Can't Lose!"* The popularity of that show inspired some to adopt this chant for themselves—and it is now part of real people's lives and helps inspire their best efforts.

Bring a Lucky Charm. When all else fails, bring a lucky charm. Do you carry a rabbit's foot, a favorite pendant, or some other good-luck charm when you are about to do something important? What are these but simple ways to bolster confidence? The ace baseball pitcher Cole Hamels wears a neckband and wristband infused with secret "hologram" technology created by a company called EFX Performance. He won his first five starts in August 2012 after he started wearing these items and believes they help him focus. "It makes my body feel in sync," he reports.

Many professional sports stars wear similar gear.

Lucky charms do not bend reality to your will, but they do sometimes make you feel more relaxed and in control. And you will most likely perform better when you are relaxed than when you are tense.

When it comes to confidence building, my philosophy is simple: do what works.

CONCLUSION
....

A glance at any newspaper or news website quickly shows that the world is, in reality, a very hostile and random place. There is a great deal we do not control, some of it good and much of it bad. In the face of all this uncertainty and risk, successful people need the right kind of self-confidence to make their way. The right kind of confidence is always built on activities that present a reasonable chance of failure.

Learning to fail is an art. If you take foolish and unnecessary risks—or strive for achievements far beyond your capabilities—you will fail often, accomplish little, and earn even less respect by showing such consistently poor judgment. On the other hand, if you play every game to "avoid losing" and refuse to try anything new for fear you will fail, your growth will stop and your days will become a repetitive cycle of boring experiences. Life will lose its savor.

Mastering the art of failure calls on two levels of self-confidence. Level One Confidence in yourself gives you a sense of control over your life. Some people forge their Level One Confidence from a "rite of passage" such as military service or a similar test of grit and character. Other people gain it from "You can do it!" messages in their youth that are subsequently tested by real-world events. Sometimes Level One Confidence comes from (and is maintained by) faith in powers beyond ourselves.

The second, more applied form of confidence (Level Two) allows you to learn and improve specific skills. Once again, the possibility of failure is crucial to making progress, and research convincingly shows that people willing to risk falling short consistently outperform those who may have more natural ability at the outset but who refuse to challenge themselves.

Finally, self-confidence, like motivation, is a renewable resource. You need to maintain a set of techniques and relationships that you can rely upon in moments of discouragement. Indeed, feeling "down" is part of the cycle of success. Remember Zig Ziglar's mantra from chapter 6: *"You haven't really lost if you learn from a defeat!"*

We are nearing the end of our success journey—we have only a couple of stops to go. On our next one, we examine the power of setting and maintaining focus on long-term goals—the ones that motivate you most deeply and call on you to apply all of your mental powers. You have four players on your inner achievement team: passion, imagination, intuition, and reason. You are the coach. Your job is to get your team to work as a unit.

But first, buckle your seatbelt. Our next chapter begins on an airplane.

Success Step #7

CULTIVATE SELF-CONFIDENCE

Somewhere between timidity and arrogance is the state of mind you need to succeed: self-confidence. If you do not believe in yourself, why should anyone else believe in you?

Level One Confidence is your basic belief in yourself as a capable, honorable person. It comes from hearing people you trust say, "You can do it!" and from surviving the rites of passage that allow you to say, "If I could do that, then I can do anything." Faith in a higher power can also help you maintain faith in yourself.

Level Two Confidence is your attitude as you engage in specific activities. A success "mindset" includes the willingness to learn, challenge your skills, focus on effort more than results, and treat failure as a stage on the journey rather than as the end of the road.

Focus Your Mind:
Passion, Imagination, Intuition, and Reason

[H]ere is the prime condition of success, the great secret:
concentrate your energy, thought, and capital exclusively
upon the business in which you are engaged . . . put all your
eggs in one basket, and watch that basket.

—ANDREW CARNEGIE

On a beautiful, clear autumn evening, a young pilot was making a mail run from St. Louis to Chicago. The nice weather meant a boring flight. It was, he later wrote, "an evening for beginners." As his mind drifted from his career plans to problems in the aviation industry to some experimental aircraft he had recently read about, he suddenly got an idea. If he could get his hands on one of these new planes, perhaps he could become a test pilot, breaking world records for speed, endurance, or range of flight. That would be something—to make a name for himself piloting experimental planes, and then use that reputation to create a career at the forefront of aviation.

The vision stirred his imagination. And, as he later remembered it, the next idea that entered his mind changed his life forever. If he could stay aloft long enough, "possibly—my mind is startled at its thought—I could fly nonstop between New York and Paris."

Every notable achievement begins as an idea. This particular idea happened to be the beginning of one of the twentieth century's greatest adventure stories. The young pilot's name, as you probably guessed, was Charles Lindbergh. It was September 1926. He was a twenty-four-year-old stunt pilot flying for a mail-delivery service. He had no money, no access to any experimental planes, and no rich friends. He knew full well that, only a few days earlier, a team attempting to take off in a three-engine aircraft to make the historic transatlantic flight (and claim the $25,000 Orteig Prize on offer to the first person to achieve this feat) had exploded on a runway in New York. The landing gear collapsed from the weight of the extra fuel onboard. Two of the four crew members died instantly.

As his new idea took root, Lindbergh began mentally testing it for feasibility. The flying, he noted, "couldn't be more dangerous or the weather worse than flying the night mail in winter." Before he landed in Chicago, his excitement had crystallized into a clear, definite goal. From there, he began sketching out how to "translate [the idea] into an actual plane flying over the Atlantic Ocean to Europe and to France . . . to lay a plan and then follow it step by step no matter how small or large each one by itself may seem."

On May 20, 1927, a mere eight months later, he took off in a $10,000 (roughly $127,500 in today's currency), one-of-a-kind plane he helped to design—and flew it into history.

How did he pull this off? Through a masterful focusing of his mental powers. His simple achievement process—which utilized all four facets of the mind in the service of a crystal-clear goal—will form the outline for this chapter. This process invites you to

- consult your passions to identify a worthy goal,
- let your imagination and intuition generate ideas,
- commit to a specific, challenging plan,
- break it down into small steps, and
- improvise and adjust—then close the deal.

Understanding Lindbergh's get-it-done achievement system will provide you with a useful road map for making progress on your own important projects. It starts with goals. A Gallup survey of highly accomplished professionals once asked how important "well-defined personal goals" were to their success at home as well as in their careers. On a ten-point scale (where ten represented the highest level of importance), 32 percent rated focused goals as a critical success factor (a nine or ten), and another 46 percent gave well-defined goals a six to eight rating. Thus, a total of 78 percent rated goal setting highly.

But having goals is only part of the achievement story. Lindbergh's epic adventure also demonstrates the power of focus in getting truly significant things done. Many people understand that setting goals is a useful way to prime the achievement engine. But far fewer realize the costs of having too many goals at the same time.

One of my students turned in his final paper for the Success class with an appendix detailing more than one hundred goals he had set for his life. His list included goals he wanted to achieve by the time he was twenty-five, thirty, thirty-five, forty, and fifty years old. He wanted to own his own business, travel to more than fifty countries, become a multimillionaire, buy a ranch in Texas, write and publish a book, and, before he was fifty, "save someone's life." He even had a goal to annually reevaluate his goals.

I was impressed with my student's planning skills, but I worried about the long-term effects of his shotgun approach to goal setting. As one team of goal-setting scholars has summarized it, "Each unfulfilled goal remains active [at some level of consciousness], intruding into one's thoughts and attention, seeking to recapture [attention] so as to move toward fulfillment. Because of this competition, the persistent intrusions into attention from unfulfilled goals can impair pursuit of other . . . tasks." This mental crowding is known as the Zeigarnik effect, after the Russian psychologist who documented the cluttering effects of unmet goals and uncompleted tasks on human consciousness.

The efficiency guru David Allen (*Getting Things Done: The Art of Stress-Free Productivity*) has made a career out of the mental chaos that ensues from having too many unresolved goals. His productivity system is built around the idea that you can clear your mind and improve your life by taking each open goal and either doing it, delegating it, deferring it (with a specific plan for the next step needed to advance it), or dropping it. His system has one goal—to reach a magic place called "zero." This is where your mind is finally at rest after you have resolved the status of your current goals and know exactly what you will do next on each one that remains outstanding.

Lindbergh was a master of both his mind and the power of focus.

To understand his achievement, you need to first become better acquainted with the four mental forces you have at your command. Then we will check back in with Lindbergh's remarkable adventure.

WELCOME TO YOUR MIND

You can measure, weigh, scan, and operate on a brain. Neuroscientists are hard at work mapping exactly which parts of the brain do which tasks. But to talk about the "mind," you need a metaphor.

The Greek philosopher Plato conceptualized the mind as a charioteer driving a team of horses. The charioteer was the human "soul" and the two horses pulling the chariot were "reason" and "passion." The soul's daily challenge was to keep these two horses—one obedient and the other unruly—pulling in the same direction.

In more recent times, the psychologist Jonathan Haidt has offered a metaphor that harks back to Plato, but with an important twist. Haidt suggests that the mind is like a small human rider (representing reason) sitting atop a large, appetite-driven, impulsive elephant.

Stanford University's Chip Heath and his brother Dan elaborated on Haidt's image in their bestselling book *Switch: How to Change Things When Change Is Hard*. As they explain it, "[T]he Rider holds the reins and seems to be the leader, but the Rider's control is precarious. . . . Any time the six-ton Elephant and the Rider disagree about which direction to go, the Rider is going to lose. He's completely overmatched."

The rider-and-elephant metaphor is not as flattering to human nature as Plato's soul-driven chariot, but the elephant idea helps explain how easily fear can overpower reason and why diets are so hard to keep. The Heath brothers give the following types of commonsense advice to keep your "elephant" under control: if you are on a diet, don't keep ice cream in the house ("shape the path" for the elephant); if you want to stay on track, offer yourself incentives ("motivate the elephant"); be clear when you talk to yourself about your goals ("point to the destination"); and go for small changes before tackling big ones ("shrink the change").

The students in my Success class take one more lesson away from the rider-and-elephant metaphor: don't expect self-control miracles. Each of them spends the entire semester on a self-selected "elephant control" challenge—from eating fewer nachos to exercising more and gossiping less. Their track records are decidedly mixed. So unless you are prepared to engage in relentless, painful training, the best strategy may be to get to know your elephant better—and then make peace with it.

Plato's horses and Haidt's elephant do good jobs of capturing the basic division of labor between our reasoning abilities and less rational appetites. But neither metaphor helps much if you are investigating the process of successful human achievement. Lindbergh's quest to be the first person to fly nonstop across the Atlantic Ocean was not just a battle between his courage and his fear. His imagination and intuition—two powers that reside in the mysterious, subconscious place where new ideas and dreams come from—also played critical roles.

So I suggest we forget about animal metaphors and speak directly about the four distinct personal powers everyone uses to get things done. We start with the two dominant forces—Passion and Reason—and then add the two additional elements I mentioned above: your powers of Imagination and Intuition. Finally, I would like to bring Plato's soul back into the picture. The way I see it, "you" stand somewhat apart from your thoughts, feelings, and other mental abilities. So your conscious identity (the sense of your "true self" we explored in the preceding chapter, on self-confidence) gets to play an important role as the decider, arbiter, and orchestrator.

If you still need a metaphor, think of the four forces of **P**assion, **I**magination, **I**ntuition, and **R**eason (PIIR—pronounced "peer") as your achievement team—a group made up of four talented specialists each offering something unique and valuable. When it is aroused, your Passion is the strongest, most dominant member. As we have seen throughout the book, your basic needs, fears, and desires provide the impetus for everything you do—and play special roles in keeping you excited about long-term projects and pushing you across the finish line. Reason contributes the analytic, logical planning skills you need to craft and carry out the goals your Passions dictate. Imagination and Intuition provide creative and integrative talents. They help you envision the future, create new solutions, and make lightning-quick adjustments when unexpected problems arise.

A DEEPER LOOK AT INTUITION

Chapter 6 explored Passion as a source for motivation. Reason and Imagination are familiar companions in your day-to-day life. But what, exactly, is Intuition?

Malcolm Gladwell's book *Blink* calls it the power of "thinking without thinking." Intuition is what helps a speaker sense when she is losing her audience, a firefighter escape a burning building before it collapses, a parent suspect that her child is lying, and an employee recognize instantly that her new boss is going to be trouble. It provides you with "snap judgments" and "instinctive" reactions to situations and people. Intuition and imagination combine in the world of subconscious dreams, daydreams, and fantasy.

How does Intuition work? According to the Nobel Prize–winning social scientist Herbert Simon, the experience is triggered when something distinctive happens that sets your unconscious mind on a search for linkages between this immediate experience and items stored in your long-term memory. The feeling of "having an intuition" is the pattern-recognition moment when the past connects to the present and you have a hard-to-explain sense of "understanding"—of what is going on or what to do next. The more extensive your experience with a given type of situation, the more refined are your intuitions about it.

During waking life, as parts of your primitive survival system, your five senses constantly scan your reactions to your surroundings for signs of the familiar and unfamiliar. Your Intuition busily integrates all that data and uses it to help you recognize threats and opportunities in your everyday experience—usually without your being consciously aware of it.

Because intuition does most of its work beyond your conscious awareness, you cannot see how it is putting together its insights. Thus, you often need to exercise judgment before placing complete faith in your "gut feelings." This is especially true when you are engaged in focused, long-term projects that involve a series of decisions, only some of which involve deadlines. Two key considerations can help guide you in using judgment to weigh your Intuitions.

1. Too Little Versus Too Much Information.

Intuitive processing works swiftly—so it often fires off an insight before there is a sound basis for one. This means you have to constantly remind yourself that your Intuition is only as good as the information that forms its foundation. Social scientists refer to quirks in intuitive mental processing as "cognitive" or "decision" biases. Researchers have identified more than forty such systematic errors, with additional ones being discovered and labeled every year as experiments continue to focus on this area. These biases include feeling too confident based on too little information, being overly attracted to information that is vivid or easy to remember, paying selective attention to facts that confirm your beliefs, being swayed more by the first or last data presented in a long series, and reaching different hunches based solely on how information is framed, contrasted, or presented to you.

You can find detailed reports on these and many other biases—most of which concern the problem of drawing incorrect conclusions too quickly—in books such as Christopher Chabris and Daniel Simons's *The Invisible Gorilla, and Other Ways Our Intuitions Deceive Us*, Dan Ariely's *Predictably Irrational*, Jonathan Baron's *Thinking and Deciding*, and Max Bazerman's and Don Moore's *Judgment in Managerial Decision Making*.

As you learn to seek more or better data, however, you also need to understand that the mind can be led astray by the opposite problem—the desire to eliminate all uncertainty and risk before acting on an Intuition. When the risks are high or there are simply too many options to choose from, it is easy to slip into "analysis paralysis."

In *The Paradox of Choice: Why More Is Less*, the Swathmore psychologist Barry Schwartz makes the case that we often have too much information about too many everyday choices—leaving us exhausted by the effort of sifting the data.

Consider the case of Dan Shi, an American high-school student who visited fifty-five schools in three countries (the United States, Canada, and the United Kingdom) in his effort to find the "perfect" college. After his marathon of campus visits, he applied to twenty-four schools and was accepted at nine. He wrote twenty unique essays, spent over $2,000 on application fees, and stayed in more motels and guesthouses during his college tour than his parents cared to count.

In the end, he enrolled in the fifty-fifth school he visited—a small urban school called Macalester College in St. Paul, Minnesota. Was this a good school for Shi? He told a reporter for *The New York Times* that he was very happy with his choice. Was it the only small urban college in the United States he could have attended and felt good about? Almost certainly not. In fact, it appears to me that Dan Shi fell for one of the cognitive biases mentioned above. This one is called the "recency effect." When you absorb a lot of data over a prolonged period of weeks or months, your mind often recalls more readily and vividly the most recent data you have been exposed to—and overweights them in your decision.

The ready availability of cheap information has made the "perfect" choice the enemy of the "good enough" decision. As Schwartz notes, "The alternative to maximizing is to be a satisficer. To satisfice is to settle for something that is good enough and not worry about the possibility that there might be something better."

Lesson: in the search for more and better information to inform your Intuition, you need to strike a balance between too little and too much. As Andy Grove, the legendary former CEO of Intel, once advised, "dive deep into the data, then trust your gut," when you are making a decision based on complex inputs. Unless you are one of the mission controllers on a Mars launch, it may not be worth the effort to eliminate all risk or uncertainty.

2. Patterns, Patterns, Everywhere. But Do They Really Exist?

An especially pervasive problem with Intuition derives from its essential function: moving at light speed to create meaning out of the chaos of sense experience. As a pattern-seeking machine, your Intuition sometimes sees patterns that are not there.

A study published in the *Journal of Neuroscience* sheds light on how Intuition can lead you into error in some very predictable circumstances. In the study, researchers tested to see how often people make gambling decisions based on illusory, short-term patterns they perceive when looking at random data. Sadly, it turned out to be the norm. The experimenters gave subjects a chance to place bets on any one of four slot machines, all of which were programmed to deliver random payoffs. Facing a complex and hard-to-predict problem, people quickly developed a simple, intuitive rule of thumb to govern their decisions. They placed their next bet based on how much a given machine had paid off on the two most recent spins.

There was one group of experimental subjects, however, who adopted the wiser practice of placing their bets on the average payoffs for all the machines and not on imagined short-term payoff patterns. These were people who had suffered brain damage to the portion of their frontal cortex that is responsible for pattern-seeking, intuitive thinking. In other words, these brain-damaged people had become "smarter" at gambling by virtue of having lost the services of their Intuition.

The stock market expert Jason Zweig, who writes The Intelligent Investor column for *The Wall Street Journal*, once drew a parallel between this experiment and investing in the stock market. He noted that average individual investors often make the same intuition-based mistake investing money in the stock market as did the normal subjects betting on the random slot machines. They buy when they detect a recent pattern of rising stock prices and sell when they see a pattern of falling prices. This is, of course, an excellent way to lose money. The smart investor does the opposite: selling into rising markets and buying when stocks are getting cheaper.

To overcome this problem, Zweig advises investors to follow a 100 percent Reason-based strategy that relies on checklists of objective criteria that signal when to buy or sell. He also suggests continuing to track the results of any investment you sell so you can compare those results with the new assets you invested in.

Your Intuition, in short, is not your whole mind. It is part of a team. An important aspect of your success is gaining enough self-understanding to know when to listen to Intuition and when to weigh it against Reason. Overall, when your Passion, Imagination, Intuition, and Reason are all working in harmony, toward a focused goal that is consistent with your basic values and beliefs, you will experience the kind of coherence that got Charles Lindbergh safely across the Atlantic in his single-engine plane.

With these four mental powers at your command, and with you at the controls, let's get the achievement process under way. As we shall see below, different stages of the achievement process often require special attention to one power more than the others. And now that we have had this introduction, I will stop capitalizing the words passion, imagination, intuition, and reason so you can focus on their operation rather than their labels.

Step #1: Consult Your Passions—Identify a Worthy Goal

The first step in achievement usually involves identifying a specific problem worth solving. Sometimes someone will simply hand you the problem and tell you to figure it out. But the search for genuine success, sooner or later, requires you to be proactive, to discover and act on problems you yourself select based on what you want. That process often starts, as chapter 4 on meaningful work suggested, when you acknowledge that you are dissatisfied with some aspect of your life. What do you want that could make your life more fun, purposeful, interesting, or challenging?

On that clear night in September 1926, as he was flying the mail to Chicago, Lindbergh was looking for more challenge. Running in the back of his mind was the steady hum of his mental powers at work on a question: what is something new and exciting I can do in aviation? He knew he was passionate about flying, but he was frustrated by how long it was taking for commercial aviation to become an accepted business.

Identifying a specific problem to work on is a vital step in the achievement process because your team of mental powers needs focus in order to work effectively. As Charles Kettering, the inventor of the first electric starter for automobiles, once said, "A problem well stated is a problem half solved."

You are looking for a goal that is neither too broad nor too narrow. The mind works by running through rapid-fire sequences of associations between the problems put to it and the data it retrieves to work on those problems. If you frame a problem too broadly, you will trigger more scattered and less useful mental associations. The question "How can I be happy?" (as we saw in chapter 2) may provoke some interesting philosophical debates, but it is probably too abstract to bring you more of whatever happiness is.

On the other hand, if you pitch the problem too narrowly—such as "Should I quit my job?"—your mind may fail to consider options that could better solve the true, underlying issue you face: what should you do next to further your career? Many achievement stories start when people ask friends or colleagues to help them shape a specific, actionable problem out of a general area of dissatisfaction.

Step #2: Let Your Imagination and Intuition Generate Ideas

As Lindbergh's mind considered his next career move, it clicked through a set of associations, moving from thoughts about piloting experimental aircraft to the types of experimental planes being used in the race to win the Orteig Prize—and finally to the startling insight that he could solve his career problem by entering that race himself. It was, like many ideas your subconscious mind generates, outrageous— even a little crazy.

As this example shows, your intuition excels at combining things that your conscious reason has kept in separate buckets and then using these disparate items to create new ideas. These subconscious powers have no "rationality" check. They just put things together to see what happens, creating the raw materials from which you can construct your goals. The product designer Henry Thorne, who invented the self-navigating delivery carts you now find in many hospitals, put it this way: "If you define what you're trying to achieve clearly enough, then the ideas [simply] present themselves to you." You just have to be patient.

The moments when these ideas pop up may seem random, but they often occur when the intentional parts of your mind either are shut down entirely or are in a distinctly relaxed state. For example, it was no accident that Lindbergh stumbled onto his idea to go for the Orteig Prize while piloting a boring midnight flight.

Here are some other common situations when your imagination and intuition are likely to present you with new ideas.

Sleep. The ancient philosopher Heraclitus once noted, "Even a soul submerged in sleep is hard at work." Google cofounder Larry Page once told a story at the University of Michigan in which he described how the powers of his unconscious mind helped him think up the idea behind the Google search engine. He was a twenty-three-year-old graduate student at Stanford and was searching for a Ph.D. thesis topic. One night, he woke up with a vivid thought left over from a dream. "I was thinking: What if we could download the whole Web and just keep the links? I grabbed a pen and started writing. . . . I spent the middle of that night scribbling out the details and convincing myself that it could work." The next day, he took his idea to his Ph.D. adviser at Stanford, Terry Winograd, who encouraged him to work on it. Eventually, he and fellow student Sergey Brin came up with a way to link his dream to a method for ranking web pages, and the Google search engine was born. Page concluded his talk with a piece of advice: "When a really great dream shows up, grab it."

In her book on dreaming and creativity, *The Committee of Sleep*, Harvard Medical School professor Deirdre Barrett tells the story of how Paul McCartney of the Beatles wrote one of the most widely played songs of all time—"Yesterday"—based on a dream. At age twenty-two, McCartney was staying at his mother's house in London while the band was filming the movie *Help!* He woke up one morning with the sound of a string ensemble playing a melody in his head. There was a piano in his bedroom, and he got out of bed and ran through the chord progression for the song he had dreamed. "I liked the melody a lot, but because I'd dreamed it, I couldn't believe I'd written it," he later said. He spent months checking it out to make sure it was really his and not a song he had heard elsewhere. He called the tune "Scrambled Eggs" and the lyrics that helped him remember it went, "Scrambled eggs, oh, my baby, how I love your legs. . . ." Eventually, the song—with greatly improved lyrics—found its way onto the *Sgt. Pepper's Lonely Hearts Club Band* album.

Other famous dreams have yielded major scientific breakthroughs. For example, Dmitri Mendeleev credited a dream for his discovery of chemistry's periodic table, and Friedrich August Kekulé discerned the ring shape of the organic chemical compound benzene in a dream of a snake biting its tail.

Research confirms what these examples suggest: that sleep is a reliable source of what psychologists call "offline" consolidation and learning by the subconscious mind. A study reported in *Psychological Science* demonstrated that people who were given goals and then asked to "sleep on them" were better at both remembering the goals and completing them than were people given the same goals and asked to work on them later the same day. The researchers concluded that "consolidation processes active during sleep increase the probability that a goal will be spontaneously retrieved and executed." In another study, published in the *Proceedings of the National Academy of Sciences*, people being trained in a new hand-eye coordination skill exhibited more rapid progress when two training sessions were separated by a night's sleep than when they were separated by an equal amount of waking time. The study's conclusion: "sleep after training" improves both "speed and accuracy of performance."

If you want to put your mind to work when you are asleep, formulate the problem you are working on in a simple, clear way just before you go to bed. Focus on it and imagine actually handing it off to your imagination and intuition before you drift off to sleep. Then keep something near your bed to record any thoughts that may come up either in the middle of the night or when you wake up the next day.

Relaxed Moments. In addition to the moment when you wake up from sleep, other favorite times for intuitive insights include daydreaming (Lindbergh's case), meditating, bathing, walking, and driving.

For example, the graphic designer Milton Glaser once undertook an assignment to create the graphic design for an ad campaign for the city of New York—a daunting challenge at the time (the mid-1970s) because the city was suffering from a crime wave and was almost bankrupt. The ad copy had already been written: "I love New York." Glaser's problem was to make that phrase into an iconic image. After weeks of work, he came up with a design that featured an elegant type font on a white background and received enthusiastic approval for it.

But Glaser was unable to shake the idea that the project was not over. About a week after sending the final design, Glaser was sitting in a cab stuck in traffic when his intuition struck. His mind on other things, he suddenly had a "Eureka!" moment in which he saw an entirely new design, this time with a big red heart right in the middle of it.

Thus was born, in the backseat of a taxi, one of the most memorable design campaigns of the twentieth century: "I ♥ NY."

The bottom line: to engage the powers of your subconscious mind, you need to frame a good problem, load up on data related to it, and then trust your intuitive powers to start coming up with ideas. Be ready to record the results—it is all too easy to forget good ideas (and good dreams) if you do not write them down.

Step #3: Commit to a Specific, Challenging Plan

The third step in Lindbergh's achievement process called on both imagination and reason. His idea to try for the $25,000 Orteig Prize prompted an immediate search for a specific plan to achieve this. He imagined a variety of options for crossing the Atlantic, and then subjected them to critical analysis.

After he landed his mail plane in Chicago, he went to bed, and, as he lay there, his mind started checking off the reasons why the other crews who had attempted the flight had failed. Chief among them was unnecessary weight. The most recent crash had involved a twenty-eight-thousand-pound, three-engine biplane with red leather trimmings, a bed, several radio sets, and a crew of two pilots, a navigator, and a radio operator.

From there, his mind returned to some of the experimental planes he had been daydreaming about, especially a new, high-efficiency single-engine aircraft called the Wright-Bellanca. "[I]f I can get the Bellanca, I'll fly alone," he thought that night. "That will cut out the need for any selection of crew, or quarreling. . . . I'll take only the food I need to eat and a few concentrated rations. I'll carry a rubber boat for emergency and a little extra water."

Nobody had yet attempted the New York to Paris flight alone in a single-engine plane. But the idea excited Lindbergh, and the next morning he awoke with a surge of energy. It was, he later wrote, the "dawn of a new life, a life in which I'm going to fly across the ocean to Europe!" He had convinced himself that his solo, single-engine plane idea was actually safer than the multi-engine, big crew approach everyone else was taking. If, halfway across the ocean, one engine failed on a big, three-engine plane, the crew would have to bail out anyway. There was no safety in numbers. Meanwhile, his plan dramatically reduced the risks of technical complexity, weight, and potential miscommunication among crew members.

As you move from your goal toward a specific action plan, consider a set of criteria used by many businesses called "SMART." A SMART plan is one that is Specific, Measurable, Actionable, Relevant, and Timely. In addition, think about how you can bring more commitment to your goal—typically by writing it down, talking to others about it, announcing it in public, and acquiring a sense of accountability for seeing it through. Research shows that the more committed you are to your goal, the more likely it is you will accomplish it.

Focusing on long-term goals is something my University of Pennsylvania colleague Angela Duckworth has studied in depth. She and a team of colleagues developed an achievement-related assessment called the GRIT scale that measures people's ability to stick with long-term goals. She discovered that GRIT scores do a great job of predicting which children will win national spelling bees, which cadets will complete their first (and hardest) summer training program at West Point, and which students are more likely to excel at tough urban high schools.

Duckworth's GRIT concept is a combination of two things: persistence and passion. While your personality accounts for some amount of your persistence, you can increase GRIT levels by selecting long-term goals that are well adapted to your core motivations—as the introverted Lindbergh's fly-solo action plan was to his. If you are a socially oriented person, your GRIT will increase if you pick projects that involve people. If you are more intellectual, choose projects with strong idea-based components. And if you are highly emotional, seek projects related to emotional expression, the arts, or the theater.

When you add GRIT to SMART, you get an unbeatable combination of action-plan attributes. For example, in the early 1960s, President John F. Kennedy faced a different kind of race from Lindbergh's, and he crafted one of the "grittiest" SMART goals in modern history to win it. The race was between the United States and its chief geopolitical rival, the Soviet Union, for technological supremacy. In April 1961, the Soviets shocked the world by placing the first man into orbit around the earth—something the United States was in no position to match. Far behind in the space race, President Kennedy changed the game with a dramatic announcement made before a joint session of Congress in May 1961.

He used that speech to challenge the nation to come up with a plan for "landing a man on the moon and returning him safely to the earth" by the end of the decade. He continued to amplify that goal in the months that followed by underlining the challenges it posed, including the need to find as-yet-undiscovered scientific knowledge to address the as-yet-unknown problems involved in visiting a celestial body. Kennedy's goal was difficult, specific, measurable, and actionable as an engineering challenge. It was also immediately relevant to the geopolitical situation faced by America and carried a definite deadline for execution. Finally, Kennedy's goal shared an important trait in common with Charles Lindbergh's single-engine-solo-pilot goal. It was emotionally vivid and inspiring—a key factor in triggering creativity as the implementation process moves forward.

Kennedy's goal galvanized the efforts of thousands of people in the following years, culminating in the Apollo 11 mission that landed two Americans on the moon on July 20, 1969, and returned its three-man crew safely to earth four days later. By the way, among the thousands who had gathered at the John F. Kennedy Space Center on July 16, 1969, to watch the launch of Apollo 11 was a sixty-seven-year-old former mail pilot named Charles Lindbergh. Forty-three years earlier he had set a gritty, SMART, challenging, and inspiring goal for himself—and, like Kennedy, achieved it.

Step #4: Break It Down into Small Steps

Big goals are inspiring, but they are also daunting. In Step #4, you need to break them down into small, manageable chunks. As a

Roman general, Quintus Sertorius, once noted, "Many things which cannot be overcome when they stand together yield themselves up when taken little by little."

Practically from the first moment Lindbergh conceived his idea, he was focused on the need "to lay a plan and then follow it step by step no matter how small or large each one by itself may seem." A few days after he decided to fly solo across the Atlantic, he took out a piece of paper and titled it: "St. Louis—New York—Paris." He then listed thirty-five specific items he needed to take care of to make his dream into a reality, touching everything from the need for financial backers and a plane to maps, condensed food, and a New York airfield from which to take off.

As the next few months unfolded, Lindbergh started to work on some technical skills he knew he needed to improve—such as long-distance navigation—and perfected the way he pitched his idea. He learned to talk about it as a way to make St. Louis a leading center for aviation and argued that the $25,000 Orteig Prize would more than reimburse any up-front costs his backers would need to cover. He used connections at his company and the local St. Louis airport to gain introductions to possible funding sources. He hit pay dirt when a local banker named Harold Bixby, who was the head of the St. Louis Chamber of Commerce, became interested in his project and agreed to take care of the financing. Lindbergh later wrote that "aside from a plane with performance enough to make the flight, my greatest asset lies in the character of my partners in St. Louis."

With his backers in place, he was ready to take his next step: acquiring a plane that could make the trip.

Let's pause the story at this point to take a look at what research tells us about the importance of step-by-step planning in achievement. The conclusion could not be clearer: a goal without a good plan is like a new car without any gas in the tank. It looks good, but it cannot take you anywhere.

In a notable study of academic achievement, researchers randomly selected college students who were struggling with their grades and conducted a simple intervention. Half the students were given a two-hour, web-based, goal-setting tutorial. The program led students through a five-step process to conceive, frame, and write out specific personal goals related to their future, followed by a three-step tutorial to help them lay out detailed strategies for how they would achieve the goals they had set.

The other group in the study received a two-hour series of web-based self-assessments measuring their personality traits and career aptitudes. This group of students was then given a report on the results of these assessments—but no training on how to set and act on goals.

At the end of the following semester, the researchers reviewed the academic performance of the two groups. The overall grade point average of all the students at the beginning of the study was the same: 2.2 on a 4.0 scale (roughly a C average). Four months later, however, the grades of the group that had received the goal tutorial had risen, on average, from 2.2 to 2.9, while the other group's grades rose only from 2.2 to 2.3. In addition, the members of the goal-tutorial group carried heavier course loads and felt better about themselves and their academic performance. This simple intervention, in short, had materially improved the chances for these students to graduate on time and with a new, more positive attitude.

Step-by-step implementation plans for your goals serve several important purposes related to achievement. First and most obviously, they give you the road map to follow so you can move efficiently toward your target. You don't waste time reviewing the whole project at each step on the way. Second, such plans can help shield your goals from distractions when temptations arise to divert your attention. As Lindbergh's plan got closer and closer to completion, he began getting offers worth hundreds of thousands of dollars from film companies and speakers bureaus eager to sign him up. He turned them all down without a second look—these tempting, lucrative contracts were not on his list of thirty-five action items needed to get him safely to Paris.

As you move your achievement process forward, follow Lindbergh's example. Take out a piece of paper and write down a list of the things that need to be done. Then sketch a preliminary plan that will enable you to check those items off.

Step #5: Improvise and Adjust—Then Close the Deal

When I paused the movie, Lindbergh had found his backers but did not yet have a plane. I saved this crucial part of his story for Step #5 because it illustrates the need for flexibility and shows how all four of your mental powers—passion, reason, imagination, and intuition— have roles to play as you close in on your goals.

As I noted earlier, Lindbergh had originally targeted an experimental, one-of-a-kind plane called the Wright-Bellanca for his attempt to win the Orteig Prize. At first, the owners of that plane did not want to risk it on a transatlantic flight that might end in a crash—destroying the company reputation along with the plane and the pilot. That set

Lindbergh to work trying to find a company that would build an experimental plane for him. As time passed and the excitement of Lindbergh's idea sank in, however, the owners of the Bellanca changed their minds. They named a $15,000 price for the aircraft and asked Lindbergh to come to New York with a check.

When he arrived, however, he was greeted by someone he had never met—an entrepreneur named Charles A. Levine. Levine, it appeared, had slipped between Lindbergh and his goal—he had purchased the Bellanca and wanted to enter the race with a crew of his own. But he was more than willing to shift the financial risk to the St. Louis team. He offered Lindbergh and his backers the chance to buy the plane, but he thought Lindbergh was too young and inexperienced for the mission. So Levine agreed to sell only if he could name the pilot for the historic flight.

Lindbergh walked away from this insulting offer, so discouraged that he told his group he was giving up his quest. That's when his team stepped up to supply the passion and motivation Lindbergh was starting to lose. They told him to keep working on the plan to build a plane of his own. He had previously made contact with an unknown aircraft company in San Diego, California, called Ryan Airlines that had said it could build his plane for $6,000 (not including the engine) within the three-month deadline he had set. Lindbergh contacted Ryan again, placed his order, and moved to San Diego.

Working hand in glove with a top aircraft designer at Ryan, he set out to "build my own experience into the plane's structure." The aircraft that emerged, the *Spirit of St. Louis*—now residing in the National Air and Space Museum at the Smithsonian in Washington, D.C.—was built for a single pilot, wing tanks full of fuel, one engine, and little else. It had no front windshield and carried no parachute, night-flying equipment, raft, or radio, or even a navigation sextant. So concerned was Lindbergh about the plane's weight that he even tried to rig the landing gear so it would drop off after takeoff, requiring him to land the plane in Paris on its belly. But his backers, alarmed for his safety, refused to allow it.

The plane ultimately cost a little over $10,000 and was equipped with the same high-efficiency Whirlwind engine that powered the Wright-Bellanca. Thus, as sometimes happens, Lindbergh's setback had turned out to be a blessing in disguise—he got to use the same, best-in-class engine he had wanted all along but in a plane that was as custom-made to his needs as a well-tailored suit. His trip between San Diego and New York's Roosevelt Field set a speed record for a coast-to-coast flight. A few days later, more than thirty thousand people showed up at the airfield, generating a circus-like atmosphere as they gawked at Lindbergh and his competitors (who included Charles Levine with the Wright-Bellanca) getting ready to take off for Paris.

The race was on—if only a late-May foul-weather system over the Atlantic would clear.

A MOMENT OF DECISION "BEYOND
THE CONSCIOUS MIND"

In every achievement story, there comes a point where someone has to make a critical decision. And it is in such moments that all four mental powers weigh in—each one battling for the last word. Reason lobbies to reduce risk; passion seeks glory and reward; imagination probes the future to see what it might hold; intuition nudges first one way and then another.

On May 19, 1927, late-night reports broke that the weather might be improving. Lindbergh, caught off guard, went to bed late and slept poorly. When he arrived at the field early the next morning, he was surprised to find that his competitors were not preparing to take off. He also heard that Charles Levine's team was in disarray, still bickering over who would pilot the Bellanca.

Incredibly, he had a chance to jump ahead of his competition—to take off for Paris before the others could get organized. But questions filled his mind. With so much fuel, would the struts supporting the landing gear weaken or snap? Would the humid air affect his engine's performance? Would the soft, wet runway under his wheels slow him down? Would the weather forecast hold? Lindbergh faced his big moment—go or no go?

He weighed every factor but realized that reason could not tell him what to do. This is how he later described his state of mind in *The Spirit of St. Louis*:

> The limits of logic are passed. Now, the intangible elements of flight—experience, instinct, intuition—must make the final judgment, place their weight upon the scales. In the last analysis, when the margin is close, when all the known factors have been considered, after equations have produced their final, lifeless numbers, one measures a field with an eye, and checks the answer beyond the conscious mind.

As his intuition whirred into action, he also called on his imagination to envision the future and test how his plane might respond to these unique conditions. "Something within you disengages itself from your body and travels ahead with your vision to make the test," he wrote. "You can feel it make the jump as you stand looking."

He suddenly felt his uncertainty give way to conviction. It was "go."

He nodded to his crew, throttled up his engine, and rumbled down the short runway, the plane rising into the air and then bumping roughly back to the ground several times from the weight of the extra fuel in his wings. With the runway getting short, the plane finally heaved itself upward and was airborne.

As he settled back into his cockpit, Lindbergh felt a rush of relief. His preparations had paid off, one of the most dangerous parts of his journey was behind him, and he was flying again—in a very special plane that seemed, he sensed, "to form an extension of my own body, ready to follow my wish as the hand follows the mind's desire."

Thirty-three hours and thirty minutes later, he landed in Paris, greeted by tens of thousands of people who had heard of his progress on the radio as he passed over Ireland and England. One small, single-engine plane had made it from New York to Paris without stopping—and the world's first truly global media celebrity had been born.

THE NEED TO ADJUST

Focused planning works because it creates the best conditions for adjustment and improvisation. Napoleon famously summed up his genius as a military strategist with eight words: "You engage, and then you wait and see." The more complex, interactive, and lengthy a plan of action is, the more improvisation will be required for you to reach the goal. Step-by-step plans are necessary, but adhering to them too rigidly closes your mind to opportunities.

Lindbergh was ready to quit when he lost the plane that he had expected to fly. It took his backers to remind him that an even better plane awaited him—one that did not yet exist—if only he would adjust his expectations, improvise, and keep moving forward.

Virtually all the stories we have encountered so far in this book have illustrated how rarely life works out exactly as we plan it. Successful people understand that chance and serendipity play an important part in life. They put themselves in motion, alert for every opportunity that may arise.

By focusing your mind on a basic problem in a relatively (but not completely) open-ended way, you leave your imagination and intuition free to seek a variety of possible solutions when you hit an obstacle. If the flight you expected to take is canceled, you immediately set to work finding another way to get where you are going. What is true for a single journey is also true about life. When one plan falls through, step back, remember your focus, and take another path.

THE FOCUS EXERCISE:
REVIEW YOUR OWN ACHIEVEMENT PROCESS

As we conclude this chapter, I would like to challenge you to think back to an especially notable achievement of a long-term goal from your past. It could be related to your education, a career success, or something you did for your family or community. Then I would like you to outline the focused achievement process you used to get your result. As you review this event, consider how you sequenced and combined your passion, reason, imagination, and intuition to get it done. Chances are, this episode holds some lessons for the next achievement challenge you might want to undertake—and for your search to find your next success in life.

1. Notable achievement:

_____

_____

_____

_____

2. What desires, passions, or emotions inspired this project? What motivated you to undertake it? Did someone assign it to you or did you proactively seek it out?

_____

_____

_____

_____

3. How, if at all, did goal setting and planning play roles in this achievement? Did you apply achievement practices more systematically and, if so, how?

_____

_____

_____

_____

4. Did you need to improvise your tactics and adjust your plans to make this project work out? How?

_____

_____

_____

_____

5. Which of your four mental powers—passion, imagination, intuition, and reason—did you rely on most in this achievement process? Give specific examples of how you used each power.

Passion:

_____

_____

_____

_____

Imagination:

_____

_____

_____

_____

Intuition:

_____

_____

_____

Reason:

_____

_____

_____

CONCLUSION

Lindbergh's story of focused achievement is inspiring. But attaining goals is not the only or even the most important measure of success. Lindbergh's famous flight gave him a place in history, yet when we discuss his story in the Success class, students often debate whether he was a truly "successful" person. When you examine his life as a whole, you quickly discover that it was filled with sadness and controversy. One of his children was kidnapped and murdered; he maintained several secret families with different women on different continents; he played a leading role on the America First Committee that lobbied to keep the United States out of the war against Hitler before the Pearl Harbor attack; he was accused by many, for this and other reasons, of being anti-Semitic; and he spent most of his later years working in relative obscurity to protect endangered species and indigenous peoples around the world.

Lindbergh himself concluded near the end of his life that his New York to Paris flight was much less important than it had seemed at the time. He concluded that "all the achievements of mankind have value only to the extent that they preserve and improve the quality of life."

The Beatle John Lennon warned about the trap of putting too much stock in achievement goals when he wrote the song "Beautiful Boy (Darling Boy)." As he put it, your life is what is happening around you while "you're busy making other plans." It is all too easy to let urgent but unimportant goals take priority over issues and values that are more genuinely important. Remember this the next time you are tempted to run a red light—putting your own life and others' lives at risk—in order to get to a business meeting on time. In your haste to relentlessly check off the little goals that pop up in your life every day like so many Whac-a-Moles, you may forget that one of the truest measures of success in your life is how you live it, not just what you accomplish.

For example, in a research study conducted at the Princeton Theological Seminary, psychologists gave students an assignment to prepare a sermon about the parable of the Good Samaritan (a Bible story about stopping to help people in need). Each student had a precise time slot for delivering the sermon but was set up to be running late. The experimenters then staged their test. To enter the chapel where the sermon would be delivered, each student had to literally step over the slumped body of a disheveled man in obvious need of assistance. Driven by their urgent goal to get to the chapel on time, only 10 percent of the students stopped to offer help to the distressed man.

In the rush to address urgent goals, therefore, do not forget what is really important in your life: family, health, and taking care of others.

Finally, the success industry likes to make a mystery of the mental powers we use to achieve things. Only true believers, the success books say, can access these magical powers to make the future unfold as we would like. But, as Teller, the quieter half of the professional magician team Penn & Teller, once said, "There is nothing special. . . . The magic is coming from your mind." Scientists may not be able to tell us exactly how we form a thought, experience a feeling, or imagine the future, but every child can do these things. As Lindbergh's story shows, there are no "secrets" to success—just clarity of purpose, hard work, focus, and persistence.

With that thought in mind, let's move to our final chapter. You have a worthy goal and have made a plan to execute it. But how are you going to influence others to help you get where you want to go?

Turn the page. We started this chapter on a single-engine plane. The next one begins with a shipwreck.

Success Step #8

FOCUS THE POWERS OF YOUR MIND TO ACHIEVE LONG-TERM GOALS

There are a lot of success gurus who talk about the "secret" powers of the mind. But there are no secrets. Everyone has passion, imagination, intuition, and reason. To succeed, you need to find long-term goals that inspire these four faculties to work together in a sustained, creative way.

Here is a process you can use to harness these forces for maximum impact.

Consult your passions—identify a worthy goal.

Let your imagination and intuition generate ideas.

Commit to a specific, challenging plan.

Break it down into small steps.

Improvise and adjust—then close the deal.

Influence Others:
Credibility and Dialogue

Always do right. This will gratify some people and astonish the rest.

—MARK TWAIN

On May 25, 1927, in a deep fog just off Nantucket Island south of Cape Cod, Massachusetts, the SS *Malolo*—the largest merchant ship yet built in America—was rammed broadside at full speed by an oncoming Norwegian freighter. The collision sliced a vertical gash two feet wide and fifteen feet high into the *Malolo*'s hull just at the point where the engine and boiler rooms were located. As people would later note, it was exactly the same type of collision that sank the British ocean liner *Empress of Ireland* in 1914 at a cost of over one thousand lives. This was a hull breach every bit as devastating to the ship's structural integrity as the one suffered by the *Titanic* when she collided with an iceberg in the North Atlantic in 1912. With seven thousand tons of seawater flooding into its engine rooms that foggy May morning, the *Malolo* was doomed.

Or it would have been had its designer, William Francis "Willy" Gibbs (who was onboard the *Malolo* at the time the accident occurred), been anything less than an obsessive perfectionist when it came to ship safety. As it was, Gibbs's revolutionary new hull design saved the day. The *Malolo* never listed more than five degrees from vertical after its collision, remained comfortably afloat as it was towed back to New York Harbor, and was soon repaired. It proudly sailed the seas for another fifty years.

Willy Gibbs's hull design became the standard in the industry—and immediately established his credibility as the premier naval architect of his generation. His firm, Gibbs & Cox, eventually grew to one thousand employees and designed 63 percent of all merchant ships over two thousand tons and 74 percent of all American naval vessels used in World War II. He was so important to the war effort that, as Americans battled the Japanese for control of the Pacific island of Guadalcanal and Hitler launched the Nazi attack on Stalingrad, *Time* magazine featured Willy Gibbs on the cover of its September 28, 1942, issue in a story titled "Ship Designer Gibbs: Yankees Again Are Experts at Sending Ships Down to the Sea."

After the war, he personally designed and supervised the construction of his lifelong dream ship—the fastest, safest, and largest American-made luxury liner ever built: the SS *United States*, which launched in 1952. Gibbs's firm, which he owned and operated as a two-man partnership with his younger brother, remains a thriving business today, the most successful independent naval architecture firm in the market.

As the historian Steven Ujifusa chronicled in his book, *A Man and His Ship: America's Greatest Naval Architect and His Quest to Build the S.S. United States*, few men have ever succeeded as thoroughly as Gibbs did in the shipbuilding business. Gibbs's secret? Three things.

First, like many people you have met in this book, he devoted his life to something that interested him. The shipbuilding business captured his imagination from the day he first witnessed, at the age of eight, the pomp and ceremony accompanying the launch of the ocean liner *St. Louis* at a Philadelphia shipyard. "[F]rom that day forward," Gibbs later said, "I dedicated my life to ships."

Second, although he was obedient to his family until his midtwenties, he did not let his family's expectations keep him from the work he longed to do. His father insisted that he become a lawyer. In the service of this goal, Gibbs went first to Harvard, dropped out when his father's businesses crashed in a financial panic, and finally ended up working his way through Columbia and Columbia Law School. He was grateful, he later said, that financial necessity had taught him the value of hard work. But he practiced law for only a single year after graduation.

In fact, no matter where he was in school, he always ended up retreating to his room to tinker with ship designs. Even in law school, he studied engineering on his own at night to advance his shipbuilding dream. "That's the way to really learn things—by *yourself*," he declared. His real life began after he quit the law job he hated and became an apprentice to a top naval architect. After that, he never looked back.

Gibbs's third success secret relates to the special question we address in this chapter—how he handled the social aspects of success. He was committed to being himself when it came to dealing with other people. He had one of the most disagreeable, cranky personalities in his industry and violated just about every rule proposed by the most popular success book of his generation, Dale Carnegie's *How to Win Friends and Influence People*. Gibbs rarely smiled, did not bother learning people's names, and abhorred flattery. "This business of being popular and having everybody like you is for the birds," he told *Fortune* magazine in an interview. "I think people thank God I'm no worse than I am."

He was not, in short, a nice man. But he succeeded because he was an authentic one. In the rough-and-tumble world of shipbuilding, this was what he needed to establish his professional credibility.

He even applied his unapologetic, I-am-what-I-am philosophy to wooing his future wife. He married late, perhaps because it took a long time for him to find someone who could put up with his personality. He was forty-one when he met Vera Cravath, the glamorous, socially prominent daughter of one of New York's leading lawyers. The two could not have been more different, but Gibbs's single-mindedness sparked the interest of this thirty-one-year-old, recently divorced woman who had seen more than her share of socially smooth but thoroughly shallow men in New York society. She explained that when she first met Gibbs at a dinner party in 1927, "I thought him rather strange, but I was fascinated. It may sound trite, but he knew what he was going to do with his life. He wanted to build ships."

They eloped one month later, shocking friends and families. Vera remained his devoted partner and biggest fan until his death in 1967. She proved as passionate in her own interests as he was in his. A lifelong opera fan whose mother was an opera singer, she eventually became the first president of the New York Metropolitan Opera Guild.

As we will see later, the social side of Gibbs's personality failed him in one critically important aspect of his life, but his credibility got him very far indeed. His story gives hope to all who think that their lack of social skills presents a barrier to fulfilling their dreams.

This chapter, then, will give you a chance to reflect more deeply on the social side of your success capabilities. In a salute to Dale Carnegie's classic book, which is one of my favorites in the success literature (even if Willy Gibbs did not follow its advice), the chapter will follow the outline Carnegie used. We'll start with friendship, and then move to influence and credibility as sources of success in interpersonal life.

I have written on subjects related to this chapter in two earlier books: *Bargaining for Advantage: Negotiation Strategies for Reasonable People* and (with my colleague Mario Moussa) *The Art of Woo: Using Strategic Persuasion to Sell Your Ideas.* This chapter will not be covering the specialized details of bargaining or persuasion, but if these topics are of particular interest to you, I recommend exploring them by consulting these works.

WINNING FRIENDS AND INFLUENCING PEOPLE

As the psychiatrist and *New York Times* contributor Paul Steinberg has noted, "Given that humans are social animals, interpersonal intelligence is perhaps the most important natural human skill—as valuable as, or more valuable than, verbal-linguistic intelligence and logical-mathematical intelligence." Thus, there is a clear answer to the question this chapter tackles.

Must you win friends and influence people in order to succeed? Yes.

But each of us does this in our own, unique way. The number of friends and amount of influence you need depends on the path you follow to success. Willy Gibbs's story suggests there are as many ways to navigate the social aspects of life as there are people and personalities. Like Gibbs, you can build influence without winning a large number of friends. Or like his wife, Vera, you can develop extensive social networks to accomplish your goals.

Before we can dig deeper into the social aspects of success, however, we need to understand what we mean by two key words: "friend" and "influence." The word "influence" is the easier of the two to define. As I see it, your influence is your capacity, without using bribes, threats, or violence, to affect the actions of other people.

Sometimes you have influence by virtue of your authority. At other times it may be due to your expert knowledge or your proven ability to do something. In many cases, a test of whether someone will allow themselves to be influenced by you relates to trust.

As Willy Gibbs's career developed, he eventually gained influence using all of these influence factors. He started with knowledge about the shipbuilding business, slowly developed his design skills, proved his ability by succeeding on several big projects, founded his firm and gained authority, and finally achieved trust by earning an industry-wide reputation for ethical dealing and reliability. All of these factors accumulated over the decades of his life to make him a powerful man when it came to affecting others' actions. But few people liked him.

The word "friend" is more of a puzzle. The advent of social media has also added new layers to the variety of social relations. Can you count as a friend someone you have never met but who loyally follows your blog on the Internet? To remain friends with someone, how often must you respond to their social media postings and comments?

One ancient authority on social life—Aristotle—divided friendships into three distinct categories: friends of pleasure, utility, and virtue. These classifications sometimes help my students parse out important differences among their friends—as well as appreciate the richness of those friendships that span all three of these domains.

Your friends of pleasure are your partners in leisure activities—whether these activities include watching sports, shopping, book or film club meetings, or barhopping. The people you interact with mainly to "get things done" at work or elsewhere are your friends of utility.

Aristotle felt that your deepest and most interesting relationships are your friends of virtue. These are the people with whom you share your innermost thoughts and feelings, perhaps over a long period of time, and with whom you always seem to be able to pick up a conversation about life, family, purpose, ideas, or passions exactly where you left off the last time you met. Although most of this chapter is directed mainly at relationships with friends of utility, I will offer you a chance near the end of the chapter to survey your life, identify the person or people you would include in your inner "virtue" circle of social relations, and review why these people have made this important list.

One thing is sure: however you define true friendship, it depends more on your authenticity as a person than on your social technique or facility with instant messaging. But being real—and accepting the inevitable flaws in your friends—is not as easy as it sounds. It requires a secure sense of self-confidence—a subject we explored in chapter 7—as well as the ability to trust other people.

Willy Gibbs's few friends forgave his crankiness rather than labeling it as offensive. They saw it as his way of protecting his very private, introverted self from having to waste time in idle chitchat and empty social rituals. Because they knew him well, they understood why he acted as he did and simply left him alone when he became too irritating. One of the few people he could relax with, the New York actress Katharine Cornell, commented that Gibbs's perfectionism at work cut him off from most people: "He was very economical with his friends . . . [but] if he liked you, he was very helpful in anything you were interested in, and he was always very generous."

When it comes to dealing with the larger set of working relationships that make up your friends of utility, however, some social role-playing is necessary. As we will see, even Willy Gibbs could turn on social charm when he absolutely had to, if only for short bursts.

MAKING FRIENDS OF UTILITY: RAPPORT

A large part of your success in dealing with other people derives from your awareness of the automatic, semiconscious reflexes that enable humans to signal to one another that they are willing to engage in everyday cooperation. Common courtesy and civility form the baseline. That usually means being willing to ask other people to talk about themselves. According to a *Wall Street Journal* report, Harvard University neuroscientists have discovered that when people talk about themselves, their needs, and their views of the world, the act "triggers the same sensation of pleasure in the brain as food or money." Said a researcher interviewed for the story, Diana Tamir: "People were even willing to forgo money in order to talk about themselves." If you have ever been curious why self-disclosure-oriented social media such as Facebook and Twitter are so popular, these brain studies suggest an answer. A tweet or a new posting about your pets on Facebook produces a form of pleasure—like finding a dollar on the street or popping a bonbon into your mouth.

With the information you gain from people, the psychological mechanisms of similarity, liking, reciprocity, and, ultimately, trust can begin to work. In the next few pages, we will examine some additional science underlying the automatic social processes that establish rapport.

Inherent in understanding these processes, however, is the paradox involved in adapting your social presentation to accomplish whatever your personal agenda might be. If you make too little effort to adjust your social style to suit a particular purpose, you risk coming across as clueless, socially unskilled, or arrogant. You may get away with this if you have the drive and credibility of a Willy Gibbs or Steve Jobs, but it is a high-risk path. On the other hand, if you try too hard to fit in, adjusting your social strategy to suit too many different audiences, you may lose people's respect and trust—a very high price in terms of your overall success.

How Much Is Your Smile Worth?

Willy Gibbs's few genuine friends came from the world of theater (he helped to found the still-thriving American Place Theatre in New York). These people appreciated Gibbs's quasi-theatrical skills when it came to managing other people's impressions of him. Actress Katharine Cornell once commented: "His wonderful dour expression—it was just a pose on his part. I don't know whether it arose from shyness; but it was absolutely marvelous [because] people were so enchanted to see him smile." Gibbs was a deeply introverted, private man. But he had enough social intelligence to know that a well-timed smile is worth a lot.

Smiles are important because they suggest that people are about to engage in a cooperative interaction. Daily life is full of potential barriers and threats. It is a relief to feel things will go well rather than badly in even the most trivial social exchange. And when the social moment is truly consequential—at a job interview, a first date, or a big sale—the total lack of a smile suggests something is wrong.

Yale psychology professor Marianne LaFrance summarized the research on smiling in her book *Lip Service: Smiles in Life, Death, Trust, Lies, Work, Memory, Sex, and Politics*. In recounting how smiles are used in social interactions to hide as well as reveal genuine feelings, she notes that smiling often causes the person smiling to feel better. In addition, if you lose your ability to smile or frown owing to injuries or Botox treatments, you may also compromise your ability to empathize with others. Our unconscious tendencies to mimic the expressions we see on others' faces help us imagine what they are feeling. When you lose the ability to mimic, you lose this source of insight.

Emotional Labor

Gibbs did not need to smile often because he was in a line of work—shipbuilding—that did not require a lot of what psychologists call "emotional labor." The same is true for many technical or knowledge-based fields such as engineering, technology, writing, accounting, or finance.

But work in the vast service-based side of the global economy—from fast-food restaurants and real estate sales to luxury hotels and consulting—requires literally hundreds of millions of people to display reassuring, positive emotions every day. The New York television news anchor Pat Kiernan once neatly summed up what emotional labor involves: "There is a lot of acting in what I do. You have to be the same person every day, regardless of how you feel." For some, jobs like these can be exhausting. For others, they require no special effort at all.

Psychologists have distinguished two different mechanisms employees use to fulfill demands for emotional work: "surface acting" and something they call "deep acting." Researchers have shown that customers pay more for services and give bigger tips when the service providers display more authentic positive emotions as part of the service experience. If you are a socially skilled extrovert, you will have an easier time getting away with mere "surface acting" to fulfill these expectations. If you are more introverted and socially reserved, you will need to dig deeper to earn your pay.

Look up from the page right now, hold your hand out, and smile at it. That is what surface acting feels like. It is a pure manipulation of your facial muscles without any genuine motivation. High school and college yearbooks, as well as candid shots taken at cocktail parties and weddings, are filled with such smiles. When the cashier at a fast-food restaurant smiles, you are most likely being treated to surface acting.

Deep-acting smiles spring from an altogether different source. You actually have to feel a touch of the real emotion that gives rise to the smile. A French doctor named Guillaume Duchenne, working in the mid-1800s, was the first scientist to study the differences between smiles. He discovered that the most convincing smiles involve activation of both the involuntary muscles around the eyes and the more voluntary muscles around the mouth. This type now bears his name—Duchenne smiles.

Did you define yourself as an extrovert on the SAME personality profiler in chapter 5? If so, you have an advantage in delivering Duchenne-style emotional labor because you actually enjoy meeting strangers. Introverts do not get paid any more than extroverts for doing service jobs, but they have to work harder to smile.

Some of my more introverted students have, at one time or another, worked as waiters or waitresses in restaurants—and they report that tips are higher when they can deliver personalized service that involves some emotional labor. How do they do it? Some imagine their customers to be members of their extended families and try to treat them "as if" they cared about them. Others, before they go to work, silently remind themselves of the importance of earning good tips to pay tuition bills or achieve some other important goal. They prepare to exert the emotional effort the job will demand and then count on their strong motivation to bring the right feelings to their customer interactions. When customers become offensive or rude, of course, introverted types can be driven to tears. No wonder introverts sometimes get exhausted by jobs that call on them to meet social rather than substantive expectations.

I worked for several years as a consultant to one of the top luxury hotel and resort chains in the world, the Four Seasons. One of the things I immediately noticed about everyone who worked for this firm—from the CEO to the desk clerks at various properties where I stayed—was their socially subdued but notably warm style of relating to people. I asked about this and was told that Four Seasons is very, very careful about whom they hire for any job that involves customer interface. Hotel staff members are, in essence, performers. Hiring is as much an audition as an interview. The senior vice president in charge of hotel operations once explained to me what is involved in running a luxury hotel: "It is like producing a Broadway show, with a cast of hundreds, that runs 365 days a year—perfectly. Everyone has their role, and we help them learn and practice it. The curtain goes up every morning and comes down long after midnight every night. It takes a special kind of person to be able to sustain that performance."

Surface acting does not cut it at the Four Seasons. The staff gets paid for reaching deeper to find their positive emotions at work, and many have been rewarded for it. On my first day consulting with them, I met the property manager for a major resort in Asia who had started his Four Seasons career as a towel boy at the pool. His smile, and the passion for customer service that lay behind it, had been worth many hundreds of thousands of dollars to him and his family.

SIMILARITY AND LIKING:
SHOULD YOU TRY TO FIT IN?

Social life is tribal. We like people more when we share something in common with them.

The research shows that virtually any common experience can trigger an automatic empathetic response. If you are traveling in a remote country and meet someone who speaks your language, you bond with him or her. At bars throughout the world, everyone who cheers for the same professional sports teams form (for a time) tribes of loyal and vocal supporters.

A study once asked subjects who had never met to team up in pairs to tap out musical tones on sensors. In some pairs, the experiment was rigged so the teammates tapped their tones in synchrony. Other teams tapped out random tones that did not match up. Later, one teammate in each pair was unfairly accused of cheating on another aspect of the test and given an onerous puzzle task to complete—but with an opportunity for his or her teammate to help out. Result: the teams that tapped together were significantly more likely to help one another and to do so for much, much longer (seven minutes of help for the synchronized groups compared with one minute for the other teams). Similar experiments have shown that commonalities as trivial as sharing a birthday, an academic major, or a taste in food with another person can increase your motivation to engage in a team-based project with them.

Thus, in most social encounters, a few steps past the opening smiles are the initial probes to find what psychologists call "similarity"—with its hoped-for "liking" effects. You probably initiate social exchanges, even with people you know reasonably well, by seeking out some recent experiences to start your conversation. The "chitchat" about movies, jobs, backgrounds, current events, or trips that Willy Gibbs so despised and his wife, Vera, so loved is especially important in establishing rapport with people you do not know well.

These social engagement rituals tend to be especially challenging for introverts. The informal, face-to-face worlds of cocktail parties, alumni reunions, or wedding receptions are stressful to those who prefer small-group interactions with people they know well. Avoiding such gatherings altogether, however, sends the signal that you do not care about the causes or people hosting these events.

How to cope? Marti Olsen Laney, the author of *The Introvert Advantage: How to Thrive in an Extrovert World*, provides some specific strategies to ensure that a social event will not drain you too quickly:

- Preparation. Think through your social strategies before any event you think might be stressful.
- Create smaller social circles within the larger gathering. Look for a quiet corner where you can sit with a few people you have found some common ground with (who will, in all likelihood, be fellow introverts).
- Come with three current topics you can steer conversations toward.
- Gravitate toward people who like to talk, use your listening skills to keep them occupied with conversations, and seek interactions with the quieter people your group attracts.
- Prepackage a few transitions. Come prepared with a few excuses ("Excuse me, I need to make a quick call home to check on . . .") so that you can drop out of conversations that

are obviously going nowhere. Use them to make your exit
before you burn out.

- Play a defined role, such as helping the host or hostess with
food, drinks, music, a restless child, or greeting people.

If you think that giving this much attention to preparing for social
events seems a bit extreme, consider how strategic the "public" aspects
of extroverted social life can get. For example, few institutions in modern life pay more systematic attention to the art of conveying and assessing similarity than the social sororities that dot the landscapes of
American colleges and universities. Indeed, consulting firms have
sprung up to counsel young college-bound women on how, as one article put it, "to be perfect for ten minutes."

Perfect at what? The facial expressions, body language, dress, and
conversational skills that will put the "rush" candidate forward as both
a "great fit" for the sorority in terms of similarity and interestingly different in terms of adding social value. One sorority-rush consultant,
Samantha von Sperling, operates out of New York and also does personal coaching for top executives. She took on sorority work at the re-
quest of her Wall Street clients, whose daughters were stressing out
over membership. "It is [essentially] the same kind of coaching I do on
Wall Street," she told a reporter. She charges $8,000 for an intensive
Friday-to-Sunday sorority-rush workshop.

All this practice at being "perfect yet different" may pay dividends
when job recruiting comes along. Major consulting firms often seek
these same social qualities when they are recruiting college and graduate students. They have what they call the "airport test." After interviewing a candidate and assessing his or her résumé and intelligence,
they ask themselves: could we share an all-day airport delay with this
person? If so, the candidate probably has the social skills to make it
with clients and colleagues.

Sorority rush preparation sounds vaguely disturbing to people who
have no interest in joining a sorority. But when membership in a new
group or development of a new relationship is sufficiently important,
most people take similar care to prepare—anticipating ways to establish "similarity" in order to trigger that hoped-for "liking response" that
makes social relations smooth.

Trying Too Hard

The similarity ritual goes bad as soon as the other person senses you
are trying too hard. As media and communications professor Jeff

Pooley has said, "The best way to sell yourself is not to appear to sell yourself." Research on employment settings shows that people who engage in too much "interpersonal spin"—that is, major adjustments made to please others—lose the respect of coworkers. Indeed, in one study, employees reported that they engaged in fewer social activities with coworkers whom they saw as social chameleons. The more they got to know these people, the less they trusted them and the more they avoided them.

There is another potential cost if you try too hard to please. You can lose your personal bearings. The seventeenth-century philosopher La Rochefoucauld put it this way several hundred years ago: "We [can become] so accustomed to disguising ourselves from other people that in the end we disguise ourselves from ourselves."

For example, in my Success class I had an exceptionally amiable student named Bill who fell into this category. He smiled whenever he spoke. If he started to speak and a classmate interrupted him, he always insisted on deferring his comment. It was no surprise, therefore, when I learned that he belonged to one of the top social fraternities on campus and that he had chosen to make this the center of his student life.

As the class progressed, however, he confided to me that he was experiencing a deep conflict about his social identity. He had recently realized he was gay, something that had an obvious effect on his sense of who he was. But that was not the source of his conflict. What bothered him—and what he was seeking my advice on—was how to deal with the fact that he had failed to speak out against his fraternity's well-known homophobic culture. Should he make an issue of this with his fraternity brothers or simply move on to graduation and forget about his lost college years?

His final Success paper for me was titled "I Am Not You," and, with counseling and input from his true friends, his final act as a student was to stand up at his fraternity's annual senior dinner and, with his few fraternity allies tipped off in advance, come out. His voice shaking, he called for the fraternity to change its attitude about gays. As a popular member of his class, he was the perfect person to show them how wrong their stereotypes were. He told them to stop speaking of people "like me" in offensive terms. The stunned silence that met this short speech was followed rapidly by applause from his friends and, ultimately, a standing ovation from everyone.

It was a signature moment that marked the beginning of Bill's adult life. His authenticity had at last triumphed over his habit of trying too hard to fit in.

Social life is a constant balancing act between your authentic individuality and your need to belong. You are the only one who can decide where that balance should be struck as you confront different situations and people. But your overall success will depend on avoiding the extremes. People who cling to eccentric forms of authenticity often live lonely lives. Those who defer too much to social norms they do not believe in may, as my student Bill did until his senior dinner breakthrough, feel like impostors.

GETTING THINGS DONE THROUGH WORKING RELATIONSHIPS: CREDIBILITY

If emotional signals, similarity, and liking set the tone for social life, the most important single factor in getting things done is credibility. Up to now, we have been talking mainly about the semiautomatic aspects of social life. But to influence someone about an important idea, you need something more than rapport. You need the substance that comes with having credibility. As I suggested at the beginning of the chapter, credibility arises from other people's perceptions of four things:

- your formal and informal authority
- your knowledge
- your reputation for getting things done
- your trustworthiness

Think of credibility as a chair supported by four legs. The more secure your credibility is on each of its four supporting columns, the easier it is for your audience to take you seriously on an important matter. Your influence starts to wobble—or collapses altogether—as you take away each leg of the chair. If your audience thinks you lack relevant authority, are poorly informed about a subject, have never handled a similar problem, or cannot be trusted, then you will have a much harder time being heard.

Credibility was where Gibbs excelled.

As we saw in the previous section, Gibbs took care of the people who worked for him, going out of his way to show that he cared about their welfare. That, in turn, generated a high level of mutual trust within his organization and helped to create a sense of shared purpose. For example, on December 8, 1941, the day after the Japanese attack on Pearl Harbor, Gibbs wrote to everyone who worked for him: "I have always been proud of you, but never more than in this hour when we face together this solemn responsibility. I know I can count on each of you to do his utmost." As noted earlier, Gibbs & Cox went on to design most of the ships that the United States built during World War II.

After his successes in World War II (and his appearance on the cover of *Time* magazine in 1942), Willy Gibbs enjoyed tremendous influence within his industry. He was the CEO of the largest and most successful naval architecture firm in the world; he was well known as one of the world's experts in ship safety and design innovations—and he had others working for Gibbs & Cox equally renowned in specialized aspects of shipbuilding, such as turbine design, propellers, and construction. His reputation for competence had been established back in 1927, when the Gibbs-designed SS *Malolo* successfully survived the ship-to-ship collision that ripped a *Titanic*-sized gash in her hull. That reputation continued to grow.

Finally, his integrity was unquestioned. Based on erroneous rumors about his firm's profitability, Congress investigated Gibbs & Cox in 1944. The hearings ended in triumph for him, with the committee chairman declaring that Gibbs personally "rendered to the country outstanding service" while the government's top witness testified that Gibbs & Cox "has been an essential factor in the overall war effort of the country." This accolade cemented Gibbs's reputation for the rest of his life.

The kind of credibility Gibbs enjoyed may be the goal, but most of us will never be as well known or well regarded as he was. And when you have a credibility deficit because people do not know enough about you, you need to make adjustments. The best moves usually involve ways to help your audience become more familiar with what you have to offer.

For example, a few years ago one of my students came to me for advice on an influence problem. Still an undergraduate (majoring in both engineering and business), he had started his own software development firm and was trying to gain funding to test a new system for tracking the preferences of customers who buy consumer goods on the web. He had performed very well as an intern for a large consumer products firm the summer before our conversation. Now he sought my advice on how he might approach this company to get them to invest in his start-up. He was a personable young man and had built some relationships to help open a few doors. But as a twenty-year-old former intern with no proven products, he had an obvious credibility problem if he approached this encounter as an investment pitch or even a product sale. He had demonstrated his "whiz kid" expertise and had delivered exceptionally well on his internship assignments, but he was too young to be taken seriously as a vendor or a business partner.

As we talked, it became clear that what he really needed was not money but a rigorous testing ground for perfecting his software—he could do most of the actual code work himself. So I advised him to structure his pitch as a "no-risk experiment" for the company. If the firm would give him the proprietary information he needed to test and tweak his program and some computing resources, he would give them a right of first refusal to license the resulting software (assuming it worked) or, at their option, the chance to invest in his firm. Using his relationships, he was able to get an audience with the Internet commerce unit and, by asking for something modest that his limited credibility would support, he gained the firm's cooperation. The firm ended up buying his software system and employing him full-time to keep improving it.

Credibility Stepping Stones

If you lack credibility on any of its four dimensions, you can strengthen it by bringing endorsements or introductions from people who have the credibility you lack. For example, at the age of twenty-nine and still working as a lawyer to fulfill his promise to his father, Willy Gibbs won the financial backing of a much more influential man, banker J. P. "Jack" Morgan Jr., to build the thousand-foot, state-of-the-art ocean liner he had been dreaming of since childhood. The way the unknown Willy Gibbs achieved access to the most important banker of his era illustrates how this process can work for a young person with a great idea and no resources.

Gibbs started by finding a college friend who could give him an introduction to the chief engineer at General Electric, a man named William LeRoy Emmet. Emmet's team made huge electric turbines, and GE was trying to find a way to get these turbines into ship engines it could sell to the U.S. Navy. Gibbs's expertise in ship design immediately impressed Emmet. Steven Ujifusa, Gibbs's biographer, writes, "After years of dealing with the Navy bureaucracy, here was a young man who not only understood marine design, but had a vision for something really grand."

Emmet then made it possible for Gibbs to meet with Rear Admiral David W. Taylor, the navy's number one person for ship design and construction. Taylor was immediately sold on Gibbs's daring plan to combine GE's new engine with a commercial ship design that rivaled the best and biggest European vessels. Taylor agreed to build a scale model of Gibbs's ship for testing at the Washington Navy Yard.

The final piece of the puzzle was to secure financing. For this, Gibbs turned first to Ralph Peters, the president of the Long Island Railroad. Gibbs had done his homework and knew that Peters was searching for a way to build an Atlantic ship terminal in Montauk, on Long Island's south shore, that could link to his railroad line. Gibbs and his brother visited Peters's office, telling his secretary as they walked in that they were there to "talk about ships from Montauk to England." When the secretary told Peters that these young men wanted to talk about his pet project, he ushered his uninvited guests into his office. There he quickly reviewed the elaborate plans Gibbs had made and saw that two big players in the industry were behind them—Emmet and Taylor. Peters then picked up the phone and called Jack Morgan.

Gibbs's meeting with Morgan was remarkably short. Now working with the endorsement of Peters as well as Emmet and Taylor—and with an elaborate scale model of his ship being tested at the Washington Navy Yard—he made a no-nonsense presentation that conveyed his careful planning and bold vision. His project called for the construction of two $30 million ships and a $15 million shipping terminal in Montauk to accommodate them. He was also offering Morgan a chance to wipe out the legacy of his father's backing of the ill-fated *Titanic* and revive Morgan's moribund shipping division, International Mercantile Marine, Inc.

Morgan listened to Gibbs, left the room, and came back twenty minutes later. A taciturn man, Jack Morgan then spoke six words that were some of the sweetest Gibbs would ever hear.

"Very well, I will back you."

Thus, in preparing for any important influence encounter, it helps to have both relationships and credibility—and to make sure all four legs of your credibility chair are as strong as possible. Credibility and influence will get your audience's attention. After that, you need to find ways into their hearts and minds.

Connecting Credibility to Passion: Persuasion and Dialogue

With both healthy working relationships and credibility established, you are ready to connect at a deeper level with others through persuasion. Persuasion involves offering arguments, justifications, and inducements your audience will find compelling. Professionals in the persuasion business, such as lawyers, advertisers, and politicians, train themselves in the tactical arts of advocating for preestablished positions. As a former lawyer myself, I know both the benefits and the limits of this approach. In relatively formal settings, where logic and reason are the appropriate vehicles for establishing a point and winning an argument, skill in the art of rhetoric is a valuable tool.

But if you are to be truly persuasive in the pivotal moments of your life, I believe emotion must play an appropriate role in the way you communicate. You need to connect your credibility to your passions.

The bestselling book *Crucial Conversations: Tools for Talking When Stakes Are High* by a team from the organizational training firm Vital-Smarts, Inc., points out that when you are genuinely trying to connect with someone, persuasion is best thought of as dialogue—a two-way exchange—rather than as one person convincing another to do or think something. The reality is that people are seldom persuaded about something important just because you make an argument. In an insightful article for the journal *Science,* titled "How We See Ourselves and How We See Others," Princeton psychologist Emily Pronin spells out in more detail why others have such trouble seeing the world from our point of view. The basic problem comes from the hardwired limits on human perspective taking.

Your internal world—your own thoughts and feelings—is extremely vivid. You have direct experience of your intentions, hopes, and desires. You can report and explain them. But what do you really know about other people's internal worlds? Only what you observe externally. Try as you might, you cannot peer inside them. So you are forced to infer thoughts, feelings, intentions, and motivations from what others do or say—and how they say it. And that is all the data they get about you, too.

Thus, what is really happening in an important persuasion moment is not one person "overcoming" the other with a brilliant argument. Instead, other people are *persuading themselves* that your ideas are worth accepting. That means they go through the following three-step process. They

- hear and consider the reasons you offer,
- assess the power of your emotional commitment to those reasons, and then
- reframe your ideas into reasons they themselves can accept.

You, in turn, need to be open enough to the point of view you hear from another person so you can go through the same process yourself.

Crucial Conversations has a nice phrase for this process. The authors call it creating a "pool of shared meaning." The goal is to develop a common understanding about a situation and then work together to find ways to resolve or advance it. More often than many people realize, especially in the consequential personal and professional moments on which your genuine success will depend, this calls for you to speak from the heart about what is really important to you. By being vulnerable in this way, you show other people you are serious about engaging with them.

Let's look at an example.

Speaking from the Heart, Saving a Life

Not long ago the news services carried a remarkable story about a single mother and struggling drug addict named Ashley Smith. A failure by most measures, she demonstrated exceptional skills for engaging in dialogue in the most stressful and unlikely circumstances.

Walking home from a nearby convenience store one night at about 2:30 A.M., Smith was taken hostage by Brian Nichols, a cold-blooded killer who was the target of one of the largest manhunts in Georgia state history. Earlier the day before, in downtown Atlanta, Nichols had shot and killed the presiding judge and a court reporter at his rape trial. As he was fleeing the scene, he killed a police deputy and then, a few hours later, a federal agent.

Nichols picked Smith at random as a hostage outside her apartment building and forced her to take him into her unit. Once inside, she recognized him as the fugitive whose face had been all over the television news. She was terrified, but she kept her composure and, through the power of creating a "pool of shared meaning" in the hours that followed, a minor miracle occurred.

In the tense initial moments of the encounter, Smith's first words were to beg Nichols not to kill her and leave her five-year-old daughter as an orphan. "Your little girl—where is she?" Nichols asked. Smith explained that her daughter was spending the night elsewhere and she expected to see her in the morning. Smith told him her husband had been murdered a few years back and had died in her arms from knife wounds. If Nichols killed her, the little girl would be alone.

As the first hour or two passed, Nichols began to open up. He told Smith he had been wrongly accused of raping his girlfriend and that he would do almost anything to avoid going back to prison. Smith sympathized. She had been to prison, too. He said he was exhausted. He did not want to hurt anyone else.

As the time dragged on, Nichols asked her if she had any mari-
juana. She didn't but she had some "ice" (crystal meth) in her room.
She had been using it for years. She was an addict. The rapport between these two damaged, very different people deepened.

As Nichols began taking the drugs, however, Smith started to see
her situation in an entirely new, transformative light. Her life had been
a series of failures and false starts due to these drugs. She had not been
able to hold down a steady job, and she had given up custody of her
daughter to her aunt. When Nichols asked her to join him in taking
meth, she found herself saying, "No way. That stuff ruined my life."

She later recounted this experience in her book: "Suddenly, looking down at my drug pouch, I realized that I would rather have died
in my apartment than have done those drugs with Brian Nichols. If
the cops were going to bust in there and find me dead, they were not
going to find drugs in me when they did the autopsy. I was not going
to die and stand before God, having done a bunch of ice up my nose."
She helped him to "hot line" the drug by snorting it, but took none
herself.

Instead, she asked Nichols if it would be all right for her to read a
book while they waited out the night. She had been reading Pastor
Rick Warren's *A Purpose Driven Life* before bed and was on chapter 32.
She brought it out and Nichols asked her to read it aloud. The passage she had marked, which Nichols asked her to read twice, begins
as follows: "God deserves your best. He shaped you for a purpose, and
he expects you to make the most of what you have been given."

Nichols asked Ashley, "What do you think your purpose is?" And
they began talking about God, about those they were put on earth to
serve, and about the families of the men Nichols had shot the previous day. These people were feeling loss just as Smith herself had felt
loss when her husband was murdered. "After I started to read to
him . . . I guess he saw my faith and what I really believed in," Smith
later told reporters. Nichols responded that there was nothing to
hope for: "Look in my eyes. I am already dead." Smith pushed back.
"You are not dead. You are standing right in front of me." She asked
him to consider it a miracle that he had found his way to her apartment so he could hear from her what God's purpose might be for
him. Meanwhile, in her own heart, she had begun seeing him as a
messenger from God sent to end her addiction—if only he would let
her live.

As dawn broke, she cooked him pancakes and drove behind him
in her own car to help him ditch the pickup truck he had used as a
getaway car from the courthouse. She later said she did not try to

escape at that point because she wanted to avoid the possibility of a public shootout that might hurt others. Finally, at 9:30 A.M., Nichols allowed her to leave the apartment alone to pick up her daughter. She dialed 911 at the first stop on her route, and Nichols was quickly and safely taken into custody. "I believe God brought him to my door," she told reporters. Nichols was later convicted on fifty-four criminal counts and given multiple life-without-parole sentences. The jury deadlocked on the death penalty.

Ashley Smith, meanwhile, went on to write a book about her experience, remarry, have another child, and become a professional hospital technician. She speaks frequently at evangelical events and drug-recovery programs. She has been drug-free since March 12, 2005, the date Brian Nichols took her hostage.

I find this story worth reflecting on not so much because of its religious content—though that certainly attracted attention in the evangelical community—but because it shows how two flawed people, drawn at random into a relationship with each other, were able to connect, create a common understanding, and alter the future. Such moments are exceptional, of course, but they are more important than many of the more obvious occasions when we craft a clever argument without putting ourselves and our beliefs on the line. The author Stephen R. Covey has called these the "defining moments in our lives and careers that make all the difference"—the conversations where "the decisions made take us down one of several roads, each of which leads to an entirely different destination." You can never predict exactly when such conversations will happen—you can predict only that they are sure to occur and that they will require you to be "in the moment" and authentic.

I credit Ashley Smith for being ready to speak from the heart when her moment came. And I credit her religious faith, too, for giving her the confidence in her beliefs that allowed her to communicate so sincerely and with such feeling. Her reward for engaging in dialogue with Brian Nichols had two dimensions. Not only did she save his life and hers, but she also discovered something she did not expect—the inner strength to overcome her addiction.

THE INNER DIMENSION OF SOCIAL LIFE:
YOUR FRIENDS OF VIRTUE
....

Friends are as companions on a journey, who ought to aid
each other to persevere in the road to a happier life.

—PYTHAGORAS

Most of this chapter has been concerned with winning friends and
influencing people who fall into Aristotle's category of "friends of
utility"—those relationships that can help you achieve the outer dimensions of success. But Ashley Smith's story confirms that social
interactions can affect inner dimensions just as surely as they do the
more obvious, outer ones. Before we conclude, therefore, I want to
help you salute the inner dimensions of your most important relationships.

Near the beginning of the chapter, I noted that Aristotle reserved
a special place in his list of social relationships for what he called
"friends of virtue." These are the few people who, for one reason or
another, you feel closest to and whom you trust the most to be "watching your back." Aristotle describes them in his *Nicomachean Ethics* as
those people who want only what is good for you (as you want only
what is good for them) and with whom you have a relationship not for
some ulterior motive but only for the sake of supporting each other.
These friendships are fewer in number than friends of pleasure or
utility; they take more effort to maintain and renew; and they tell you
a lot about your own inner character and interests.

I think of friends of virtue as the people who know your flaws and
yet focus on the person you are (or can be) at your best. In fact, they
are the people who make you even better than you could otherwise
be by virtue of your relationship.

Thus, before concluding this chapter on the social aspects of success, I want to give you a chance to reflect on the truest friends you
have made in your life thus far. They are the short list of people who,
as Pythagoras said, serve as your steadfast "companions" on your
journey. With them, it is always about more than just having a good
time or getting work done.

Take a minute to list the few people you would put at the top of
this list and think for a moment about why you have put them there.
And, if you have not contacted them recently, reach out and tell them
how important they are in your life.

My Friends of Virtue | What They Contribute to My Life

1. _____

2. _____

3. _____

4. _____

5. _____

6. Continue your list on your own.

CONCLUSION

This chapter gave you a chance to reflect on the social side of success. We reviewed the science of first impressions and rapport, and we saw how relationships can open the door to influence. Credibility based on perceived authority, knowledge, ability, and trustworthiness can give weight to your words. Meanwhile, when you bring conviction along with credibility to the art of persuasion, it is possible to transform relationships, taking both you and the other person to a more successful place than either of you could have found alone.

There is one form of relationship we did not discuss, however, and I want to close with that one. I mentioned earlier that Willy Gibbs was successful despite his disagreeable personality in all but one aspect of his social life. He had a devoted wife, a successful career, and, from all reports, some close friends.

But he made a mess of his life with two people—his two sons, Frank and Christopher.

Most success stories have a darker side, and Gibbs's tale was no exception. When he married Vera Cravath, she already had one son and they went on to have two boys together. Gibbs succeeded as a naval architect but he failed as a father to his two boys. The family grew apart as the years went on. As adults, his sons seldom spoke of their father even to their own children. His younger son, Christopher, refused to attend Gibbs's funeral in 1967.

If a meaningful family life is one of your criteria for success, then this is a gash in Gibbs's life as deep and wide as the one that the SS *Malolo* suffered in 1927. Whether it sinks him, of course, is your call to make.

What went wrong?

Perhaps it was Gibbs's famously acid personality. But the evidence is clear that he could alter that if he really wanted to for the special people in his life. So I have another theory. I think Gibbs, lacking a role model for fatherhood from his own youth, missed his opportunity for the kind of dialogue we talked about in this chapter with his two boys. Instead of engaging them as equals with an open mind, he treated them the way his own father had treated him—as footnotes in his own, grand life story.

As we have seen throughout this book, people who become too preoccupied with the outer dimensions of success often pay a high price on the inner dimension. Willy Gibbs may have been, to bring back a term we used in chapter 3, a Hungry Ghost for Fame. He could not get enough of the world's acclaim, so he missed the chance to earn his sons' respect and love.

With the end of this chapter, we end the second part of the book. Part 1 asked how you would define success for yourself. Part 2 asked how you would achieve it. In answer, I have suggested five steps.

- Discover what you do better than most by taking inventory of your unique capabilities.
- Set yourself on fire by combining your satisfaction-based and reward-based motivations.
- Earn self-confidence through trial and error; learn to fail.
- Focus the four powers of your mind—passion, imagination, intuition, and reason—on goals that inspire you.
- Influence others by establishing credibility and engaging them in genuine dialogue.

With these success tools sharpened and ready, and with your own, authentic vision of what success means to guide your steps, all that remains is to take action.

The road ahead is open.

Success Step #9

ENGAGE OTHERS: EXERCISE INFLUENCE

Nobody achieves success alone. Sooner or later, you will need to influence other people to make things happen. When you do, the most important tools you bring will be your credibility and your ability to engage others in genuine, give-and-take dialogue.

Credibility is something you must earn and renew every day of your life. As people come to see you as a person who can be trusted and who has authority, knowledge, and competence, they will be much more willing to cooperate with you. Credibility can take a lifetime to build and, in the case of trust, only a moment to destroy. Never compromise your credibility.

Dialogue is what happens when people actually listen to one another and create a "pool of shared meaning" that is richer than the points of view they started with. Treasure moments when this happens. They can change your life.

| CONCLUSION |

The Right Answers

The only true measure of success is the ratio between what
we might have done and what we might have been on the
one hand, and . . . the things we have made of ourselves on
the other.

—H. G. WELLS

The last day of my Success course is always bitter-
sweet. I collect the students' final papers on what
they have decided success means to them, and we say
our good-byes. As the class concludes, we share a sense that we have
experienced something special together. They have had the chance to
read and debate the success theories of CEOs, preachers, gurus, and
psychologists, not to mention Socrates and Aristotle. More important,
the class has given them the freedom to discuss and get feedback on
their deepest goals. As for me, I have gotten to know another group of
unique, talented people who have bright futures ahead of them. As the
semester unfolds, I take time to communicate with each student in the
class about his or her goals. I have learned about the obstacles they
face—from family and culture as well as their own fears—and I have
my fingers crossed that they will find the courage to overcome these
barriers and find their own way.

For the students, most of whom are in their final semester, the end of
class means the beginning of life after school—a transition we have
been talking about all semester. The room is filled with a complex mixture of excitement and anxiety. Everyone is anticipating the future.

Sometimes I take a moment to read them a note from a former graduate of the course reporting on how his or her Odyssey is progressing. I like to show my current students that the course has given them tools—and self-awareness—that can survive the last day of class.

For example, I once got an e-mail from a Wharton alumnus in the Philippines named Evan Chen, who had taken the Success class a year earlier. He was a devout Christian, although he never made a big issue of this in class discussions. I had noticed this theme in his papers, however, and talked with him about how important his faith might be in his search for meaningful work. He did not land a job before he graduated, so he returned home to the Philippines to see what he could find.

During his job search in Manila, he happened to meet the founders of a new nonprofit organization—an offshoot of the highly successful Teach For America that was called Teach For the Philippines. Like Teach For America, the new group planned to recruit talented college seniors and ask them to teach in local Philippine primary schools for two years. The start-up phase for the organization was just coming to an end. It had won recognition from the Teach For America network (called Teach For All) and had already forged relationships with the schools where its young teachers could be placed. It was getting ready to take applications from its first incoming class of new teachers.

Chen was interviewing for some corporate jobs when the Teach For the Philippines team called him and offered him the position of director of training and support. Among other things, he would be responsible for planning the program's eight-week summer institute to make sure the teacher-recruits were ready to enter their classrooms each fall. The job did not pay as well as the corporate positions he was seeking, and there was the risk that the organization's mission—which works well in a country like the United States—might not take hold in a culture like that of the Philippines. He told them he would think about it. He was worried that taking a risky nonprofit job right out of college might limit his options down the road.

As he reflected on his choice, he remembered some of the discussions in the Success class. "In one of our sessions," he wrote in his note to me, "I clearly recalled thinking that one of my dreams in life was to support others in making their dreams come true. I looked back at the different journals and notes I wrote, and I found a record of my thoughts and your comments. You mentioned that I might one day be able to live this dream through coaching, counseling, or human resource management.

You commented that 'It is also a mission you can embrace through your faith. Go for it!' "

With those memories in mind, he consulted one of his mentors in the Philippines. "He asked me to imagine that I was 30 and going to a school reunion. 'What would you want to tell your classmates about? The management training job you are interviewing for or your role in helping to start up a new organization?' He did not tell me what he thought I should do, but he did say that I should go where my heart was leading me."

Evan's message concluded with a reference to our class discussion of meaningful work. "I did not expect it to happen so quickly," he wrote, "but I found a job that pays, a job I am passionate about, and hopefully a job I'm good at (I still have to prove that)."

My purpose in writing this book has been to give you the same opportunity this former student had to think about your life, relationships, talents, and future goals. That kind of reflection, when focused on the right subjects, almost always yields substantial dividends. It can help you recognize, as Evan Chen did, which pathways have a better chance of leading you toward your own vision of success. He is just starting out, so this is neither the last job he will ever hold nor the final life-changing decision he will ever make. But he has established a good precedent for the future. He has made a choice that reflects his genuine success values. As long as he keeps doing that, I think he will have an interesting life.

In just the same way, I hope that the work you have done in this book will help you recognize your own path when it opens in front of you.

To conclude the book, I would like to revisit the nine key "Success Steps" I provided at the end of each chapter. I will highlight them with some of the quotes and examples you encountered to help you remember the basic points.

THE FIRST QUESTION: WHAT IS SUCCESS?

The first four chapters investigated the question "What is success?" I offered you answers that challenged you to examine the roots of your success beliefs.

Step #1: Balance the Two Sides of Success

We started with the Six Lives Exercise. Can you recall which life you ranked as number one? You might take a glance back at the chapter now to see if you would still stick with your vote.

That exercise makes the point that success always involves trade-offs. It is neither achievement nor happiness, but some mix of both. There are the outer, socially defined aspects of success and the inner, fulfillment-oriented aspects. As you craft your life and set your goals, you need to constantly balance these two sides.

How? Through greater self-awareness. Chapter 1 began with a quotation from Michel de Montaigne: "There is no one who, if he listens to himself, does not discover in himself a pattern all his own, a ruling pattern." Listening to yourself involves noticing what genuinely excites you and paying attention when you are dissatisfied with where your life is headed. For example, the Stone Mason in the Six Lives Exercise (who, by the way, is a real person named Carl Murray Bates) was happy in his work because he understood what he liked about it. "It's a good day laying brick or stone," he said. "It's hard work, but you get interested in fitting each piece in just its right spot and the day is over before you know it." And the social entrepreneur Eric Adler, whose story opened chapter 1, could not begin his personal success journey toward the SEED schools until he admitted to himself that he was dissatisfied with the career he had started in business consulting.

Finally, it helps to notice that you are becoming too preoccupied with what other people think about you instead of what you, yourself, find exciting and interesting. The Roman emperor Marcus Aurelius, who made his first appearance here in chapter 1, summed this up well in a quote that many students in my class find one of the most memorable. "I have often wondered," he wrote, "how it is that every man loves himself more than all the rest of men, yet sets more value on others' opinions than on his own." I quoted Steve Jobs's famous 2005 Stanford graduation speech in the introduction. He echoed this sentiment. "Don't let the noise of others' opinions drown out your own inner voice. And, most important, have the courage to follow your heart and intuition," he said. "They somehow already know what you truly want to become."

Step #2: Define Happiness for Yourself

Chapter 2 focused on the inner dimension of success. I started with a story about an elderly working-class man who visited a Wharton School seminar on happiness. I nicknamed him the Wise Angel because his simple words resonated so deeply with me. "As I see it," he said to the seminar presenter, "happiness is just three things: good health, meaningful work, and love. You have that, you are happy."

This chapter challenged you to craft a definition of happiness for yourself. Many others have tried their hand at this before you. Here are three additional examples this chapter featured:

Roman philosopher Epicurus: "Everything we need to be happy is easy to obtain."

Nobel Prize–winning psychologist Daniel Kahneman: "It is only a slight exaggeration to say that happiness is the experience of spending time with people you love and who love you."

Rabbi Akiva Tatz: "The experience of the soul that comes when you are doing what you should be doing."

"Happiness" is a word we all understand in our own way.

What is your definition?

Step #3: Gain Perspective on Your Family and Your Cultural Beliefs

Chapter 3 challenged you to become aware of how your family and your culture drive your beliefs about what it means to be successful. Once you identify these forces, many of which are unconscious, you gain more control over your own goals.

The chapter began with a story that entrepreneur Carl Bolch Jr. told my class. It is a story that describes what it feels like to wake up in midcareer and realize that your whole life has been spent on a quest driven by cultural goals you did not fully endorse. A lawyer Carl Bolch knew once told him, "I worked in high school to get into a great college. Then I worked in college to get into a great law school. Then I worked at law school to get a job at a top-flight law firm. Then I worked at the law firm to make partner. I've finally figured out that it is all just a big pie-eating contest. You win, and the prize is always . . . MORE PIE. Who wants that?"

Some of your success beliefs originate with desires to please your parents or other authority figures. As Rainer Maria Rilke wrote, children sometimes "dance to the unlived lives of their parents." To help you consider whether the commonly held view that professional status, celebrity, and great wealth are the best measures of a successful life, I challenged you to take the Lottery Exercise. This test asked you to assume that you had already attained status, fame, and fortune. Now what? What would you do next?

We heard from the California lottery winner Cynthia Stafford, who collected $112 million and then did a remarkable thing with it: put the money to good use. "I'm comfortable with myself," Stafford told an interviewer from *The Huffington Post*. "My life is pretty much the same [as before the lottery]. I just have more resources to do what I love to do." The children and senior citizens benefiting from her theater programs at the Geffen Playhouse are glad she has maintained her balance, even after her life was turned upside down by sudden wealth. Fame and fortune can ruin a life unless it is already grounded. And if your life has such a grounding, do you need fame or fortune to tell you that you are successful?

Step #4: Seek Meaningful Work

The quotation that opened chapter 4 came from a German online employment website: "Life's too short for the wrong job." To help you escape the fate of getting stuck in the wrong kind of work, chapter 4 gave you the opportunity to reflect on the differences between jobs and careers, and between careers and "callings." I argued that the phrase "meaningful work" was a better way to label the last of these three categories because the religious connotations of a "calling" sometimes confuse people.

Where can you find meaningful work? I suggested that it is located at the intersection of three overlapping circles—the jobs that will pay you something, the jobs that use your talents and strengths, and the jobs that ignite your passions and sense of purpose.

By far the hardest of the three circles to grasp is the third—the one that encompasses work you find emotionally satisfying. Chapter 4 discussed two ways to figure this out. First, there was the path taken by the Georgetown computer science professor Cal Newport. Embrace a field you have an aptitude for, master it fully, and let the meaning emerge from your career. Second, there was Po Bronson's pathway of "deeply felt experiences" that can guide you toward activities that resonate with your life story. I elaborated on this by showing you seven types of meaning you can bring to your projects. These formed the acronym PERFECT. Which of the following list of values did you find most inspiring?

- Personal growth and development
- Entrepreneurial independence
- Religious or spiritual identity
- Family
- Expressing yourself through ideas, invention, or the arts
- Community—serving a cause, helping people in need
- Talent-based striving for excellence

In the end, the owner of an art gallery tour company I met in New York named Rafael Risemberg gave a succinct definition of what it feels like to have meaningful work. He had tried to fulfill his parents' dream for him to become a doctor and given up when he realized he hated being around sick people. Next he had made a career as a tenured professor in arts education. Finally, he found his sweet spot when he launched his own arts-related business. "It has become the greatest intellectual and emotional passion I have ever known," he said. "I literally leap out of bed each morning. My definition of meaningful work is waking up with a feeling of excitement about what each day will bring." What is your definition?

THE SECOND QUESTION:
HOW WILL I ACHIEVE IT?

The second part of the book turned from your definition of success to the unique talents and abilities you can summon to achieve the success you desire. These five chapters asked you to investigate your capabilities, motivations, sources of self-confidence, mind powers, and social skills.

Step #5: Look Inside to Find Your Unique Combination of Capabilities

Chapter 5 began with the story of the legendary chef Julia Child as well as a Danish folk saying: "You must bake with the flour you have." It is tempting to look outside yourself for the capabilities that will make you successful. "If only I could . . ." is a mantra that has kept many talented people from achieving their potential. But this chapter argued that your achievement skills are always close at hand. One of Julia Child's insights was to notice what she enjoyed doing and then do more of it.

"The more I cook, the more I like to cook," she said.

The chapter featured a classic success speech from nineteenth-century America given thousands of times by the Reverend Russell

Conwell, founder of Temple University. The speech was called Acres of Diamonds and carried the simple lesson that everything you need for success is right in your backyard if you will only take the time to look.

The chapter then helped you search for these four diamonds within your heart and mind. They included

- your interests and passions,
- your aptitudes and skills,
- your past experience, and
- your personality strengths.

One of the key parts of this chapter was the SAME personality profiler. When you know yourself well, you have a much better chance of choosing activities that suit your strengths, energize your motivations, and accelerate your learning. Which of these four personality foundations turned out to be dominant for you: Social, Action-Oriented, Mindset, or Emotional Temperment? By taking your key personality traits and using them as screens to consider possible occupations, you may find your way to success more quickly.

Step #6: Energize Yourself by Combining Satisfaction-Based and Reward-Based Motivations

Chapter 6 linked motivation to personality. What does it take to "set yourself on fire" as you work to achieve your goals? We looked at the inner, satisfaction-based forms of motivation—the drives that the author Daniel Pink has described as those for "freedom, challenge, and purpose"—as well as the more traditional, reward-based motives that come when people offer you money, status, praise, and recognition. Many writers in the success field say that you should ignore reward-based motivation and focus only on the satisfaction-based drives. I disagree. I think you need to combine and balance both sources of motivation if you are to do your best. Satisfaction-based motivation is best for endurance. Reward-based energy is best for sprints.

In addition to helping you investigate your motivations, I provided some ideas for renewing your energies when they flag. Nobody can stay motivated all the time, so everyone has some private techniques that help them relight their fires. We talked about the value of making yourself accountable, connecting with role models, creating motivational rituals, competing with yourself, proving someone wrong, and channeling your strongest survival emotions.

Finally, I asked you to contemplate the number 32,850. That is the number of days you will get to live if you are lucky enough to reach the age of ninety. Your limited time on earth, I suggested, is perhaps the most powerful motivator of them all. I quoted Steve Jobs again. The fact of his own, inevitable death, he said, is "the most important tool I've ever encountered to help me make the big choices in life. Because almost everything—all external expectations, all pride, all fear of embarrassment or failure—these things just fall away in the face of death, leaving only what is truly important. . . . You are already naked. There is no reason not to follow your heart."

Do you know what motivates you most? Find out. Then stay on course by returning to these sources of energy each and every day.

Step #7: Cultivate Self-Confidence

Chapter 7 asked you to consider the sources of your self-confidence. It began with a provocative quote by Alfred Binet, the inventor of the IQ test. "It is not always the people who start out the smartest," he said, "who end up the smartest." Intelligence, in short, is something you cultivate, not just something you "have." That is true for almost every talent you have been endowed with. Your confidence is what gives you the courage to try, fail, learn, grow, and, ultimately, succeed. By the same token, as the psychologist William James put it, "There is but one cause of human failure. And that is man's lack of faith in his true self."

The chapter introduced you to two levels of self-confidence. Level One Confidence springs from your basic and deepest sense of your "true self"—the belief in your own autonomy, moral character, and ability to take action in the world. The seeds of your Level One Confidence are often sown by people you trust and admire—parents, teachers, coaches, or mentors—who affirm that "you can do it." When others believe in you, you begin to believe in yourself. In addition, people acquire the "I can do it" spirit through rites of passage that test their character and, for some, by acquiring faith in powers beyond their own.

Level Two Confidence relates to specific skill-based activities. Professor Carol Dweck's growth mindset includes the willingness to learn, challenge your skills, focus on effort more than results, and treat failure as a stage on the journey rather than as the end of the road.

Do you have the right kind of confidence?

Step #8: Focus the Powers of Your Mind to Achieve Long-Term Goals

There is a lot of hocus-pocus written by success gurus about the powers of your mind. Authors such as Rhonda Byrne (*The Secret*) suggest that there is a magical "Law of Attraction" that will, like a genie in a bottle, deliver all your hopes and dreams if you will just think about them in a positive way. Of course, if this were true, everyone would win the lottery whenever they wanted to and your favorite sports team would defeat its opponents week after week—as would your best friend's teams (and all their friends' teams, too).

The reality of the mind is much more complex and interesting. Things happen that we do not want or expect, and many things we dream of remain out of reach. It is nevertheless possible to achieve long-term goals by harnessing the four genuine mental powers at your command—your passion, imagination, intuition, and reason—and focusing them on a target you believe in.

The chapter traced the story of a remarkable twentieth-century achievement, Charles Lindbergh's first nonstop flight across the Atlantic. Lindbergh used all four of his mental powers at the appropriate times. Do you think his systematic approach to achievement can work for you?

- Consult your passions—identify a worthy goal.
- Let your imagination and intuition generate ideas.
- Commit to a specific, challenging plan.
- Break it down into small steps.
- Improvise and adjust—then close the deal.

Step #9: Engage Others—Exercise Influence

Chapter 9 began with a quote from Mark Twain, "Always do right. This will gratify some people and astonish the rest." I offered this quotation because it underlines why credibility is such an important asset as you begin engaging other people to help you on your journey. When you "do right," you establish the basis for trust—and trust is what prompts other people to offer their enthusiastic cooperation.

The chapter featured the story of William Francis "Willy" Gibbs, one of the most influential naval architects in American history—and one of the most disagreeable people of his era. His example allowed us to see how it is possible to be socially effective even when your personality makes it hard for you to be liked by more than a few close friends. That raised the issue of what the word "friend" actually means, and Aristotle proved helpful by delineating the differences among friends of "pleasure," friends of "utility," and friends of "virtue." I asked you to consider your own personal relationships and reflect on Aristotle's categories.

To help advance your social skills with "friends of utility," I outlined the science of smiling, building rapport, and establishing positive feelings through connections of similarity. But I also warned that your success in social relations often depends on your finding a good balance between your skills at social adjustment and your ability to convey a sense of authenticity. A good way to find this balance is to emphasize credibility rather than glad handing as a social strategy. Credibility consists of other people's impressions of your formal and informal authority, knowledge, reputation for getting things done, and trustworthiness.

Finally, I suggested that in your most important personal encounters, success will come from being able to engage in the genuine give-and-take of dialogue. This requires an ability to listen as well as persuade. The goal is to create a "pool of shared meaning" between the people in the dialogue. I offered the example of a young drug addict named Ashley Smith, who was able to escape a harrowing hostage situation at the hands of a murderer by genuinely connecting with her captor. Are you prepared to share your true feelings in crucial conversations?

A FINAL WORD

As we close out the Success class, the students turn in their papers that answer the two questions you have investigated for yourself in this book.

What is success? How will I achieve it?

They come to as many different conclusions about success as there are students in a class. I have shared some of their ideas with you in the book. In chapter 3, you met J. J. Fliegelman, who devised his theory about how people who become preoccupied with seeking "recognition respect" often get lost in a quest for fame and fortune—losing sight of the more important search for informed respect from a smaller audience.

Then there was the student you met in chapter 8, who wrote about more than one hundred goals he had set for each stage of his life.

You and I can both be thankful that you do not have to turn in a paper, but you do have to decide how you will live your life going forward. That has been the point of all our work together. What, in the end, do you think success really is? And with that idea in mind, what specific steps can you to take to achieve it? These are the big questions, and I hope you are now prepared to think about them, talk about them, and, if you like, even write about them so people you trust can help you make your way.

At the very end of class, we take a group snapshot. The students have spent three months sharing their goals, fears, stories, and success theories. They have learned things about one another that even their closest friends may not know. They are thrilled to be graduating, but they are also sad to say good-bye to friends and a little terrified of what awaits them as they step into what they often refer to as the "real world." The picture captures a special moment.

For myself, I always feel as if I am watching close friends leaving for a very long journey. I am on the dock, waving to them as their ships sail. The students don't really understand this, but for me, my classroom *is* the real world. And they are leaving it.

I want to bid you a similar farewell. As I mentioned in the book's introduction, writing this book has been one of the hardest things I have ever done. The subject is daunting, of course, but the hardest part has been not being able to look up from these pages to see you— the person whose hopes, dreams, and fears have been sitting next to me all along the way. I hope that the exercises, surveys, and assessments have given you the same chance my students have to customize the learning experience.

My goal has been to make this experience a living workbook about you, your goals, and your life. If you have learned something useful, I have accomplished my purpose. Because, for me, success is about helping others find and make progress along their own unique paths. Teaching and writing are my ways of striving to achieve that success.

Acknowledgments

Writing a book about a time-honored subject such as success is like walking on a wobbly tightrope across a great chasm. Look to one side and all you see are the depths of the genre's clichés. On the other side lurk the temptations of a self-indulgent memoir. If I have made it across this canyon without falling too often into either extreme, it is only because so many people kept me focused and helped me maintain my balance.

My wife, Robbie, always comes first on the list when it comes to acknowledgments, and this book is no exception. It was she, at a lunch with our close friends Simon and Rosalie Auster, who first said, "I think your next book ought to be about success." Her patient and constructive editing, nudging, and brainstorming over every aspect of this project kept me going on even the most difficult of days. Similar thanks go to my two sons, Ben and Ned, who took time to read and comment on chapters, offer encouragement, provide helpful criticism, and remind me that their generation thinks about success in terms slightly different from mine. My family is proof that happiness, hard work, honest talk, love, and mutual support are all possible under a single roof.

Next in line are the students in my Literature of Success class, to whom the book is dedicated. They have challenged and inspired me for nearly a decade to keep looking inside myself to answer the same questions about success I ask them to consider every year. Their insistence that I "walk the talk" and write my own final paper explaining my personal theory of success brought this project into focus. Their stories are everywhere in this book, and their commitment to their own journeys keeps me motivated on my own.

Special thanks go to five former students. First, Eric Adler kindly allowed me to use his story to start the book. Eric is one of those people who defines the word "success" with every action he takes, and I count myself lucky that he sought me out at office hours so many years ago. Second, J. J. Fliegelman wrote one of the best final papers I have ever encountered in any course and allowed me to cite it and use his ideas in chapter 3. He also read the entire book in draft form, commented extensively on its organization and table of contents, and set me straight regarding all passages that touched on Jewish custom, practice, and vocabulary. I consider J.J. a true collaborator on this project. Third, John Picasso, a passionate consumer of success books, proposed the Andre Agassi example that appears in chapter 3 and worked with me to create the SAME personality profiler that appears in chapter 5. Fourth, Catherine Wei, a student who launched her own Asian Odyssey soon after graduation, read a number of chapters several times. She offered excellent advice on breaking up certain topics and highlighting key ideas. Finally, the writer and brand consultant Jeremy Hildreth, a member of one of the first classes of Penn students I ever taught, generously gave time and thought to the book and helped me brainstorm about the title.

My wonderful friends (and godfathers to our two sons) Guthrie Sayen and Simon Auster provided some especially timely comments and perspectives at a time when I most needed them. They read chapters, offered support, and were patient and kind in their critiques. In addition, Salmon River Capital's founder, Josh Lewis, gave the entire manuscript a complete reading just when I needed it most—before the final edit—and provided valuable comments. My friend and Penn colleague Professor Angela Duckworth, one of the world's foremost research psychologists on achievement, also helped me over many years to develop my ideas about success, co-led our Penn Success Seminar, and continues to provide a role model for a careful, research-based approach to this field. As this book started to jell, she generously gave her time, counsel, research perspectives, and encouragement.

My long-standing publishing partnership with my agent, Michael Snell, expanded during this project to include Pat Snell, his talented partner. As usual, Michael was a source of inexhaustible good humor, positive energy, imagination, and perspective as the book made its way from concept to proposal to finished product. My e-mail inbox overflowed with so many messages about possible titles for this book that I had to create a separate file to hold them all. This is the kind of support from an agent that every author should have but few enjoy.

My partners at Portfolio and Penguin used this project to prove, once again, why authors seek out great publishers. Simply put: imprints such as these employ editors who add significant value to the process of writing and producing a book. Special thanks to Adrian Zackheim for seeing the promise of this project and acquiring it. In addition, Editor Jillian Gray oversaw the earliest and most tentative drafts. Finally, Senior Editor Maria Gagliano picked up the project near the end to move it to completion. Her comments on the final draft sharpened the focus throughout, and her enthusiasm for the final product provided a welcome burst of energy as the book reached its final stages.

Last but not least, I want to thank the sterling set of research assistants who, over a period of ten years, helped me accumulate the materials that went into this book. The evidence of their tireless work can be found in the notes and bibliography sections for readers interested in diving deeper into the sources that form the foundation for the project. The list starts in 2002 with outstanding work on goal setting and expectations by Claudio Waller, then an MBA student and now a management consultant and executive coach. Picking up the baton was Eileen Cella, now a Broadway Equity actress and rising star. Eileen assembled a complete set of psychological research articles on every aspect of this project. She also digested and summarized countless books, book chapters, and stories related to success. Ellen Fu, a current student at Wharton, patiently and thoroughly worked through the piles of papers, clippings, articles, books, and notebook entries for each chapter and helped me assemble the final endnotes and bibliography. She provided the disciplined focus on detail that this kind of project needs as it moves from draft to final form. MBA student Katie Farrel assembled several focus groups of her MBA colleagues to read and discuss every chapter of the book in the final months of its revision. The comments that emerged from these groups inspired the last set of revisions.

To all of the above, plus the author of my favorite success book and founder of my university, the ever-fascinating Benjamin Franklin, my heartfelt thanks.

Notes

Opening Quotations

ix **A man saw a ball of gold:** Stephen Crane, *Black Riders and Other Lines* (Boston: Copeland and Day, 1896), p. 36.

ix **It is only when we have the courage to face things exactly as they are:** *The I Ching or Book of Changes* 2nd ed., Richard Whilhelm Translation rendered into English by Cary F. Baynes (Princeton, NJ: Princeton University Press, 1966), p. 25.

Introduction
Two Big Questions

1 **"Ralph Waldo Emerson":** This conversation took place in Emerson's home in 1852 and was noted by a visitor named John Albee. See Robert D. Richardson Jr., *Emerson: The Mind on Fire* (Berkeley: University of California Press, 1995), pp. 281–82. See also Walter Harding, *The Days of Henry Thoreau* (New York: Alfred A. Knopf, 1970), p. 51.

2 **the "Odyssey Years":** David Brooks, *The Social Animal: The Hidden Sources of Love, Character, and Achievement* (New York: Random House, 2011), pp. 190–92. Recent research also shows that the brain is still developing in people during their twenties and that they may be "better equipped to make major life decisions in their late-20s than earlier in the decade." See Melinda Beck, "Delayed Development: 20-Somethings Blamed the Brain," *Wall Street Journal*, August 21, 2012, p. D1 (discussing research conducted by Jay Giedd at the National Institute of Mental Health; Giedd says, "It's a good thing that the 20s are becoming a time for self-discovery").

6 **"The voyage of discovery":** Marcel Proust, *Remembrance of Things Past*, vol. 5, *La prisonnière*, trans. C. K. Scott Moncrieff and Terence Kilmartin, (New York: Random House, 1981), p. 62. The original text is in French, but this is the most common English translation.

7 **"the most useful life is led by one who is fully awakened":** Master Ku San is the author of a book on Buddhist doctrine. See Ku San Sunim, *Nine Mountains: Dharma-Lectures of the Korean Meditation Master Ku San*, 4th ed. (Rangoon: International Meditation Center, 1982).

8 **living with uncertainties:** In a letter in 1817, the poet John Keats described a state of mind he called "negative capability" as "when a man is capable of being in uncertainties, mysteries, doubts, without any irritable

reaching after fact and reason." The sum of my traveling experiences had taught me something very much like the attitude Keats described. See Nathan Scott, *Negative Capability: Studies in the New Literature and the Religious Situation* (New Haven, CT: Yale University Press, 1969).

8   **"the end of all our exploring will be to arrive where we started":** T. S. Eliot, *The Complete Poems and Plays, 1909–1950* (New York: Harcourt, Brace & World, 1952), p. 145. The quotation comes from "Little Gidding," the last of Eliot's *Four Quartets.*

9   **established the field of positive psychology:** For a detailed look at the history and activities of Professor Seligman's center, see www.ppc.sas .upenn.edu.

9   **the meaning of success today:** There are many editions of Benjamin Franklin's *Autobiography*; see, e.g., Benjamin Franklin, *Autobiography* (New York: Macmillan, 1962).

9   **call it "Success" for short:** For a look at the syllabus for this course, see http://lgstdept.wharton.upenn.edu/shellric/teaching.htm.

11   **The "story of success":** Malcolm Gladwell, *Outliers: The Story of Success* (Boston: Little, Brown, 2008).

12   **"When have any":** A clip containing this quote is at http://www .filmoa.com/video/voldemort-knows-harry-potter-and-the-deathly -hallows-part-2.

13   **explosion of research on happiness in recent decades:** For good summaries of positive psychology research on happiness and other topics, see Christopher Peterson, *A Primer in Positive Psychology* (New York: Oxford University Press, 2006); Corey L. M. Keyes and Jonathan Haidt, *Flourishing: Positive Psychology and the Life Well-Lived* (Washington, DC: American Psychological Association, 2002); P. Alex Linley and Stephen Joseph, *Positive Psychology in Practice* (Hoboken, NJ: John Wiley & Sons, 2004).

14   **"Believe in yourself!":** Norman Vincent Peale, *The Power of Positive Thinking* (New York: Prentice-Hall, 1952), p. 1.

15   **"Your time is limited":** Steve Jobs's famous 2005 commencement address at Stanford University is available in text and on video at http:// news.stanford.edu/news/2005/june15/jobs-061505.html

Chapter 1
The First Answer: Choose Your Life

19   **"There is no one who":** Michel de Montaigne, *The Complete Essays of Montaigne* (Palo Alto, CA: Stanford University Press, 1958), p. 615. *Essays* is the title of a collection of 107 essays written by Montaigne over his lifetime (1533–92).

21   **Eric's story was turning out to be much more interesting:** The details of the story of Eric Adler in this chapter include materials from *Washington Jewish Week*, March 5, 2009, http://washingtonjewishweek. com/print.asp?ArticleID=10352&SectionID=4&SubSectionID=51; Sharon Crenson, "On the Education Frontier," *Wharton Alumni Magazine,* January 1, 2003, http://whartonmagazine.com/issues/winter-2003/ title/; and personal exchanges between Eric Adler and me. Mr. Adler reviewed the final text in this chapter for accuracy.

22 **The first School for Educational Evolution and Development (SEED) was born:** For a detailed look at the history and activities of the SEED Foundation, see http://www.seedfoundation.com/.

24 **"good and desirable":** For the quotation from Jean-Jacques Rousseau, see Robert Zaretsky and John T. Scott, "First Theater, Then Facebook," *New York Times,* June 17, 2012, Sunday Review, p. SR9.

24 **"I have often wondered":** Marcus Aurelius, *Meditations,* trans. Gregory Hays (New York: Modern Library, 2002), p. 162.

24 **Buddhists have a name for them:** On Hungry Ghosts generally, see Yin-shun, *The Way to Buddhahood* (Somerville, MA: Wisdom Publications, 1998). For reference to Hungry Ghosts with regard to addiction, see Gabor Mate, *In the Realm of Hungry Ghosts: Close Encounters with Addiction* (Berkeley, CA: North Atlantic Books, 2010).

26 **The Six Lives Exercise:** I use this exercise in my Success course and in executive programs. All the lives are fictional with the exception of the Stone Mason. That life, with some editorial changes that I've introduced, comes from Studs Terkel, *Working* (New York: Pantheon, 1972); see the transcript of the interview with Carl Murray Bates.

33 **act like a gravitational field on your goals:** See, e.g., H. R. Markus and S. Kitayama, "Culture and the Self: Implications for Cognition, Emotion, and Motivation," *Psychological Review* 98 no. 2 (1991): 224–53; I. Grossman, P. Ellsworth, and Y. Hong, "Culture, Attention, and Emotion," *Journal of Experimental Psychology: General* 141 no. 1 (2012): 31–36.

Chapter 2
An Easy Answer: Be Happy

35 **"Those only are happy":** John Stuart Mill, *The Autobiography of John Stuart Mill* (Minneapolis: Filiquarian Publishing, 2007), p. 110. There is a research basis for Mill's insight. See I. B. Mauss, M. Tamir, C. L. Anderson, and N. S. Savino, "Can Seeking Happiness Make People Happy? Paradoxical Effects of Valuing Happiness," *Emotion* 11 no. 4 (2011): 807–15.

36 **"During the past ten years":** Daniel Kahneman, *Thinking, Fast and Slow* (New York: Farrar, Straus & Giroux, 2011), p. 407.

38 **"the experience of the soul that comes when you are doing what you should be doing":** Rabbi Akiva Tatz , "The Thinking Jew's Guide to Life: Happiness" (lecture, 2010). Retrieved from http://www.simpletoremember.com/media/a/happiness/.

38 **words such as "flow," "flourishing" and "meaning":** For "flow," see Mihaly Csikszentmihalyi, *Flow: The Psychology of Optimal Experience* (New York: Harper & Row, 1990); for "flourishing," see Martin Seligman, *Flourish: A Visionary New Understanding of Happiness and Well-Being* (New York: Free Press, 2012); for "meaning," see Jonathan Haidt, *The Happiness Hypothesis: Finding Modern Truth in Ancient Wisdom* (New York: Basic Books, 2006).

38 **this ultimate form of happiness was *eudemonia*:** Aristotle, *Nicomachean Ethics,* trans. Terence Irwin (Indianapolis: Hackett, 1999). This translation uses the word "happiness" as the English equivalent of eudemonia.

38 **an experience marked by suffering and dissatisfaction:** The reality of
    suffering and dissatisfaction as the central fact in human experience is
    the first of the Buddha's Four Noble Truths. See, e.g., Steve Hagen,
    Buddhism Plain and Simple (Portland, OR: Broadway Books, 1998).

39 **"Everything we need to be happy is easy to obtain":** For the English
    translation of the Epicurus quotation, see Richard Schoch, *The Secrets of
    Happiness: Three Thousand Years of Searching for the Good Life* (New York:
    Scribner, 2008), p. 51.

39 **"Happiness is a warm puppy":** The comic strip is at http://www
    .gocomics.com/peanuts/1960/04/25. The quotation from Charles Schulz is
    in "Happiness Is a Warm Puppy," *Escape* blog, January 3, 2012, retrieved on
    September 15, 2012, from http://danwritesaboutbooks.blogspot.com/2012/
    01/happiness-is-warm-puppy.html; see also David Michaelis, *Schulz and
    Peanuts: A Biography* (New York: HarperCollins, 2007), pp. 336–45.

39 **defined this as the happiness of the "Experiencing Self":** Kahneman,
    Thinking, Fast and Slow, p. 381.

40 **studied Momentary Happiness through meditation:** For mindfulness,
    see, e.g., Thich Nhat Hanh, *The Miracle of Mindfulness: An Introduction to
    the Practice of Meditation,* trans. Mobi Ho (Boston: Beacon Press, 1999).
    See also B. Fredrickson, M. Cohn, K. Coffey, J. Pek, and S. Finkel, "Open
    Hearts Build Lives: Positive Emotions, Induced Through Loving-
    Kindness Meditation, Build Consequential Personal Resources," *Journal
    of Personality and Social Psychology* 95 no. 5 (2008): 1045–62.

40 **women spend about the same amount of time each week eating:**
    Kahneman, *Thinking, Fast and Slow,* p. 395. French women also spend
    less time with their children but enjoy it more (ibid., p. 394).

40 **sections of a juicy tangerine into his mouth:** Thich Nhat Hanh, *Miracle
    of Mindfulness,* pp. 8–10.

40 **"It seems as though Stevens composed poems in his head":** Quoting
    Professor Helen Vendler in Jeff Gordinier, "For Wallace Stevens,
    Hartford as Muse," *New York Times,* February 26, 2012, p. TR11.

41 **people are poor predictors of what will make them happy:** Daniel Gilbert,
    Stumbling on Happiness (New York: Vintage Books, 2005), pp. 233–57.

42 **becoming "a psychological burden" to everyone:** Quoting Carol Ryff
    in Shirley S. Wang, "Is Happiness Overrated?" *Wall Street Journal,* March
    15, 2011, http://online.wsj.com/article/SB10001424052748704893604576
    200471545379388.html.

42 **what psychologists call "adaptation":** See, e.g., M. H. Appley, *Adapta-
    tion Level Theory: A Symposium* (New York: Academic Press, 1971), pp.
    287–302.

43 **a yearlong program to make her life happier:** Gretchen Rubin, *The
    Happiness Project: Or, Why I Spent a Year Trying to Sing in the Morning,
    Clean My Closets, Fight Right, Read Aristotle, and Generally Have More Fun*
    (New York: HarperCollins, 2009). For information and quotations
    about Ms. Rubin's "Boot Camp Perfect" happy days, see pp. 277–89; for
    biggest "happiness boosters" and "you are trying to get more control
    over your life," see pp. 282 and 289.

44 **an actual question from one of these surveys:** Kahneman, *Thinking,
    Fast and Slow,* p. 396. In addition, for a variety of psychological

self-assessments related to happiness, see Ed Diener and Robert Diener, *Happiness: Unlocking the Mysteries of Psychological Wealth* (Malden, MA: Blackwell, 2008), pp. 234–43.

45   **tend to scan for memories of "peaks":** Diener and Diener, *Happiness*, p. 216 ("We recommend that people think of happiness in terms of mildly pleasant emotions that are felt most of the time, with intense positive emotions being felt occasionally").

45   **"gap" between the life they actually have and the life they hoped to have:** Ibid., pp. 99–102. See also Marne L. Arthaud-Day and Janet P. Near, "The Wealth of Nations and the Happiness of Nations: Why 'Accounting' Matters," *Social Indicators Research* 74 no. 3 (2005): 516–17.

45   **the famous Serenity Prayer:** The theologian Reinhold Niebuhr is credited with originating this prayer. See Elizabeth Sifton, *The Serenity Prayer: Faith and Politics in Times of Peace and War* (New York: W. W. Norton, 2003), pp. 7, 9–14.

45   **"most people are mildly happy most of the time":** Diener and Diener, *Happiness*, p. 129.

46   **people who score a perfect ten on the Overall Happiness surveys pay a price:** Ibid., pp. 214–15. The study reports that "people who score '8' on a cheerfulness survey earn more (20 years later) than people who score 6, 7, 9, or 10."

46   **"making the team, being promoted at work":** David Lykken and Auke Tellegen, "Happiness Is a Stochastic Phenomenon," *Psychological Science* 7 no. 3 (May 1996): pp. 186–89.

47   **you will probably adapt if you have an accident and end up in a wheelchair:** Gilbert, *Stumbling on Happiness*, pp. 100–2.

47   **achieving long-term, difficult goals increases your Overall Happiness:** Kahneman, *Thinking, Fast and Slow*, pp. 401–2.

48   **"It is only a slight exaggeration":** Quoting Daniel Kahneman in Jonah Lehrer, "Holiday Happiness? Not Under the Tree," *Wall Street Journal*, December 24–25, 2011, p. C12.

48   **"the only thing that really matters in life are your relationships":** For information on the Grant Study and the quotation from George Vaillant, see Joshua Wolf Shenk, "What Makes Us Happy?," *Atlantic* (June 2009), p. 11, http://www.theatlantic.com/magazine/archive/2009/06/what-makes-us-happy/307439/.

48   **more money does not buy you more and more Momentary Happiness:** Robert Frank, "The Perfect Salary for Happiness: $75,000," *Wall Street Journal*, September 7, 2010, http://blogs.wsj.com/wealth/2010/09/07/the-perfect-salary-for-happiness-75000-a-year/.

48   **wealth can improve your Overall Happiness:** Kahneman, *Thinking, Fast and Slow*, pp. 401–2.

49   **Another reason money may buy some Overall Happiness is cultural:** Ed Diener and Weiting Ng, "Wealth and Happiness Across the World: Material Prosperity Predicts Life Evaluation, Whereas Psychosocial Prosperity Predicts Positive Feeling," *Journal of Personality and Social Psychology* 99 no. 1 (2010): 52–61; Louis Tay and Ed Diener, "Needs and Subjective Well-Being Around the World," *Journal of Personality and Social Psychology* 101 no. 2 (2011): 354–65.

49   **"$100 more than his wife's sister's husband":** Quoted in Diener and
      Diener, *Happiness,* p. 107.
49   **Aristotle called this quality in human life eudemonia:** Aristotle,
      Nicomachean Ethics.
50   **"moving along your own road":** Quoted at http://www.atime.org/
      newsletters_pg/Summer5761/happiness.html. A TIME is a Jewish-
      oriented advocacy organization.
50   **"not entitled to a central place in any theory":** Seligman, *Flourish,*
      p. 14.
50   **an ultimate good Seligman labels as "Well-being":** Ibid., pp. 13–29.
50   **"What can you do to have a good, happy":** Haidt, *Happiness Hypothesis,*
      p. 218.
51   **"the right relationships between yourself and others":** Ibid., p. 239.
51   **"a sense of purpose and meaning will emerge":** Ibid.
51   **pessimistic people tend to see reality more clearly than optimists:**
      Professor Joseph P. Forgas is a leading researcher on the improved
      accuracy of human perception when people are in something less than
      a happy mood. For a general study of the benefits of being something
      other than happy, see Jennifer Michael Hecht, *The Happiness Myth* (New
      York: HarperCollins, 2008). See also K. Fiedler, U. Fladung, and
      U. Hemmeter, "A Positivity Bias in Person Memory," *Journal of Social
      Psychology* 17 no. 2 (1987): 243–46; J. P. Forgas, "On Being Happy but
      Mistaken: Mood Effects on the Fundamental Attribution Error," *Journal
      of Personality and Social Psychology* 75 no. 2 (1998): 318–31; J. P. Forgas,
      "When Sad Is Better Than Happy: Negative Affect Can Improve the
      Quality and Effectiveness of Persuasive Messages and Social Influence
      Strategies," *Journal of Experimental Social Psychology* 43 no. 4 (2007): 513–
      28; J. P. Forgas,
      P. Vargas, and S. Laham, "Mood Effects on Eyewitness Memory:
      Affective Influences on Susceptibility to Misinformation," *Journal of
      Experimental Social Psychology* 41 no. 6 (2005): 574–88.
51   **"To make a goal of comfort or happiness has never appealed to me":**
      Albert Einstein, *Living Philosophies* (New York: Simon & Schuster, 1931),
      p. 4.
52   **doing the right thing even if that comes at the price of our happiness:**
      For Immanuel Kant's sentiments, see Gary Gutting, "Happiness,
      Philosophy and Science," Opinionator, *New York Times,* August 31, 2011,
      http://opinionator.blogs.nytimes.com/2011/08/31/happiness
      -philosophy-and-science/.
52   **"I don't know why":** Quoting Ludwig Wittgenstein in Peter Hershey,
      The Beginning of the End (College Station, TX: Virtual bookworm.com,
      2004), p. 109.
52   **a society in which unhappiness is outlawed:** Aldous Huxley, *Brave New
      World* (New York: RosettaBooks, 1979); see p. 240 for the conversation
      between the Savage and the Controller.
53   **round-the-world tour of major religions:** For the fundamental principles
      of each religion discussed in the text, see Christopher Hugh Partridge,
      Introduction to World Religions (Minneapolis: Fortress Press, 2005).

53–54 **not about the emotion of happiness at all:** The Dalai Lama and Howard C. Cutler, *The Art of Happiness: A Handbook for Living* (New York: Riverhead Books, 1998).

54 **powerful king who tried to find the meaning of life:** Eccles. 12:13, King James Version.

55 **Research suggests that belief in *any* religion raises your level of Overall Happiness:** Sonja Lyubomirsky, *The How of Happiness: A Scientific Approach to Getting the Life You Want* (New York: Penguin Press, 2008), pp. 227–54.

60 **wait for a person named Godot to arrive:** Samuel Beckett, *Waiting for Godot: A Tragicomedy in Two Acts* (London: Folio Society, 2000), p. 74.

Chapter 3
Society's Answer: Seek Status, Fame, and Fortune

62 **"I always wanted to be somebody":** Quoted in Mark Albion, *Making a Life, Making a Living* (New York: Warner Business Books, 2000), p. 23.

62 **"I've been poor":** Leonard Lyons, "The Post's New Yorker," *Washington Post,* May 12, 1937, p. 13.

62 **An entrepreneur named Carl Bolch Jr.:** Carl Bolch is the CEO of RaceTrac Petroleum. See http://www.forbes.com/lists/2011/21/private-companies-11_RaceTrac-Petroleum_EM4F.html.

63 **They are called Hungry Ghosts:** On Hungry Ghosts generally, see Yin-shun, *The Way to Buddhahood* (Somerville, MA: Wisdom Publications, 1998). For reference to Hungry Ghosts with regard to addiction, see Gabor Mate, *In the Realm of Hungry Ghosts: Close Encounters with Addiction* (Berkeley, CA: North Atlantic Books, 2010).

64 **children often "dance to the unlived lives of their parents":** Quoted in Randy W. Roberts and James Stuart Olson, *John Wayne: American* (Lincoln: University of Nebraska Press, 1998), p. 7. See generally Rainer Maria Rilke, *Letters to a Young Poet,* trans. Stephen Mitchell (New York: Random House, 1984).

65 **Rousseau taught us that individuals take their cues about what is "good or desirable":** Robert Zaretsky and John T. Scott, "First Theater, Then Facebook," *New York Times,* June 17, 2012, Sunday Review, p. SR9.

65 **"The Kyrgyz [people]":** Edward Wong, "Two Schools in Afghanistan, One Complicated Situation," *New York Times,* April 23, 2011, p. WK5.

65 **so many images of Buddha depict him as fat:** Andrew Perry, "Why Is the Buddha Fat?," Buddhism/Taoism, Suite101.com, May 17, 2010, http://andrew-perry.suite101.com/why-is-the--buddha-fat-a238307. Fat Buddha is also a popular name for Chinese restaurants and bars.

65 **"The fashion magazine *Marie Claire*":** Abigail Haworth, "Forced to Be Fat," *Marie Claire,* July 21, 2001, http://www.marieclaire.com/world-reports/news/forcefeeding-in-mauritania.

66 **"You could call me fat and, yes, even obese":** Quoted in Jennifer Preston, "Yes, I'm Fat, and You're a Bully, Anchor Declares," *New York Times,* October 4, 2012, p. A21.

67   **"Sometimes," Obama writes:** For Barack Obama's experiences when he
was working at Business International, see Jonathan Karl, "Barack
Obama: The Story," *Wall Street Journal*, June 16–17, 2012, p. C5, which is
a book review of David Maraniss, *Barack Obama: The Story* (New York:
Simon & Schuster, 2012). See also Barack Obama, *Dreams from My Father*
(New York: Three Rivers Press, 2004), p. 136.

68   **"Eveyone needs fuel":** For the story of Kurt Timken, see Po Bronson,
What Should I Do with My Life? (New York: Random House, 2002), pp.
292–301. See also Garry Emmons, "Working the Street MBA Cop Kurt
Timken," *Harvard Business School Alumni Bulletin* (June 2004), http://
www.alumni.hbs.edu/bulletin/2004/june/timken.html.

70   **not born with a racket in his hands:** Andre Agassi, *Open: An
Autobiography* (New York: Vintage Books, 2010); for "a child who hits one
million balls" and "Hit harder!" see p. 28; for "the killer instinct," see
p. 57.

70   **he would yell, "Doesn't fit! Come on! Let's go!:** Ibid., p. 32. For Agassi's
winning a sportsmanship trophy at the national youth tournament, see
p. 56; for "hate it with a dark and secret passion" and "the good feeling
doesn't last as long as the bad," see pp. 3 and 167 ; for information on
Agassi's being able to reclaim his life through relationships and
"BELIEVE," see pp. 279–80, 327–38, 380.

72   **"Model Minority" Asian family units:** For more information on the
term "model minority," see e.g., Japanese American Citizens League,
Myths and Mirror: Real Challenges Facing Asian American Students, p. 2,
"Not Easily Defined: Sterotypes, the Model Minority Myth, and You,"
http://www.jacl.org/leadership/documents/MythsandMirrors Final.
pdf. The model minority phenomenon has attracted a great deal of
research. See, e.g., H. C. Yoo, K. S. Burrola, and M. F. Steger, "Model
Minority Phenomena: A Preliminary Report on a New Measure:
Internalization of the Model Minority Myth Measure (IM-4) and Its
Psychological Correlates Among Asian American College Students,"
Journal of Counseling Psychology 57 no. 1 (2010): 114–27; Sapna Cheryan
and Galen V. Bodenhausen, "When Positive Stereotypes Threaten
Intellectual Performance: The Psychological Hazards of 'Model
Minority' Status," *Psychological Science* 11 no. 5 (2000): 399–402.

72   **They call this period Rumspringa:** See Tom Shachtman, *Rumspringa: To
Be or Not to Be Amish* (New York: Farrar, Straus & Giroux, 2006).

73   **Not long ago:** The scandal was triggered when Jon Krakauer blew the
whistle on Mortenson in a short exposé called *Three Cups of Deceit: How
Greg Mortenson, Humanitarian Hero, Lost His Way.* (Harpswell, ME: Anchor,
2011). The exposé was featured on a *60 Minutes* segment, which is at
http://www.cbsnews.com/video/watch/?id=7363068n&tag=mncol;lst;1.
In the wake of this scandal, the Montana attorney general investigated
the Central Asia Institute and concluded that the board had failed to
supervise Mortenson's expenditures and there was a lack of financial
accountability. Mortenson reimbursed the charity nearly $1 million. He
was removed from any position involving financial oversight and the
board was expanded as part of a legal settlement. See Matt Volz, "'3
Cups' Charity's New Board," *Philadelphia Inquirer,* July 20, 2012, p. A17.

74　**"The lust for fame has taken on [a] pathological form":** Quoted in Miki Turner, "Addicted to Fame: Stars and Fans Share Affliction," August 9, 2007, *Today Entertainment,* http://today.msnbc.msn.com/id/ 20199608/ns/today-entertainment/t/addicted-fame-stars-fans-share -affliction/. See generally David Sloan Wilson, *Evolution for Everyone: How Darwin's Theory Can Change the Way We Think About Our Lives* (New York: Delacorte Press, 2007).

74　**found a niche writing about his experiences with sex and alcohol:** For the story about the writer Tucker Max, see Reeves Wiedeman, Dept. of Grownups, "A New Max," *New Yorker,* March 5, 2012, pp. 24–25.

75　**"Happiness is measured not by the number of days you live":** The original source for this aphorism is unknown. I found a version in Martin Lindstrom, "How to Be Happy Anywhere," *Fast Company,* February 28, 2012, http://www.fastcompany.com/1820974/ how-be-happy-anywhere.

75　**"We sit down with everyone":** Quoting Thom Beers in Craig Tomashoff, "Casting Reality TV? It's Now Difficult to Find Real People," *New York Times,* August 28, 2011, p. AR14.

75　**"Reality TV can be very dangerous":** Quoted in Holly McKay, "Dark Side of Reality Television Spotlighted as Networks Struggle with Growing Number of Cast Suicides," Fox News, August 17, 2011, http://www.foxnews.com/entertainment/2011/08/17/dark-side- reality-television-spotlighted-as-networks-struggle-with-growing/. This article also highlights examples of suicides by cast members of several reality television shows.

76　**"Top Ten" emperors in the long history of China:** See http://china. org.cn/top10/2010-11/30/content_21448985.htm.

76　**more satisfied with their lives two years after winning:** Ed Diener and Robert Diener, *Happiness: Unlocking the Mysteries of Psychological Wealth* (Malden, MA: Blackwell, 2008), pp. 95–97.

76　**"Wealth is a menace to happiness":** Stephen Miller, "Society Girl Who Spent 8 Decades in Seclusion," *Wall Street Journal,* May 25, 2011, p. A8.

76–77　**tried to have him killed to collect the inheritance:** For the story of William "Bud" Post, see Oren Dorell, "Lottery Winner's Good Luck Can Go Bad Fast," *USA Today,* February 26, 2006, http://usatoday30 .usatoday.com/news/nation/2006-02-26-lotteryluck_x.htm (Bill Welsh and *USA Today* research contributed to this story).

77　**"If you worship money":** Quoting the novelist David Foster Wallace in the commencement speech that he gave at Kenyon College on May 21, 2005. See the full speech at http://moreintelligentlife.com/story/ david-foster-wallace-in-his-own-words. See also David Foster Wallace, *This Is Water: Some Thoughts, Delivered on a Significant Occasion, About Living a Compassionate Life* (New York: Little, Brown, 2009).

77　**"[Gupta's] enamored with Kravis":** For the story of the scandal surrounding Raj Rajaratnam and Raj Gupta, see Holman Jenkins Jr., "A Hedge Fund's Neurotic Tipsters," *Wall Street Journal,* April 23, 2011, p. A12; Michael Rothfeld and Susan Pulliam, "Gupta

Surrenders to FBI," *Wall Street Journal,* October 25, 2011, http://online.
wsj.com/article/SB10001424052970204777904576653850379354850.
html.

77 **"The *love of* money is the root of many evils":** 1 Tim. 6:10, King James
Version.

78 **A student in my Success class:** See J. J. Fliegelman, "My 2011 Theory
of What Success Is and How to Achieve It." The paper is on file in my
office.

78 **a form that the philosopher Stephen Darwall has called "recognition
respect":** Stephen L. Darwall, "Two Kinds of Respect," *Ethics* 88 no. 1
(1977): 36–49. Professor Darwall uses the phrase "appraisal respect" for
the more substantive type of respect, but I prefer "informed respect."
See also Elias L. Khalil, "Respect, Admiration, Aggrandizement: Adam
Smith as Economic Psychologist," *Journal of Economic Psychology* 17 no. 5
(1996): 555–77.

79 **"You don't know me":** Preston, "Yes, I'm Fat," p. A21.

79 **"A lot of people have opinions":** Quoted in Darren Everson, "Only One
Gets the Golden Scissors," *Wall Street Journal,* April 3, 2010, p. D12,
http://online.wsj.com/article/SB2000142405270230487170457516002400
92619254.html.

79 **"no idol more debasing than the worship of money":** Andrew Carnegie,
"Memorandum of 1868," chap. 5 in *The Andrew Carnegie Reader,* ed. Joseph
Frazier Wall (Pittsburgh: University of Pittsburgh Press, 1992), p. 41.

81 **I keep a file on lottery winners:** The first part of Stafford's story about
how she won the lottery, and her associated quotations, comes from
David Hochman, "The $112 Million Dollar Woman," *Parade,* January 16,
2011), p. 6, http://www.parade.com/news/2011/01/16-the-112-million
-dollar-woman.html.

81 **the "Law of Attraction":** Rhonda Byrne, *The Secret* (New York: Atria
Books, 2006). The Law of Attraction is discussed on pages 1 through 25
(chap. 1, "The Secret Revealed").

82 **she chose a different path:** The second part of Stafford's story about
what she has chosen to do with her newfound lottery wealth, and
associated quotations, comes from an interview she gave to the
Huffington Post. See Vickie Karp, "Third Screen: Lotto Winner Gives
Millions to the Arts," *Huffington Post,* June 7, 2009, http://www.
huffingtonpost.com/vickie-karp/third-screen-lotto-winner_b_212378.
html. More information about Cynthia Stafford and her charitable
and other activities can be found on her website. See http://
cynthiapstafford.com/.

Chapter 4
An Inspired Answer: Find Meaningful Work

86 **"Life's too short for the wrong job":** Advertising slogan for a German
online recruiting website featured in "The Art of Getting Attention,"
Review, *Wall Street Journal,* August 27, 2011, p. C12.

86 **working for five years as the Internet sales manager:** For the story of
Robert Chambers, see Marc Freeman, *Encore: Finding Work That Matters*

in the Second Half of Life (New York: PublicAffairs, 2007), pp. 57–66. See also "Founder's Story," the More Than Wheels company website, http://www.morethanwheels.org/founders-story.

90 **how these employees thought about their work:** This framework originated with Robert N. Bellah, Richard Madsen, William M. Sullivan, Ann Swidler, and Steven M. Tipton, *Habits of the Heart* (Berkeley: University of California Press, 1985), pp. 65–66. The framework was extended in Amy Wrzesniewski, Clark McCauley, Paul Rozin, and Barry Schwartz, "Jobs, Careers, and Callings: People's Relations to Their Work," *Journal of Research in Personality* 31 no. 1 (1997): pp. 21–33. For different ways that people can transform jobs into meaningful work, see Amy Wrzesniewski and Jane E. Dutton, "Crafting a Job: Revisioning Employees as Active Crafters of Their Work," *Academy of Management Review* 26 no. 2 (2001): pp. 179–201; Bill Barnett, "Make Your Job More Meaningful," Harvard Business Review Blog Network, April 25, 2012, http://blogs.hbr.org/cs/2012/04/make_your_job_more_meaningful.html.

93 **cultural commentator Po Bronson collected:** Po Bronson, *What Should I Do with My Life?* (New York: Random House, 2002), p. 365. See also Po Bronson, "What Should I Do With My Life?," *Fast Company,* December 31, 2002, http://www.fastcompany.com/45909/what-should-i-do-my-life.

93 **"I chose this path":** Quoting Melba K. Duncan in Phyllis Korkki, "Assistants, Yes, but They Can Do It All," Jobs Section, *New York Times,* October 7, 2012, p. BU7.

94 **the many symbols and ceremonies that different professions use:** See, e.g., Peter M. Warren, "For New Medical Students, White Coats Are a Warmup," *Los Angeles Times,* October 18, 1999, http://articles.latimes.com/1999/oct/18/local/me-23619; R. M. Veatch, "White Coat Ceremonies: A Second Option," *Journal of Medical Ethics* 28 no. 1 (2002): 5–6; Kathy Rivers, "Pinning Ceremony Honors School of Nursing Students," *Reporter* (Vanderbilt University Medical Center's Weekly Newspaper), http://www.mc.vanderbilt.edu/reporter/index.html?ID=6597.

95 **diagram of three interlocking circles:** I got the idea for this figure from Jim Collins, *Good to Great: Why Some Companies Make the Leap . . . and Others Don't* (New York: HarperBusiness, 2001). See also Jim Collins, "Good to Great," *Fast Company,* October 1, 2001, http://www.jimcollins.com/article_topics/articles/good-to-great.html. Collins's three circles relate to success for an organization. I adapted them to discuss success for an individual.

96 **people who merely like rather than love their work:** Karen Burns, "Why You Don't Need to Love Your Job," On Careers, *U.S. News & World Report,* June 2, 2010, http://money.usnews.com/money/blogs/outside-voices-careers/2010/06/02/why-you-dont-need-to-love-your-job.

96 **As a laid-off human resources manager:** Quoting Yundra Thomas, in Jennifer Medina, "Long-Term Jobless Regroup to Fight the Odds," *New York Times,* August 17, 2012, p. A1.

97   **story about a self-employed carpenter:** For the story of Richard Ryder, see P. J. Reilly, "Civil War Interest Is a Big Undertaking," *Philadelphia Inquirer,* September 10, 2012, p. B6.

98   **Jacqueline Khan worked for thirty years:** Freedman, *Encore,* pp. 90–97.

99   **"Jobs are like college courses":** Holly Robinson, "Why I Told My Daughter to Quit Her Job," *Huffington Post, College,* January 18, 2012, http://www .huffingtonpost.com/holly-robinson/quitting-your-job_b_ 1211880.html.

99   **Mary Lee Herrington:** For the story of Mary Lee Herrington, see Alex Williams, "Maybe It's Time for Plan C," Sunday Styles, *New York Times,* August 14, 2011, p. ST1.

101   **In our career-obsessed:** Bertrand Russell, *Principles of Social Reconstruction* (New York: Psychology Press, 1997), pp. 159–60.

101   **"three things—autonomy, complexity, and a connection between effort and reward":** Malcolm Gladwell, *Outliers: The Story of Success* (Boston: Little, Brown, 2008), pp. 149–50.

101   **known to Indonesians as the "gatekeeper":** Stephen Miller, "Volcano's Sentry to the Very End," World News, *Wall Street Journal,* October 29, 2010, p. A12.

102   **"So guide us":** The Episcopal prayer is found in Bellah et al., *Habits of the Heart,* p. 66.

103   **parenting itself as a form of meaningful work:** Justin Coulson, Lindsay Oades, and Gerard Stoyles, "Parent's Conception and Experience of Calling in Child Rearing: A Qualitative Analysis," *Journal of Humanistic Psychology* 52 no. 2 (2012): 222–27.

103   **"Here's how I define":** "A Conversation with Malcolm Gladwell," an interview with Malcolm Gladwell by Charlie Rose, is posted on Matt Linderman's blog at http://37signals.com/svn/posts/1483-malcolm -gladwell-on-meaningful-work-and-curiosity?15#all_comments. This interview can also be found at http://www.charlierose.com/view/ interview/9855. The quote in the text is a comment about this interview posted by "Patrick Henry" on December 31, 2008.

103   **"My parents," he replied:** Andrew Goldman, "Marco Rubio Won't Be V.P.," *New York Times,* January 29, 2012, p. MM10. See also, http://www.rubio .senate.gov/public/index.cfm/about?p=biography.

104   **His graduation from law school in 1996:** Marco Rubio, *An American Son* (New York: Penguin, 2012), p. 83.

105   **"Music for me is my voice":** For the story of Dalia Moukarker, see Daniel J. Wakin and Reem Makhoul, "For Flutist in West Bank, a Rare Chance," *New York Times,* September 30, 2012, p. AR9.

105   **founder of the online payment system PayPal:** Caitlin Kelly, "Drop Out, Dive In, Start Up," Sunday Business, *New York Times,* September 16, 2012, p. BU1. See also David Brooks, "The Creative Monopoly," *New York Times,* April 23, 2012, http://www.nytimes.com/2012/04/24/ opinion/brooks-the-creative-monopoly.html.

108   **"work performed at the highest level of excellence":** H. G. Liddell and R. Scott, *A Greek-English Lexicon* (Oxford: Clarendon Press, 1961), p. 238 (arete is ἀρετή in ancient Greek).

108   **For example, Fred Beckey:** Michael J. Ybarra, "The Old Man, His Mountains," *Wall Street Journal,* November 10, 2011, p. D4.

109 **Others start with a talent:** Cal Newport, "Follow a Passion? Let It Follow You," Jobs Section, *New York Times*, September 30, 2012, p. BU 8. See also Cal Newport, *So Good They Can't Ignore You: Why Skills Trump Passion in the Quest for Work You Love* (New York: Business Plus, 2012).

109 **talent for coaching vocal speech:** Joanne Kaufman, "A Matter of Voice," *Wall Street Journal*, August 31, 2011, p. C10, http://online.wsj.com/article/SB10001424053111904787404576534690533590346.html.

111 **In past lives, he had studied:** For more about Rafael Risemberg's wonderful gallery tours, go to http://www.nygallerytours.com/about/.

111 **"hard work is a prison sentence only if it does not have meaning":** Gladwell, *Outliers*, p. 150.

Chapter 5
Discover What You Can Do Better Than Most: Capabilities

117 **"You have brains in your head":** Dr. Seuss, *Oh, the Places You'll Go!* (New York: Random House, 1960), p. 3.

117 **"You must bake with the flour you have":** G. Richard Shell, *Bargaining for Advantage: Negotiation Strategies for Reasonable People* 2nd ed. (New York: Penguin, 2006), p. 3. See also R. G. H. Siu, *Folk Wisdom and Management: 3,333 Proverbs* (unpublished, 1994), p. 13.

117 **"I am sadly an ordinary person . . . with talents I do not use":** Laura Jacobs, "Our Lady of the Kitchen," *Vanity Fair,* August 2009, http://www.vanityfair.com/culture/features/2009/08/julia-child200908; Julia Moskin, "The Gifts She Gave," Dining, *New York Times*, August 15, 2012, p. D1; Marilyn Mellowes, "Julia Child: About Julia Child," *American Masters*, PBS, June 15, 2005.

121 **"Many of these stories":** The transcript of Russell Conwell's Acres of Diamonds speech, transcribed by Michelle Moore, is found at http://www.americanrhetoric.com/speeches/rconwellacresofdiamonds.htm. See also http://www.temple.edu/about/RussellConwell.htm.

122 **people who "maximize their talents":** David Brooks, "The Talent Society," Op-Ed, *New York Times,* February 21, 2012, p. A21.

124 **Discernment is your willingness to listen for God's voice:** For information on discernment, see Timothy M. Gallagher, *The Discernment of Spirits: An Ignatian Guide for Everyday Living* (New York: Crossroad, 2005).

125 **her collection of brochures from airplane manufacturers:** Stephen Miller, "A Match for Men in the Skies," Remembrances, *Wall Street Journal*, September 3, 2011, p. A5.

125 **He won the hearts of both the crowd and the general public:** John Paul Newport, "Is Bubba's Secret No Lesson?," *Wall Street Journal*, April 13, 2012, p. A16.

126 **" 'As a kid who was short' ":** Dotson Rader, "Michael J. Fox at 50: 'I Don't Look at Life as a Battle,' " *Philadelphia Inquirer,* April 1, 2012, pp. 8, 14.

127 **has spent her life researching:** Nancy L. Segal, *Someone Else's Twin* (Amherst, NY: Prometheus Books, 2011), p. 25. See also Nancy L. Segal, *Born Together—Reared Apart: The Landmark Minnesota Twin Study* (Cambridge, MA: Harvard University Press, 2012).

127 **adult identical twins who had been reared apart:** T. J. Bouchard Jr., D. T. Lykken, M. McGue, N. L. Segal, and A. Tellegen, "Sources of

Human Psychological Differences: The Minnesota Study of Twins Reared Apart," *Science* 250 no. 4978 (1990): 223–28.

128 **"the most influential gift that parents give their children":** Bryan Caplan, *Selfish Reasons to Have More Kids: Why Being a Great Parent Is Less Work and More Fun Than You Think* (New York: Basic Books, 2011), p. 53.

128 **illustrates the relationship between genes and abilities with an example of beavers:** Richard Dawkins, *The Extended Phenotype* (London: Oxford University Press, 1999).

128 **"number sense":** Sindya N. Bhanoo, "In Future Math Whizzes Signs of 'Number Sense,' " Observatory, *New York Times,* August 16, 2011, p. D3.

129 **human genes for physical "endurance" versus physical "strength":** Matt Ridley, "When Genes Write the Athletic Playbook," *Wall Street Journal,* July 30, 2011, p. C4.

129 **Cape Cod native Liam Haveran:** Molly Driscoll, "Cape Tech Grad Followed a Strange Path to Medicine," *Cape Cod Times,* June 16, 2011, http://www.capecodonline.com/apps/pbcs.dll/article?AID=/20110616/ LIFE/106160306.

131 **I have tried a variety of tests:** For Myers-Briggs, see http://www .myersbriggs.org/. For StrengthsFinder, see http://www.strengthsfinder .com/home.aspx; Donald O. Clifton and Marcus Buckingham, *Now, Discover Your Strengths* (New York: Free Press, 2001); in addition, see a follow-up book, Tom Rath, *StrengthsFinder2.0* (New York: Gallup Press, 2007). For VIA Survey of Character Strengths, see http://www .authentichappiness.sas.upenn.edu/default.aspx. The Big Five personality factors are the dominant research paradigm for personality in modern psychology. See, e.g., P. T. Costa Jr. and R. R. McCrae, *NEO-PI-R: Professional Manual* (Odessa, FL: Psychological Assessment Resources, 1992); Sonia Roccas, Lilach Sagiv, Shalom H. Schwartz, and Ariel Knafo, "The Big Five Personality Factors and Personal Values," *Personality and Social Psychology Bulletin* 28 no. 6 (2002): 789–801. The NEO Summary is at http://www4.parinc.com/Products/Product.aspx? ProductID=NEO -PI-3&tp=neo-pi-3#Items.

132 **The exercise requires:** The "Looking-Glass Self" is discussed in Charles Cooley, *Human Nature and the Social Order* (Charleston, SC: Nabu Press, 2010).

132 **"Who is it that can tell me who I am":** William Shakespeare, *King Lear* (New Haven, CT: Yale University Press, 2007), p. 47.

132 **The SAME Personality Assessment:** A former MBA student, John Picasso, and I collaborated to construct the SAME personality assessment for use in my class by breaking down the thirty facets of the Big Five inventory, eliminating what appeared to us to be confusing overlaps among various items, and creating a simple scale for the four categories of four items each that you see in the text. The Big Five— openness, conscientiousness, extroversion, agreeableness, and neuroticism—have six facets each. A full scale of thirty items would have been too detailed for the purposes of this book. But limiting the assessment to only the Big Five categories left too much out. We took encouragement from an attempt to reduce the thirty facets to ten. See

Colin G. DeYoung, Lena C. Quilty, and Jordon B. Peterson, "Between Facets and Domains: 10 Aspects of the Big Five," *Journal of Personality and Social Psychology* 93 no. 5 (2007), pp. 880–96. The sixteen-item SAME assessment is thus our attempt to create a useful profiler for readers to get a sense of the capabilities residing within their personalities. Readers are encouraged to go more deeply into the personality question by sampling some of the popular commercial and academically tested profilers referred to above and in the bibliography at the end of the book.

137 **"The Hedgehog and the Fox":** William Barrett, "Sharp Eyes for the Multiple Things," Books, *New York Times,* February 14, 1954, http://www .nytimes.com/books/98/11/29/specials/berlin-hedgehog.html. See also Isaiah Berlin, *The Hedgehog and the Fox* (Lanham, MD: Ivan R. Dee, 1993).

140 **what positive psychologists call "flow":** See, e.g., Mihaly Csikszentmihalyi, *Flow: The Psychology of Optimal Experience* (New York: Harper & Row, 1990).

142 **illusion that great wealth is the secret to success:** Paulo Coelho, *The Alchemist* (New York: HarperCollins, 1995).

Chapter 6
Set Yourself on Fire: Motivation

144 **"Success is not the result":** Quoted in J. D. Reed, "In the Rocket's Red Glare," *Sports Illustrated,* May 17, 1976, http://sportsillustrated.cnn.com/ vault/article/magazine/MAG1091088/index.htm.

144 **When the Princeton mathematician:** For the story of Andrew Wiles, see Simon Singh, *Fermat's Enigma: The Epic Quest to Solve the World's Greatest Mathematical Problem* (New York: Walker and Company, 1997); for "I was electrified," see p. 205; for "craving for glory," see p. 208.

145 **"I would wake up with [Fermat] first thing in the morning":** Ibid., p. 211. For "One enters the first room of the mansion," see pp. 236–37. The story of Wiles's process for solving Fermat's Last Theorem is told on pp. 205–77.

147 **the promise of external rewards can even raise an IQ score:** Faye Flam, "Smart Money and IQs," *Philadelphia Inquirer,* April 27, 2011, p. A3.

147 **IBM computer named "Watson" made history:** David A. Ferrucci, "Building the Team That Built Watson," *New York Times,* January 8, 2012, p. BU7.

148 **known as the "Crespi effect":** Kent C. Berridge, "Motivation Concepts in Behavioral Neuroscience," *Psychology and Behavior* 81 no. 2 (2004): 179–209.

149 **traditionalists who think that external rewards dominate:** Daniel H. Pink, *Drive: The Surprising Truth About What Motivates Us* (New York: Riverhead Books, 2009), pp. 15–33.

149 **animals will ignore available rewards:** W. R. White, "Motivation Reconsidered," *Psychological Review* 66 no. 5 (1959): 297–333.

149 **explosion of research on so-called intrinsic motivation:** See, e.g., Richard M. Ryan and Edward L. Deci, "Intrinsic and Extrinsic Motivations: Classic Definitions and New Direction," *Contemporary Educational Psychology* 25 no. 1 (2000): 54–67.

149   **innate desires for "freedom, challenge, and purpose":** Pink, *Drive*, p. 78.

149   **the search for inner satisfactions and the quest for outer rewards:** Ibid., pp. 34–69.

149   *Modern Madness:* Douglas LaBier, *Modern Madness: The Emotional Fallout of Success* (Reading, MA: Addison-Wesley, 1986). For this book, the author conducted 230 interviews with "successful" people between the ages of twenty-five and forty-seven and chronicled the variety of dysfunctional ways in which overstressed executives coped with work pressures.

150   **different personality types require different motivational boosts:** Jane M. Von Bergen, "End Users Motivate Workers in Small Firms," *Philadelphia Inquirer,* May 2, 2011, p. C4.

151   **"The only easy day was yesterday":** Quoted at http://www.navy.org/heart_of_a_navy_seal/.

151   **To keep a promise he made:** Maria Panaritis, "Modest Man Behind Popular Snack Brand," *Philadelphia Inquirer,* April 7, 2012, p. A1.

152   **record-breaking journey around the world:** The entry for Laura Dekker's blog is at http://www.lauradekker.nl/Basis.aspx?Hmi=5042&STARTPOS=90&Sid=5042&Tid=5019.

153   **"Curiosity killed the cat—but satisfaction brought him back":** See, e.g., http://www.phrases.org.uk/bulletin_board/5/messages/291.html.

153   **people are "pattern seeking" animals:** Michael Shermer, *The Believing Brain: From Ghosts and Gods to Politics and Conspiracies—How We Construct Beliefs and Reinforce Them as Truths* (New York: Henry Holt, 2011), p. 59. Shermer writes, "Our brains are belief engines, evolved pattern-recognition machines that connect the dots and create meaning out of the patterns that we think we see in nature."

153   **As a twenty-one-year-old:** Maria Cheng, "Defying Disease, Hawking Turning 70," *Philadelphia Inquirer,* January 6, 2012, p. A13. See also Stephen Hawking, *A Brief History of Time* (New York: Bantam, 1998). For "My goal is simple" quotation, see Martin Gardner, "The Ultimate Turtle," *New York Review of Books,* June 16, 1988, http://www.nybooks.com/articles/archives/1988/jun/16/the-ultimate-turtle/?pagination=false.

154   **One of the most famous intellectual circles of the early twentieth century:** See the book review of Michael Holroyd, *A Book of Secrets* (New York: Farrar, Straus & Giroux, 2011), in Toni Bentley, "Women in Love," *New York Times Book Review,* August 7, 2011, p. 1.

155   **program that sends bright but underachieving inner-city kids to college:** Tina Rosenberg, "Beyond SATs, Finding Success in Numbers," *New York Times,* February 15, 2012, http://opinionator.blogs.nytimes.com/2012/02/15/beyond-sats-finding-success-in-numbers/.

156   **"When you have bacon and eggs":** Jim Jackson and Ed Snider, *Walking Together Forever: The Broad Street Bullies, Then and Now* (Champaign, IL: Sports Publishing LLC, 2005), p. 31.

157   **all-day Get Motivated! Seminar:** For a lineup of all the speakers who addressed the crowd on June 17, 2009, at the Wachovia Center, Philadelphia, Pennsylvania, see the Get Motivated Seminar full-page advertisement found in *the Philadelphia Inquirer,* April 28, 2009, p. C8. For an interesting article about the Get Motivated Seminars business

model, see Denny Hatch, "The Greatest Lead Generation Scheme: With Colin Powell, How Can They Lose?," *Target Marketing* 5 no. 13 (July 7, 2009), http://www.targetmarketingmag.com/article/the-greatest-lead -generation-scheme-colin-powell-can-get-motivated-lose-409400/1#. Sadly, Zig Ziglar died on Novermber 28, 2012. See Alan Duke, "Motivational Guru Zig Ziglar Dies at 86, CNN, http://www.cnn.com/ 2012/11/28/showbiz/zig-ziglar-obit

159 **Sports teams often use shared musical rituals to get pumped:** Lacey Sorenson, Daniel R. Czech, Stephen Gonzalez, James Klein, and Tony Lachowetz, "Listen Up: The Experience of Music in Sport—A Phenomenological Investigation," *Athletic Insight: The Online Journal of Sport Psychology*, http://www.athleticinsight.com/Vol10Iss2/Music .htm#ABSTRACT.

160 **"Competition can be a very strong motivation":** Mary Kay Ash, *Miracles Happen: The Life and Timeless Principles of the Founder of Mary Kay Inc.* (New York: Quill, 2003), p. 11.

160 **I go into a very happy state of mind when I am vacuuming:** See interview with Joyce Carol Oates in the *New York Times Magazine* by Deborah Solomon, April 12. 2009, http://www.nytimes.com/2009/04/ 12/magazine/12wwln-q4-t.html.

161 **The humor writer:** Will Blythe, "The Man in the Flying Lawn Chair: The Raconteur," *New York Times Book Review,* January 2, 2005, http:// www.nytimes.com/2005/01/02/books/review/02BLYTHEL.html? pagewanted=1. See also George Plimpton and Sarah Plimpton, *The Man in the Flying Lawn Chair and Other Excursions and Observations* (New York: Random House, 2004).

161 **"I have been trying to prove that guy wrong my whole adult life":** Peggy Payne, "How Insults Spur Success," Preoccupations, *New York Times,* October 16, 2011, p. BU9.

161 **"Success is not the result of spontaneous combustion":** Reed, "In the Rocket's Red Glare."

163 **he motivated himself through awareness of his own death:** The text and video of Steve Jobs's 2005 Stanford graduation speech can be found at http://news.stanford.edu/news/2005/june15/jobs-061505.html.

163 **"set yourself on fire":** Reed, "In the Rocket's Red Glare."

Chapter 7
Learn to Fail: Self-Confidence

165 **"It is not always the people who start out the smartest who end up the smartest":** Quoted in Carol S. Dweck, *Mindset: The New Psychology of Success* (New York: Ballantine Books, 2006), p. 5.

165 **In 2011, when professional golfer:** For the story of Rory McIlroy, see Christine Brennan, "Thursdays Belong to Rory McIlroy; Now to Solve Sundays," *USA Today,* June 17, 2011, http://usatoday30.usatoday.com/ sports/columnist/brennan/2011-06-16-brennan-on-the-us-open_n .htm. See also Gene Wojciechowski, "Rory McIlroy Breaks Through with No. 1," ESPN, June 19, 2011, http://sports.espn.go.com/espn/columns/ story?columnist=wojciechowski_gene&page=wojciechowski-110619& sportCat=golf.

165 **Contast McIlroy's attitude:** For more details on self-handicapping, see, e.g., Sean M. McCrea, "Self-Handicapping, Excuse Making, and Counterfactual Thinking: Consequences for Self-Esteem and Future Motivation," *Journal of Personality and Social Psychology* 95 no. 2 (2008): 274–92.

168 **"There is but one cause of human failure":** Rebecca J. Schlegel, Joshua A. Hicks, Jamie Arndt, and Laura A. King, "Thine Own Self: True Self-Concept Accessibility and Meaning in Life," *Journal of Personality and Social Psychology* 96 no. 2 (2009): 473–90.

168 **Temple of Apollo:** See, e.g., Eloise Hart, "The Delphic Oracle," http:// www.theosociety.org/pasadena/sunrise/35-85-6/me-elo.htm.

169 **"Do it, then learn how":** For the story of Bill Richmond, see Jane E. Brody, "Taking Flight, No Matter the Headwinds," *New York Times,* July 3, 2012, p. D7.

170 **discovering (or rediscovering) the true self is crucial to psychological health:** Schlegel et al., "Thine Own Self."

170 **"resourceful attainment of one's set aim in the cognizance of a clear conscience":** George Gurdjieff, *Meetings with Remarkable Men* (New York: E. P. Dutton, 1963), p. 302.

170 **Russell Wasendorf Sr.:** Jacob Bunge, Scott Patterson, and Julie Steinberg, "Peregrine CEO's Dramatic Confession," *Wall Street Journal,* July 14, 2012, p. A1.

172 **telling someone she is smart does not make it so:** See Carol S. Dweck, "Beliefs That Make Smart People Dumb," in *Why Smart People Can Be So Stupid,* ed. R. J. Sternberg (New Haven, CT: Yale University Press, 2002), pp. 24–41. See also Carol S. Dweck, *Self-Theories: Their Role in Motivation, Personality, and Development* (New York: Psychology Press, 2000).

172 **The power of suggestion is well documented by scientists in several disciplines:** The well-known medical phenomenon called the "placebo effect" is perhaps the best-known example of the power of suggestion in action. See, e.g., Anne Harrington, *The Placebo Effect* (Cambridge, MA: Harvard University Press, 1997), and Fabrizio Benedetti, *Placebo Effects* (Oxford: Oxford University Press, 2009).

172 **"He cures most in whom most are confident":** Tova Navarra, *The Encyclopedia of Complementary and Alternative Medicine* (New York: Infobase Publishing, 2004), p. 49.

172 **"Your expectations can have profound impacts on your brain and on your health":** Associated Press, "Brainpower the Best Medicine?," *CBS News,* February 11, 2009, http://www.cbsnews.com/8301-204_162 -1081624.html.

172 **Roughly 30 percent of the effectiveness of most medicines and medical procedures:** Harrington, *Placebo Effect,* pp. 44–45.

173 **the brain actually changes in response to these suggestions:** Benedetti, *Placebo Effects,* pp. 104–6. See also Associated Press, "Research Links Placebo Effects to Changes in the Human Brain," *Wall Street Journal,* November 29, 2005, p. D4 (discussing University of Michigan research showing that placebo administration led to release of endorphins).

173 **the "nocebo effect":** Robert A. Hahn, "The Nocebo Phenomenon: Scope and Foundations," in Harrington, *Placebo Effect,* pp. 56–76.

173 **inventor of a new punch-card system for the national census:** Ibid., pp. 41–42.

173 **"Pygmalion in the classroom" study:** Robert Rosenthal and Lenore Jacobson, *Pygmalion in the Classroom: Teacher Expectation and Pupils' Intellectual Development* (New York: Holt, Rinehart & Winston, 1968). One of the most famous examples of the Pygmalion effect in a classroom setting is the story of a math teacher, Jaime Escalante, which was made into the movie *Stand and Deliver*; see Ann Byers, *Jaime Escalante: Sensational Teacher* (Berkeley Heights, NJ: Enslow, 1996).

174 **"self-fulfilling prophecy":** See, e.g., Russell A. Jones, *Self-Fulfilling Prophecies: Social, Psychological, and Physiological Effects of Expectancies* (Hillsdale, NJ: Lawrence Erlbaum, 1977).

175 **If he was good enough for the Marine Corps:** Brody, "Taking Flight," p. D7.

175 **suffering-induced transformational experiences (SITEs):** See, e.g., Steve Taylor, "Transformation Through Suffering: A Study of Individuals Who Have Experienced Positive Psychological Transformation Following Periods of Intense Turmoil," *Journal of Humanistic Psychology* 52 no. 1 (2012): 30–52; Mark D. Seery, E. Alison Holman, and Roxane Cohen Silver, "Whatever Does Not Kill Us: Cumulative Lifetime Adversity, Vulnerability, and Resilience," *Journal of Personality and Social Psychology* 99 no. 6 (2010): 1025–41; Jonathan Renshon, "Stability and Change in Belief Systems: The Operational Code of George W. Bush," *Journal of Conflict Resolution* 52 no. 6 (2008): 820–49.

177 **pilgrimage to a famous chapel in Chimayo:** For more information about the chapel, see, e.g., http://www.archdiocesesantafe.org/AboutASF/Chimayo.html.

177 **"Believe in yourself! Have faith in your abilities!":** The story of the businessman is told on pp. 1–3 in Norman Vincent Peale, *The Power of Positive Thinking* (New York: Prentice-Hall, 1952).

178 **"The greatest secret for eliminating the inferiority complex is to fill your mind":** Ibid., p. 6.

178 **mind power schools:** Napoleon Hill, *Think and Grow Rich* (New York: Fawcett Books, 1937), p. 15.

178 **every human society in recorded history has had a religion:** Nicholas Wade, *The Faith Instinct: How Religion Evolved and Why It Endures* (New York: Penguin Press, 2009), p. 1.

178 **"There are more things in heaven and earth, Horatio":** William Shakespeare, *Hamlet* (Cambridge: Cambridge University Press, 1999), p. 43.

179 **The topic of self-confidence:** Albert Bandura, "Self-Efficacy: Toward a Unifying Theory of Behavioral Change," *Psychological Review* 84 no. 2 (1977): 191–215; T. A. Judge, A. Erez, J. E. Bono, and C. J. Thoresen, "The Core Self-Evaluations Scale (CSES): Development of a Measure," *Personnel Psychology* 56 no. 3 (2003): 303–31; Timothy A. Judge and Charlice Hurst, "How the Rich (and Happy) Get Richer (and Happier): Relationship of Core Self-Evaluations to Trajectories in Attaining Work Success," *Journal of Applied Psychology* 93 no. 4 (2008): 849–63.

179 **"fixed" versus "growth" mindsets:** Dweck, *Mindset*, pp. 3–14; Dweck, *Self-Theories*, pp. 1–4.

180   **children praised for their effort at solving IQ test puzzles were much more eager:** Dweck, *Self-Theories*, pp. 95–106.

180   **growth-oriented people actively take on challenges:** The subject of the growth-oriented mindset can be explored thoroughly in Dweck, *Mindset*, p. 7.

181   **the value of praising effort rather than innate talent:** Dweck, *Self-Theories*, pp. 107–26.

181   **world-class performers require ten thousand hours of deliberate practice:** K. Anders Ericsson and Paul Ward, "Capturing the Naturally Occurring Superior Performance of Experts in the Laboratory," *Psychological Science* 16 no. 6 (2007): 346–50; see also K. Anders Ericcson, ed., *The Road to Excellence: Acquisition of Expert Performance in Arts and Sciences, Sports and Games* (New York: Psychology Press, 1996). The ten-thousand-hour rule refers to the research of K. Anders Ericsson: K. Anders Ericsson, Ralf Th. Krampe, and Clemes Tesch-Römer, "The Role of Deliberate Practice in Acquisition of Expert Performance," *Psychological Review* 100 no. 3 (1993): 363–406; see also Geoff Colvin, "How Deliberate Practice Works," in *Talent Is Overrated: What Really Separates World-Class Performers from Everybody Else* (New York: Penguin, 2008), pp. 84–104. See generally Malcolm Gladwell, *Outliers: The Story of Success* (New York: Little, Brown, 2008).

182   **learning, taking risks, and improving their effort will naturally be more resilient:** See, e.g., S. R. Maddi, R. H. Harvey, D. M. Khoshaba, M. Fazel, and N. Ressurrecion, "The Personality Construct of Hardiness, IV," *Journal of Humanistic Psychology* 49 no. 3 (2009): 292–305; P. Frazier, N. Keenan, S. Anders, S. Perera, S. Shallcross, and S. Hintz, "Perceived Past, Present, and Future Control and Adjustment to Stressful Life Events," *Journal of Personality and Social Psychology* 100 no. 4 (2011): 749–65.

183   **"When I decide to write anything, I get caught up in my insecurity":** Maya Angelou, *Letter to My Daughter* (New York: Random House, 2008), p. 66.

184   **"The problem is . . . how to remain whole in the midst of the distractions of life":** Anne Morrow Lindbergh, *Gift from the Sea* (New York: Random House, 1995), p. 29.

184   **"This is my Bible: I am what it says I am":** Samuel Keith Curran, *I-Witness Devotions* (Maitland, FL: Xulon Press, 2007), p. 114.

185   **he called these his "errata":** Benjamin Franklin, *The Autobiography and Other Writings*, ed. Peter Shaw (New York: Bantam, 1982), p. 31.

185   **visualizing a body movement activates exactly the same areas:** Aymeric Guillot, Christian Collet, Vo An Nguyen, Francine Malouin, Carol Richards, and Julien Doyon, "Brain Activity During Visual Versus Kinesthetic Imagery: An fMRI Study," *Human Brain Mapping* 30 no. 7 (2009): 2157–72; Tamara van Gog, Fred Paas, Nadine Marcue, Paul Ayres, and John Sweller, "The Mirror Neuron System and Observational Learning: Implications for the Effectiveness of Dynamic Visualizations," *Educational Psychology Review* 21 no. 1 (2009): 21–30.

186   **"Before the trials":** Quoted at https://sportpsychquotes.wordpress .com/tag/michael-phelps/.

186 **the auctioneer at Sotheby's auction house:** Ellen Gamerman, "An Auctioneer's Big Night," *Wall Street Journal,* May 4, 2012, p. D6.

187 **athletes ready to compete in the Olympic games:** Daniel Chambliss, "The Mundanity of Excellence: An Ethnographic Report on Stratification and Olympic Swimmers," *Sociological Theory* 7 no. 1 (1989): 7–8.

187 **focus on a series of "small wins" in training:** Karl E. Weick, "Small Wins: Redefining the Scale of Social Problems," *American Psychologist* 39 no.1 (1984), p. 40.

187 *"Clear Eyes! Full Hearts! Can't Lose!":* See, e.g., http://www.youtube .com/watch?v=q5Z5BzNAh6Y.

187 **baseball pitcher Cole Hamels wears a neckband and wristband:** Cole Hamels, "EFX Team Athlete Cole Hamels Talks About His Experience with EFX," *Philadelphia Sports Review,* February 10, 2012, http://phillysports.info/philadelphia-sports-report/efx -team-athlete-cole-hamels-talks-about-his-experience-with-efx/. See also http://www.efxusa.com/SFNT.html.

Chapter 8
Focus Your Mind: Passion, Imagination, Intuition, and Reason

190 **"[H]ere is the prime":** Andrew Carnegie, *The Empire of Business* (Garden City, NY: Doubleday, Page, & Co., 1902), pp. 17–18.

190 **"an evening for beginners":** The full story of Charles Lindbergh's historic flight and his description of the process leading up to it can be found in his Pulitzer Prize–winning book, *The Spirit of St. Louis* (New York: Scribner Classics, 1953). For "an evening for beginners," see p. 11; for "nonstop between New York and Paris" and "flying the night mail in winter," see p. 14.

191 **"translate [the idea]":** Ibid., p. 15.

191 **asked how important "well-defined personal goals" were to their success:** George Gallup Jr. and Alec M. Gallup, *The Great American Success Story: Factors That Affect Achievement* (Homewood, IL: Dow Jones– Irwin, 1986), pp. 63–65, 215–16.

192 **"Each unfulfilled goal remains active":** Roy F. Baumeister and John Tierney, *Willpower: Rediscovering the Greatest Human Strength* (New York: Penguin Press, 2011), pp. 80–84 (discussing both David Allen's work and the mechanisms for the Zeigarnik effect). For a general source on how to gain clarity by getting your "to do" list under control, see David Allen, *Getting Things Done: The Art of Stress-Free Productivity* (New York: Penguin, 2001). See also E. J. Masicampo and Roy F. Baumeister, "Unfulfilled Goals Interfere with Tasks That Require Executive Functions," *Journal of Experimental Social Psychology* 47 no. 2 (2011): 300–11; Tali Kleiman and Ran R. Hassin, "Non-Conscious Goal Conflicts," *Journal of Experimental Social Psychology* 47 no. 3 (2011): 521–32.

193 **Plato conceptualized the mind as a charioteer driving a team of horses:** This analogy can be found in the Phaedrus dialogue in Plato, *Phaedrus* (Cambridge: Cambridge University Press, 2011).

193   **mind is like a small human rider:** Jonathan Haidt, *The Happiness Hypothesis: Finding Modern Truth in Ancient Wisdom* (New York: Basic Books, 2006), pp. 4–5.

193   **"[T]he Rider holds the reins":** Chip Heath and Dan Heath, *Switch: How to Change Things When Change Is Hard* (New York: Broadway Books, 2010), pp. 7–8.

194   **the power of "thinking without thinking":** See Malcolm Gladwell, *Blink: The Power of Thinking Without Thinking* (New York: Little, Brown, 2005).

194   **feeling of "having an intuition":** Daniel Kahneman, *Thinking, Fast and Slow* (New York: Farrar, Straus & Giroux, 2011), p. 237. See also David G. Meyers, *Intuition: Its Powers and Perils* (New Haven, CT: Yale University Press, 2002), p. 56.

195   **"cognitive" or "decision" biases:** For examples of these biases, see Max H. Bazerman and Don A. Moore, *Judgment in Managerial Decision Making* 7th ed. (Hoboken, NJ: John W. Wiley & Sons, 2013).

196   **too much information about too many everyday choices:** Barry Schwartz, *The Paradox of Choice: Why More Is Less* (New York: HarperCollins, 2005). See also Barry Schwartz, Andrew Ward, Sonja Lyubomirsky, John Monterosso, Katherine White, and Darrin R. Lehman, "Maximizing Versus Satisficing: Happiness Is a Matter of Choice," *Journal of Personality and Social Psychology* 83 no. 5 (2002): 1178–97.

196   **visited fifty-five schools in three countries:** "Extreme Campus Touring," Education Life, *New York Times,* July 22, 2012, p. 4.

196   **called the "recency effect":** See, e.g., Robert A. Bjork and William B. Whitten, "Recency-Sensitive Retrieval Processes in Long-Term Free Recall," *Cognitive Psychology* 6 no. 2 (1974): 173–89.

196   **"The alternative to maximizing is to be a satisficer":** Schwartz, *Paradox of Choice,* p. 78.

196   **"dive deep into the data, then trust your gut":** Richard Tedlow, *Andy Grove: The Life of an American* (New York: Portfolio, 2006), p. 123.

197   **how Intuition can lead you into error in some very predictable circumstances:** Jason Zweig, "Why We're Driven to Trade," *Wall Street Journal,* July 21, 2012, p. C1.

197   **individual investors often make the same intuition-based mistake:** Ibid.

198   **"A problem well stated is a problem half solved":** Douglas W. Hubbard, *How to Measure Anything: Finding the Value of Intangibles in Business* (Hoboken, NJ: John Wiley & Sons, 2010), p. 26.

199   **"If you define what you're trying to achieve clearly enough":** James R. Hagerty, "Gadget Gurus for Modern Moms and Dads," *Wall Street Journal,* November 12, 2011, http://online.wsj.com/article/SB100014240 52970204190704577026021148982082.html.

199   **"Even a soul submerged in sleep is hard at work":** Brooks Haxton, *Fragments: The Collected Wisdom of Heraclitus* (New York: Penguin, 2003), p. 57.

199   **his unconscious mind helped him think up the idea behind the Google search engine:** The transcript of Larry Page's University of Michigan commencement address from May 2, 2009, can be found at

http://googlepress.blogspot.com/2009/05/larry-pages-university-of
-michigan.html.

200 **In her book on dreaming and creativity:** Deirdre Barrett, *The Committee of Sleep* (n.p.: Oneiroi Press, 2001), pp. 66–67. Other examples are found on p. 116 (Dmitri Mendeleev) and pp. 84–87 (Friedrich August Kekulé).

200 **sleep is a reliable source of what psychologists call "offline" consolidation and learning:** Michael K. Scullin and Mark A. McDaniel, "Remember to Execute a Goal: Sleep on It!," *Psychological Science* 21 no. 7 (2010): 1028–35.

200 **"sleep after training" improves both "speed and accuracy of per-formance":** Stefan Fischer, Manfred Hallschmid, Anna Lisa Elsner, and Jan Born, "Sleep Forms Memory for Finger Skills," *Proceedings of the National Academy of Sciences* 99 no. 18 (2002): 11987–91.

201 **"I love New York":** For the Milton Glaser "Eureka" moment story, see e.g., Alastair Sooke's "Milton Glaser: His Heart Was in the Right Place," *Telegraph*, February 7, 2011, http://www.telegraph.co.uk/culture/art/art -features/8303867/Milton-Glaser-his-heart-was-in-the-right-place .html; "Chip Kidd Talks with Milton Glaser," Interview, *Believer Magazine* (September 2002), http://www.believermag.com/issues/200309/?read =interview_glaser.

202 **"[I]f I can get the Bellanca":** Lindbergh, *Spirit of St. Louis,* p. 18.

202 **a set of criteria used by many businesses called "SMART":** For more on the SMART objectives, see, e.g., G. T. Doran, "There's a SMART Way to Write Management's Goals and Objectives," *Management Review* 70 no. 11 (1981): 35–36.

202 **the more committed you are to your goal, the more likely it is you will accomplish it:** See, e.g., G. Richard Shell, *Bargaining for Advantage: Negotiation Strategies for Reasonable People* 2nd ed. (New York: Penguin, 2006), pp. 36–39; Ute C. Bayer, Peter M. Gollwitzer, and Anja Achtziger, "Staying on Track: Planned Goal Striving Is Protected from Disruptive Internal States," *Journal of Experimental Social Psychology* 46 no. 3 (2010): 505–14.

202 **achievement-related assessment called the GRIT scale:** Angela L. Duckworth, Christopher Peterson, and Michael D. Matthews, "Grit: Perseverance and Passion for Long-Term Goals," *Journal of Personality and Social Psychology* 92 no. 6 (2007): 1087–101. See also http://www.sas .upenn.edu/~duckworth/images/17-item%20Grit%20and%20Ambition .040709.pdf.

203 **"landing a man on the moon and returning him safely to the earth":** A transcript of John F. Kennedy's "Man on the Moon" address can be found at http://www.homeofheroes.com/presidents/speeches/kennedy _space.html.

204 **"Many things which cannot be overcome when they stand together":** See, e.g., John Blaydes, *The Educator's Book of Quotes* (Thousand Oaks, CA: Corwin Press, 2003), p. 185. For more information about Quintus Sertorius, see, e.g., *Encyclopedia Britannica Online Academic Edition* (Chicago: Encyclopedia Britannica, 2013), "Quintus Sertorius," http://www.britannica.com/EBchecked/topic/535908/Quintus-Sertorius.

204 **"St. Louis—New York—Paris":** Lindbergh, *Spirit of St. Louis,* p. 23.

204 **"aside from a plane":** Ibid., p. 169.

204 **selected college students who were struggling with their grades:** Dominique Morisano, Jacob B. Hirsch, and Jordan B. Peterson, "Setting, Elaborating, and Reflecting on Personal Goals Improves Academic Performance," *Journal of Applied Psychology* 95 no. 2 (2010): 255–64.

206 **"build my own experience into the plane's structure":** Lindbergh, *Spirit of St. Louis*, p. 86.

207 **"The limits of logic are passed"; "make the jump as you stand looking":** Ibid., pp. 184–85.

208 **"to form an extension":** Ibid., p. 189.

208 **"You engage, and then you wait and see":** Owen Connelly, *Blundering to Glory: Napoleon's Military Campaigns* (Lanham, MD: Rowman & Littlefield, 2006), p. ix.

211 **"all the achievements of mankind have value only to the extent that they preserve and improve the quality of life":** Susan M. Gray, *Charles A. Lindbergh and the American Dilemma: The Conflict of Technology and Human Values* (Madison, WI: Popular Press, 1988), p. 90. See also the Charles A. and Anne Morrow Lindbergh Foundation website at http://www.lindberghfoundation.org/docs/index.php/about-us/lindbergh-history/charles-lindbergh.

211 **life is what is happening around you while you're "busy making other plans":** For the lyrics of John Lennon's song "Beautiful Boy (Darling Boy)," see, e.g., http://www.lyrics007.com/John%20Lennon%20Lyrics/Beautiful%20Boy%20(Darling%20Boy)%20Lyrics.html.

212 **prepare a sermon about the parable of the Good Samaritan:** John M. Darley and Daniel Batson, "From Jerusalem to Jericho: A Study of Situational and Dispositional Variables in Helping Behavior," *Journal of Personality and Social Psychology* 27 no. 1 (1973): 100–8.

Chapter 9
Influence Others: Credibility and Dialogue

214 **"Always do right":** Mark Twain, "Note to Young People's Society in Brooklyn," February 16, 1901, in Alex Ayres, *The Wit and Wisdom of Mark Twain* (New York: HarperCollins, 2010), p. 154.

214 **William Francis "Willy" Gibbs:** For the stories and examples taken from the life of William Francis Gibbs, see Steven Ujifusa, *A Man and His Ship: America's Greatest Naval Architect and His Quest to Build the S.S. United States* (New York: Simon & Schuster, 2012).

215 ***Time* magazine featured Willy Gibbs on the cover of its September 28, 1942, issue:** Ibid., pp. 176–77. For a picture of this issue of *Time* magazine, see http://www.time.com/time/covers/0,16641,19420928,00.html.

215 **"[F]rom that day forward":** Ujifusa, *A Man and His Ship*, p. 6.

216 **"That's the way to really learn things—by *yourself*":** Ibid., p. 21.

216 **"This business of being popular and having everybody like you is for the birds":** Richard Austin Smith, "The Love Affair of William Francis Gibbs," *Fortune*, August 1957, p. 154. See also http://features.blogs.fortune.cnn.com/2012/04/15/william-francis-gibbs/.

216 **"I thought him rather strange, but I was fascinated":** Ujifusa, *A Man and His Ship,* p. 101.

217 **"Given that humans are social animals, interpersonal intelligence is perhaps the most":** Paul Steinberg, "Asperger's History of Overdiagnosis," *New York Times,* January 31, 2012, http://www.nytimes.com/2012/02/01/opinion/aspergers-history-of-over-diagnosis.html.

218 **three distinct categories: friends of pleasure, utility, and virtue:** Aristotle, *Nicomachean Ethics,* trans. Terence Irwin (Indianapolis: Hackett, 1999), chap. 3, "The Three Types of Friendship."

218 **it depends more on your authenticity as a person:** The subject of authenticity is an important one in modern ethics and philosophy. Authenticity has been defined as being honest with or true to oneself. This compares with the idea of "sincerity," which is a congruence between what you say and how you actually feel. See, e.g., Charles Taylor, *The Ethics of Authenticity* (Cambridge, MA: Harvard University Press, 1991), and Lionel Trilling, *Sincerity and Authenticity* (Cambridge, MA: Harvard University Press, 1972). Psychologists have also studied authenticity and sincerity. See, e.g., Omro Gillath, Amanda K. Sesko, Phillip R. Shaver, and David S. Chun, "Attachment, Authenticity, and Honesty: Dispositional and Experimentally Induced Security Can Reduce Self- and Other-Deception," *Journal of Personality and Social Psychology* 98 no. 5 (2010): 841–55.

218 **"He was very economical":** Ujifusa, *A Man and His Ship,* p. 338.

219 **that when people talk about themselves:** Robert Lee Hotz, "Science Reveals Why We Brag So Much," *Wall Street Journal,* May, 7, 2012, p. D1.

220 **"His wonderful dour expression":** Ujifusa, *A Man and His Ship,* p. 338.

220 **Smiles are important because they suggest that people are about to engage in a cooperative interaction:** Marianne LaFrance, *Lip Service: Smiles in Life, Death, Trust, Lies, Work, Memory, Sex, and Politics* (New York: W. W. Norton, 2011). See also, Carol Tavris, "And the Whole World . . . ," *Wall Street Journal,* August 6, 2011, p. C7 (review and summary of *Lip Service*).

220 **what psychologists call "emotional labor":** See, e.g., D. J. Beal, J. P. Trougakos, H. M. Weiss, and S. G. Green, "Episodic Processes in Emotional Labor: Perceptions of Affective Delivery and Regulation Strategies," *Journal of Applied Psychology* 91 no. 5 (2006): 1053–65; M. Groth, T. Hennig-Thurau, and G. Walsh, "Customer Reactions to Emotional Labor: The Roles of Employee Acting Strategies and Customer Detection Accuracy," *Academy of Management Journal* 52 no. 5 (2009): 958–74.

220 **"There is a lot of acting":** Katia Bachko, "Talk of the Town: 'Deus Ex Machina Dept.—Explainer,' " *New Yorker,* May 21, 2012, p. 21.

221 **"surface acting" and something they call "deep acting":** Nai-Wen Chi, Alicia A. Grandey, and Jennifer A. Diamong, "Want a Tip? Service Performance as a Function of Emotion Regulation and Extraversion," *Journal of Applied Psychology* 96 no. 6 (2011): 1337–46.

221 **first scientist to study the differences between smiles:** Martin E. P. Seligman, *Authentic Happiness: Using the New Positive Psychology to Realize Your Potential for Lasting Fulfillment* (New York: Free Press, 2002), p. 5.

221 **they have to work harder to smile:** Chi et al., "Want a Tip?" See also
R. E. Lucas and F. Fujita, "Factors Influencing the Relation Between
Extraversion and Pleasant Affect," *Journal of Personality and Social Psychology*
79 no. 6 (2000): 1039–56; A. A. Grandey, G. M. Fisk, A. S. Mattila, K. J.
Jansen, and L. A. Sideman, "Is 'Service with a Smile' Enough? Authenticity
of Positive Display During Service Encounters," *Organizational Behavior and
Human Decision Processes* 96 no. 5 (2005): 38–55.

222 **"It is like producing a Broadway show":** Personal conversation between
the author and Craig Reid, then the Four Seasons' senior vice president
for hotel operations in the Americas. The conversation took place in
July 2009 at the Wharton School.

222 **any common experience can trigger an automatic empathetic
response:** This study is discussed in David DeSteno, "Compassion Made
Easy," *New York Times*, July 15, 2012, p. SR12.

223 **what psychologists call "similarity"—with its hoped-for "liking"
effects:** For "similarity" and "liking" effects, see Robert B. Cialdini,
Influence: The Psychology of Persuasion rev. ed. (New York: Quill, 1993),
pp. 167–207; Gregory M. Walton, Geoffrey L. Cohen, David Cwir, and
Steven J. Spencer, "Mere Belonging: The Power of Social Connections,"
Journal of Personality and Social Psychology 102 no. 3 (2012): 513–32.

223 **strategies to ensure that a social event will not drain you too quickly:**
Marti Olsen Laney, *The Introvert Advantage: How to Thrive in an Extrovert
World* (New York: Workman, 2002), pp. 159–86.

224 **"to be perfect for ten minutes":** Abigail Sullivan Moore, "Pledge Prep:
How to Be Perfect, for at Least Ten Minutes," Education Life, *New York
Times*, July 22, 2012, pp. 28–29.

225 **"The best way to sell yourself is not to appear to sell yourself":**
Stephanie Rosenbloom, "Authentic? Get Real," *New York Times*,
September 11, 2011, p. ST1.

225 **too much "interpersonal spin":** S. Côté, D. S. Moskowitz, and D. C.
Zuroff, "Social Relationships and Intraindividual Variability in
Interpersonal Behavior: Correlates of Interpersonal Spin," *Journal of
Personality and Social Psychology* 102 no. 3 (2012): 646–59.

225 **"We [can become] so accustomed":** Joseph Epstein, "Puncturing Our
Pretensions," *Wall Street Journal*, September 24, 2011, http://online.wsj
.com/article/SB10001424053111904060604576574670901055418.html.

227 **"I have always been proud of you, but never more than in this hour
when we face together this solemn responsibility":** Ujifusa, *A Man
and His Ship*, p. 173.

227 **"rendered to the country outstanding service":** Ibid.

227 **"has been an essential factor in the overall war effort of the country":**
Ibid., p. 188.

228 **Gibbs won the financial backing of a much more influential man,
banker J. P. "Jack" Morgan Jr.:** For the story of how Gibbs obtained his
funding from Morgan, see ibid., pp. 55–62.

230 **persuasion is best thought of as dialogue:** Kerry Patterson, Joseph
Grenny, Ron McMillan, and Al Switzler, *Crucial Conversations: Tools for
Talking When Stakes Are High* (New York: McGraw-Hill, 2002), p. 20.

230 **why others have such trouble seeing the world from our point of view:** Emily Pronin, "How We See Ourselves and How We See Others," *Science* 320 no. 5880 (2008): 1177–80.

231 **creating a "pool of shared meaning":** The authors of *Crucial Conversations* introduced the concept of "pool of shared meaning" on pp. 21–25 and summarized their technique for engaging in "dialogue" (three-step process) on pp. 179–92.

231 **story about a single mother and struggling drug addict named Ashley Smith:** Ashley Smith tells her story, with Stacy Mattingly, in her book *Unlikely Angel: The Untold Story of the Atlanta Hostage Hero* (Grand Rapids, MI: Zondervan, 2005).

231 **"Your little girl—where is she?":** Ibid., p. 18.

232 **"No way. That stuff ruined my life" She later recounted:** Ibid., p. 83.

232 **"God deserves your best. He shaped you for a purpose":** Ibid., p. 149.

232 **"What do you think your purpose is?":** Ibid., p. 150.

232 **"After I started to read":** Smith gave this quotation to reporters soon after her encounter with Brian Nichols. See Edward Wyatt, "Spiritual Book Helped Hostage Mollify Captor," *New York Times,* March 15, 2005, http://www.nytimes.com/2005/03/15/national/15book.html.

232 **"You are not dead. You are standing right in front of me":** Smith, *Unlikely Angel,* p. 181.

233 **"God brought him to my door":** See "Faith Helped Hostage," http://www.foxnews.com/story/0,2933,150323,00.html.

233 **"defining moments in our lives and careers that make all the difference":** Stephen R. Covey, foreword in Patterson et al., *Crucial Conversations,* p. xi.

234 **"Friends are as companions on a journey":** Quoted in Richard C. Lamb Jr., *The Pursuit of God in the Company of Friends* (Downers Grove, IL: InterVarsity Press, 2003), p. 96.

235 **his two sons, Frank and Christopher:** Ujifusa, *A Man and His Ship,* pp. 242–44.

Conclusion
The Right Answers

238 **"The only true measure of success":** Quoted in John C. Maxwell, *Success 101: What Every Leader Needs to Know* (Nashville: Thomas Nelson, 2008), p. 8.

Topical Bibliography

Achievement: Family

Caplan, Bryan. *Selfish Reasons to Have More Kids: Why Being a Great Parent Is Less Work and More Fun Than You Think.* New York: Basic Books, 2011.

Chua, Amy. *Battle Hymn of the Tiger Mother.* New York: Penguin Press, 2011.

Freeman, Joan. *Gifted Lives: What Happens When Children Grow Up?* New York: Routledge, 2010.

Holroyd, Michael. *A Book of Secrets.* New York: Farrar, Straus & Giroux, 2011.

Howe, Michael J. A., ed. *Encouraging the Development of Exceptional Skills and Talents.* Leicester, UK: British Psychological Society, 1990.

———. *The Origins of Exceptional Abilities.* Oxford: Basil Blackwell, 1990.

Lareau, Annette. *Unequal Childhoods: Class, Race, and Family Life.* Berkeley: University of California Press, 2003.

Segal, Nancy L. *Born Together—Reared Apart: The Landmark Minnesota Twin Study.* Cambridge, MA: Harvard University Press, 2012.

———. *Someone Else's Twin.* Amherst, NY: Prometheus Books, 2011.

Shachtman, Tom. *Rumspringa: To Be or Not to Be Amish.* New York: Farrar, Straus & Giroux, 2006.

Tough, Paul. *How Children Succeed.* Boston: Houghton Mifflin Harcourt, 2012.

Achievement: Psychology

Allen, David. *Getting Things Done: The Art of Stress-Free Productivity.* New York: Penguin, 2001.

Gallup, George, Jr., and Alec M. Gallup. *The Great American Success Story: Factors That Affect Achievement.* Homewood, IL: Dow Jones–Irwin, 1986.

Howe, Michael J. A. *The Psychology of High Abilities.* New York: New York University Press, 1999.

LaBier, Douglas. *Modern Madness: The Emotional Fallout of Success.* Reading, MA: Addison-Wesley, 1986.

Autobiographies/Biographies

Agassi, Andre. *Open: An Autobiography.* New York: Vintage Books, 2010.

Ash, Mary Kay. *Miracles Happen: The Life and Timeless Principles of the Founder of Mary Kay Inc.* New York: Quill, 2003.

Byers, Ann. *Jaime Escalante: Sensational Teacher.* Berkeley Heights, NJ: Enslow, 1996.

Carnegie, Andrew. *The Andrew Carnegie Reader.* Joseph Frazier Wall, ed. Pittsburgh: University of Pittsburgh Press, 1992.

Connelly, Owen. *Blundering to Glory: Napoleon's Military Campaigns.* Lanham, MD: Rowman & Littlefield, 2006.

Franklin, Benjamin. *Autobiography.* New York: Macmillan, 1962.

———. *The Autobiography and Other Writings.* Peter Shaw, ed. New York: Bantam, 1982.

Gray, Susan M. *Charles A. Lindbergh and the American Dilemma: The Conflict of Technology and Human Values.* Madison, WI: Popular Press, 1988.

Harding, Walter. *The Days of Henry Thoreau.* New York: Alfred A. Knopf, 1970.

Isaacson, Walter. *Steve Jobs.* New York: Simon & Schuster, 2011.

Lindbergh, Charles. *The Spirit of St. Louis.* New York: Scribner Classics, 1953.

Maraniss, David. *Barack Obama: The Story.* New York: Simon & Schuster, 2012.

Michaelis, David. *Schulz and Peanuts: A Biography.* New York: HarperCollins, 2007.

Mill, John Stuart. *The Autobiography of John Stuart Mill.* Minneapolis: Filiquarian Publishing, 2007.

Obama, Barack. *Dreams from My Father.* New York: Three Rivers Press, 2004.

Plimpton, George, and Sarah Plimpton. *The Man in the Flying Lawn Chair and Other Excursions and Observations.* New York: Random House, 2004.

Rubio, Marco. *An American Son.* New York: Penguin, 2012.

Singh, Simon. *Fermat's Enigma: The Epic Quest to Solve the World's Greatest Mathematical Problem.* New York: Walker and Company, 1997.

Smith, Ashley, with Stacy Mattingly. *Unlikely Angel: The Untold Story of the Atlanta Hostage Hero.* Grand Rapids, MI: Zondervan, 2005.

Spears, Lynne. *Through the Storm: The Real Story of Fame and Family in a Tabloid World.* Nashville: Thomas Nelson, 2008.

Tedlow, Richard. *Andy Grove: The Life of an American.* New York: Portfolio, 2006.

Terkel, Studs. *Working.* New York: Pantheon, 1972.

Ujifusa, Steven. *A Man and His Ship: America's Greatest Naval Architect and His Quest to Build the S.S. United States.* New York: Simon & Schuster, 2012.

Whitaker, Mark. *My Long Trip Home: A Family Memoir.* New York: Simon & Schuster, 2011.

Careers/Meaningful Work

Albion, Mark. *Making a Life, Making a Living.* New York: Warner Business Books, 2000.

Bellah, Robert N., Richard Madsen, William M. Sullivan, Ann Swidler, and Steven M. Tipton. *Habits of the Heart.* Berkeley: University of California Press, 1985.

Bronson, Po. *What Should I Do with My Life?* New York: Random House, 2002.

Collins, Jim. *Good to Great: Why Some Companies Make the Leap . . . and Others Don't.* New York: HarperBusiness, 2001.

Freeman, Marc. *Encore: Finding Work That Matters in the Second Half of Life.* New York: PublicAffairs, 2007.

Lore, Nicholas. *The Pathfinder: How to Choose or Change Your Career for a Lifetime of Satisfaction and Success.* New York: Fireside, 1998.

Lore, Nicholas (with Anthony Spadafore). *Now What? The Young Person's Guide to Choosing the Perfect Career.* New York: Fireside, 2008.

Post, Stephen G. *The Hidden Gifts of Helping: How the Power of Giving, Compassion, and Hope Can Get Us Through Hard Times.* San Francisco: Jossey-Bass, 2011.

Quinn, Ryan, and Robert E. Quinn. *Lift: Becoming a Positive Force in Any Situation.* San Francisco: Berrett-Koehler, 2009.

Salaman, Graeme. *Community and Occupation: An Exploration of Work/Leisure Relationships.* London: Cambridge University Press, 1974.

Snodgrass, Mary Ellen. *Late Achievers: Famous People Who Succeeded Late in Life.* Westport, CT: Libraries Unlimited, 1992.

Tieger, Paul D., and Barbara Barron. *Do What You Are: Discover the Perfect Career for You Through the Secrets of Personality Type.* New York: Little, Brown, 1992.

Evolution/Science

Dawkins, Richard. *The Extended Phenotype.* London: Oxford University Press, 1999.

Hawking, Stephen. *A Brief History of Time.* New York: Bantam, 1998.

Wilson, David Sloan. *Evolution for Everyone: How Darwin's Theory Can Change the Way We Think About Our Lives.* New York: Delacorte Press, 2007.

Happiness

Anchor, Shawn. *The Happiness Advantage: The Seven Principles of Positive Psychology That Fuel Success and Performance at Work.* New York: Crown Business, 2010.

Appley, M. H. *Adaptation Level Theory: A Symposium.* New York: Academic Press, 1971.

Ben-Shahar, Tal. *Happier.* New York: McGraw-Hill, 2007.

The Dalai Lama and Howard C. Cutler. *The Art of Happiness: A Handbook for Living.* New York: Riverhead Books, 1998.

Diener, Ed, and Robert Diener. *Happiness: Unlocking the Mysteries of Psychological Wealth.* Malden, MA: Blackwell, 2008.

Ehrenreich, Barbara. *Bright-Sided: How the Relentless Promotion of Positive Thinking Has Undermined America.* New York: Metropolitan Books, 2009.

Gilbert, Daniel. *Stumbling on Happiness.* New York: Vintage Books, 2005.

Haidt, Jonathan. *The Happiness Hypothesis: Finding Modern Truth in Ancient Wisdom.* New York: Basic Books, 2006.

Hecht, Jennifer Michael. *The Happiness Myth.* New York: HarperCollins, 2008.

Lyubomirsky, Sonya. *The How of Happiness: A Scientific Approach to Getting the Life You Want.* New York: Penguin Press, 2008.

McMahon, Darrin M. *Happiness: A History.* New York: Atlantic Monthly Press, 2006.

Myers, David G. *The Pursuit of Happiness: Discovering the Pathway to Fulfillment, Well-Being, and Enduring Personal Joy.* New York: Quill, 1992.

Nettle, Daniel. *Happiness: The Science Behind Your Smile.* Oxford: Oxford University Press, 2005.

Rubin, Gretchen. *The Happiness Project: Or, Why I Spent a Year Trying to Sing in the Morning, Clean My Closets, Fight Right, Read Aristotle, and Generally Have More Fun.* New York: HarperCollins, 2009.

Schoch, Richard. *The Secrets of Happiness: Three Thousand Years of Searching for the Good Life.* New York: Scribner, 2008.

Seligman, Martin E. P. *Authentic Happiness: Using the New Positive Psychology to Realize Your Potential for Lasting Fulfillment.* New York: Free Press, 2002.

———. *Flourish: A Visionary New Understanding of Happiness and Well-Being.* New York: Simon & Schuster, 2012.

Wilson, Eric G. *Against Happiness: In Praise of Melancholy.* New York: Sarah Crichton Books, 2008.

Identity/Consciousness

Blackmore, Susan. *Consciousness: An Introduction.* New York: Oxford University Press, 2011.

Cooley, Charles. *Human Nature and the Social Order.* Charleston, SC: Nabu Press, 2010.

Humphrey, Nicholas. *Soul Dust: The Magic of Consciousness.* Princeton, NJ: Princeton University Press, 2011.

Rogers, Carl R. *On Becoming a Person.* New York: Houghton Mifflin, 1961.

Rosenberg, Morris. *Conceiving the Self.* New York: Basic Books, 1979.

Wegner, Daniel M. *The Illusion of Conscious Will.* Cambridge, MA: Massachusetts Institute of Technology, 2003.

Wilson, Timothy D. *Strangers to Ourselves: Discovering the Adaptive Unconscious.* Cambridge, MA: Harvard University Press, 2004.

Life Stories

Angus, Lynne E., and John McLeod. *The Handbook of Narrative and Psychotherapy: Practice, Theory, and Research.* Thousand Oaks, CA: Sage Publications, 2004.

Birren, James E., and Kathryn N. Cochran. *Telling the Stories of Life Through Guided Autobiographical Groups.* Baltimore: Johns Hopkins University Press, 2001.

Lieblich, Amia, Dan P. McAdams, and Ruthellen Josselson. *Healing Plots: The Narrative Basis of Psychotherapy.* Washington, DC: American Psychological Association, 2004.

Madigan, Stephen. *Narrative Therapy.* Washington, DC: American Psychological Association, 2011.

Morgan, Richard L. *Remembering Your Story: Creating Your Own Spiritual Autobiography.* Nashville: Upper Room Books, 2002.

White, Michael, and David Epson. *Narrative Means to Therapeutic Ends.* New York: W. W. Norton, 1990.

Literary Works

Angelou, Maya. *Letter to My Daughter.* New York: Random House, 2008.

Beckett, Samuel. *Waiting for Godot: A Tragicomedy in Two Acts.* London: Folio Society, 2000.

Eliot, T. S. *The Complete Poems and Plays, 1909–1950.* New York: Harcourt, Brace & World, 1952.

Huxley, Aldous. *Brave New World.* New York: RosettaBooks, 1979.

Krakauer, Jon. *Three Cups of Deceit: How Greg Mortenson, Humanitarian Hero, Lost His Way.* Harpswell, ME: Anchor, 2011.

Lindbergh, Anne Morrow. *Gift from the Sea.* New York: Random House, 1995.

Miller, Arthur. *Death of a Salesman.* New York: Dramatists Play Service, 1980.

Montaigne, Michel de. *The Complete Essays of Montaigne.* Palo Alto, CA: Stanford University Press, 1958.

Plato. *Phaedrus.* Cambridge: Cambridge University Press, 2011.

Proust, Marcel. *Remembrance of Things Past.* Translated by C. K. Scott Moncrieff and Terence Kilmartin. New York: Random House, 1981.

Rilke, Rainer Maria. *Letters to a Young Poet.* Translated by Stephen Mitchell. New York: Random House, 1984.

Scott, Nathan. *Negative Capability: Studies in the New Literature and the Religious Situation.* New Haven, CT: Yale University Press, 1969.

Shakespeare, William. *Hamlet.* Cambridge: Cambridge University Press, 1999.

———. *King Lear.* New Haven, CT: Yale University Press, 2007.

Wallace, David Foster. *This Is Water: Some Thoughts, Delivered on a Significant Occasion, About Living a Compassionate Life.* New York: Little, Brown, 2009.

Mind: Intuition, Creativity, Conscious and Unconscious Thought

Barrett, Deirdre. *The Committee of Sleep.* N.p.: Oneiroi Press, 2001.

Bazerman, Max H., and Don A. Moore. *Judgment in Managerial Decision Making.* 7th ed. Hoboken, NJ: Wiley, 2013.

Benedetti, Fabrizio. *Placebo Effects.* Oxford: Oxford University Press, 2009.

Berdik, Chris. *Mind Over Mind: The Surprising Power of Expectations.* New York: Penguin, 2012.

Bristol, Claude M. *The Magic of Believing.* New York: Pocket Books, 1948.

Cousins, Norman. *Anatomy of an Illness as Perceived by the Patient.* New York: W. W. Norton, 1979.

———. *The Healing Heart: Antidotes to Panic and Helplessness.* Boston: G. K. Hall, 1983.

Csikszentmihalyi, Mihaly. *Flow: The Psychology of Optimal Experience.* New York: Harper & Row, 1990.

Dweck, Carol S. *Mindset: The New Psychology of Success.* New York: Ballantine Books, 2006.

———. *Self-Theories: Their Role in Motivation, Personality, and Development.* New York: Psychology Press, 2000.

Gladwell, Malcolm. *Blink: The Power of Thinking Without Thinking.* New York: Little, Brown, 2005.

Hanh, Thich Nhat. *The Miracle of Mindfulness: An Introduction to the Practice of Meditation.* Mobi Ho, trans. Boston: Beacon Press, 1999.

Harrington, Anne. *The Cure Within: A History of Mind-Body Medicine.* New York: W. W. Norton, 2008.

———. *The Placebo Effect.* Cambridge, MA: Harvard University Press, 1997.

Jones, Russell A. *Self-Fulfilling Prophecies: Social, Psychological, and Physiological Effects of Expectancies.* Hillsdale, NJ: Lawrence Erlbaum, 1977.

Kahneman, Daniel. *Thinking, Fast and Slow.* New York: Farrar, Straus & Giroux, 2011.

Kahneman, Daniel, Paul Slovic, and Amos Tversky, eds. *Judgment Under Uncertainty: Heuristics and Biases.* New York: Cambridge University Press, 1982.

Lynn, Steven Jay, and Irving Kirsch. *Essentials of Clinical Hypnosis: An Evidence-Based Approach.* Washington, DC: American Psychological Association, 2006.

Meyers, David G. *Intuition: Its Powers and Perils.* New Haven, CT: Yale University Press, 2002.

Murphy, Joseph. *The Power of Your Subconscious Mind.* Rev. ed. New York: Bantam, 2000.

Peale, Norman Vincent. *The Power of Positive Thinking.* New York: Prentice-Hall, 1952.

Rosenthal, Robert, and Lenore Jacobson. *Pygmalion in the Classroom: Teacher Expectation and Pupils' Intellectual Development.* New York: Holt, Rinehart, & Winston, 1968.

Schwartz, Barry. *The Paradox of Choice: Why More Is Less*. New York: HarperCollins, 2005.

Shermer, Michael. *The Believing Brain: From Ghosts and Gods to Politics and Conspiracies—How We Construct Beliefs and Reinforce Them as Truths*. New York: Henry Holt, 2011.

Tan, Chade-Meng. *Search Inside Yourself: The Unexpected Path to Achieving Success, Happiness (and World Peace)*. New York: HarperOne, 2012.

Willingham, Daniel T. *Why Don't Students Like School? A Cognitive Scientist Answers Questions About How the Mind Works and What It Means for the Classroom*. San Francisco: Jossey-Bass, 2009.

Wilson, Timothy D. *Strangers to Ourselves: Discovering the Adaptive Unconscious*. Cambridge, MA: Harvard University Press, 2004.

Motivation

Cowen, Tyler. *Discover Your Inner Economist: Use Incentives to Fall in Love, Survive Your Next Meeting, and Motivate Your Dentist*. New York: Dutton, 2007.

Deci, Edward, and Richard Flaste. *Why We Do What We Do: Understanding Self-Motivation*. New York: Penguin, 1996.

Jackson, Jim, and Ed Snider. *Walking Together Forever: The Broad Street Bullies, Then and Now*. Champaign, IL: Sports Publishing LLC, 2005.

Pink, Daniel H. *Drive: The Surprising Truth About What Motivates Us*. New York: Riverhead Books, 2009.

Skinner, B. F. *Science and Human Behavior*. New York: Free Press, 1965.

Vroom, Victor. *Work and Motivation*. San Francisco: Jossey-Bass, 1994.

Personality Psychology

Barondes, Samuel. *Making Sense of People: Decoding the Mysteries of Personality*. Upper Saddle River, NJ: FT Press, 2011.

Brown, Brene. *The Gifts of Imperfectionism: Let Go of Who You Think You're Supposed to Be and Embrace Who You Are*. Center City, MN: Hazelden, 2010.

———. *I Thought It Was Just Me: Telling the Truth About Perfectionism, Inadequacy, and Power*. New York: Gotham Books, 2008.

Cain, Susan. *Quiet: The Power of Introverts in a World That Can't Stop Talking*. New York: Crown, 2012.

Clifton, Donald O., and Marcus Buckingham. *Now, Discover Your Strengths*. New York: Free Press, 2001.

Costa, P. T., Jr., and R. R. McCrae. *NEO-PI-R: Professional Manual*. Odessa, FL: Psychological Assessment Resources, 1992.

Helgoe, Laurie. *Introvert Power: Why Your Inner Life Is Your Hidden Strength*. Naperville, IL: Sourcebooks, 2008.

LaFrance, Marianne. *Lip Service: Smiles in Life, Death, Trust, Lies, Work, Memory, Sex, and Politics.* New York: W. W. Norton, 2011.

Laney, Marti Olsen. *The Introvert Advantage: How to Thrive in an Extrovert World.* New York: Workman, 2002.

Myers, Isabel Briggs. *Gifts Differing: Understanding Personality Type.* 2nd ed. Boston: Nicholas Brealey, 1995.

Tieger, Paul D., and Barbara Barron. *Do What You Are: Discover the Perfect Career for You Through the Secrets of Personality Type.* New York: Little, Brown, 1992.

Philosophy

Aristotle. *Nicomachean Ethics.* Terence Irwin, trans. Indianapolis: Hackett, 1999.

Bakewell, Sarah. *How to Live—or—a Life of Montaigne: One Question and Twenty Attempts at an Answer.* New York: Other Press, 2010.

Berlin, Isaiah. *The Hedgehog and the Fox.* Lanham, MD: Ivan R. Dee, 1993.

Einstein, Albert. *Living Philosophies.* New York: Simon & Schuster, 1931.

Haxton, Brooks. *Fragments: The Collected Wisdom of Heraclitus.* New York: Penguin, 2003.

Marcus Aurelius. *Meditations.* Gregory Hays, trans. New York: Modern Library, 2002.

Montaigne, Michel de. *The Complete Essays.* London: Penguin Press, 1991.

Russell, Bertrand. *Principles of Social Reconstruction.* New York: Psychology Press, 1997.

Taylor, Charles. *The Ethics of Authenticity.* Cambridge, MA: Harvard University Press, 1991.

Trilling, Lionel. *Sincerity and Authenticity.* Cambridge, MA: Harvard University Press, 1972.

Positive Psychology

Keyes, Corey L. M., and Jonathan Haidt. *Flourishing: Positive Psychology and the Life Well-Lived.* Washington, DC: American Psychological Association, 2002.

Linley, P. Alex, and Stephen Joseph. *Positive Psychology in Practice.* Hoboken, NJ: John Wiley & Sons, 2004.

Peale, Norman Vincent. *The Power of Positive Thinking.* New York: Prentice-Hall, 1952.

Peterson, Christopher. *A Primer in Positive Psychology.* New York: Oxford University Press, 2006.

Religion

Gallagher, Timothy M. *The Discernment of Spirits: An Ignatian Guide for Everyday Living.* New York: Crossroad, 2005.

Hagen, Steve. *Buddhism Plain and Simple.* Portland, OR: Broadway Books, 1998.

Hanh, Thich Nhat. *The Miracle of Mindfulness: An Introduction to the Practice of Meditation*. Mobi Ho, trans. Boston: Beacon Press, 1999.

Holy Bible, King James Version.

Partridge, Christopher Hugh. *Introduction to World Religions*. Minneapolis: Fortress Press, 2005.

Sifton, Elizabeth. *The Serenity Prayer: Faith and Politics in Times of Peace and War*. New York: W. W. Norton, 2003.

Sunim, Ku San. *Nine Mountains: Dharma-Lectures of the Korean Meditation Master Ku San*. 4th ed. Rangoon: International Meditation Center, 1982.

Wade, Nicholas. *The Faith Instinct: How Religion Evolved and Why It Endures*. New York: Penguin Press, 2009.

Yin-shun. *The Way to Buddhahood*. Somerville, MA: Wisdom Publications, 1998.

Self-Control

Baumeister, Roy F., and John Tierney. *Willpower: Rediscovering the Greatest Human Strength*. New York: Penguin Press, 2011.

Duhigg, Charles. *The Power of Habit: Why We Do What We Do in Life and Business*. New York: Random House, 2012.

Heath, Chip, and Dan Heath. *Switch: How to Change Things When Change Is Hard*. Broadway Books: New York, 2010.

McGonigal, Kelly. *The Willpower Instinct: How Self-Control Works, Why It Matters, and What You Can Do to Get More of It*. New York: Avery, 2012.

Mate, Gabor. *In the Realm of Hungry Ghosts: Close Encounters with Addiction*. Berkeley, CA: North Atlantic Books, 2010.

Possada, Joachim de, and Ellen Singer. *Don't Eat the Marshmallow . . . Yet! The Secret to Sweet Success in Work and Life*. New York: Berkley Books, 2005.

Wilson, Timothy D. *Redirect: The Surprising New Science of Psychological Change*. New York: Little, Brown, 2011.

Social Skills: Dialogue, Influence, and Negotiation

Carnegie, Dale. *How to Win Friends and Influence People*. Rev. ed. New York: Pocket Books, 1936.

Cialdini, Robert B. *Influence: The Psychology of Persuasion*. Rev. ed. New York: Quill, 1993.

Kovecses, Zoltan. *Metaphor: A Practical Introduction*. New York: Oxford University Press, 2002.

Lakoff, George, and Mark Johnson. *Metaphors We Live By*. Chicago: University of Chicago Press, 1980.

Mnookin, Robert. *Bargaining with the Devil: When to Negotiate, When to Fight*. New York: Simon & Schuster, 2010.

Nichols, Shaun, and Stephen P. Stich. *Mindreading: An Integrated Account of Pretence, Self-Awareness, and Understanding Other Minds.* Oxford: Clarendon Press, 2003.

Patterson, Kerry, Joseph Grenny, Ron McMillan, and Al Switzler. *Crucial Conversations: Tools for Talking When Stakes Are High.* New York: McGraw-Hill, 2002.

Shell, G. Richard. *Bargaining for Advantage: Negotiation Strategies for Reasonable People.* 2nd ed. New York: Penguin, 2006.

Shell, G. Richard, and Mario Moussa. *The Art of Woo: Using Strategic Persuasion to Sell Your Ideas.* New York: Portfolio, 2007.

Success: General

Brooks, David. *The Social Animal: The Hidden Sources of Love, Character, and Achievement.* New York: Random House, 2011.

Byrne, Rhonda. *The Secret.* New York: Atria Books, 2006.

Canfield, Jack. *The Success Principles: How to Get from Where You Are to Where You Want to Be.* New York: HarperCollins, 2005.

Coelho, Paulo. *The Alchemist.* New York: HarperCollins, 1995.

Covey, Stephen R. *The 7 Habits of Highly Effective People: Powerful Lessons in Personal Change.* New York: Free Press, 1989.

Gallup, George, Jr., and Alec M. Gallup. *The Great American Success Story: Factors That Affect Achievement.* Homewood, IL: Dow Jones–Irwin, 1986.

Gladwell, Malcolm. *Outliers: The Story of Success.* Boston: Little, Brown, 2008.

Gurdjieff, George. *Meetings with Remarkable Men.* New York: E. P. Dutton, 1963.

Hill, Napoleon. *Think and Grow Rich.* New York: Fawcett Books, 1937.

Huber, Richard M. *The American Idea of Success.* New York: McGraw-Hill, 1971.

Maxwell. John C. *Success 101: What Every Leader Needs to Know.* Nashville: Thomas Nelson, 2008.

Talent and Expert Practice

Colvin, Geoff. *Talent Is Overrated: What Really Separates World-Class Performers from Everybody Else.* New York: Penguin, 2008.

Ericcson, K. Anders, ed. *The Road to Excellence: Acquisition of Expert Performance in Arts and Sciences, Sports and Games.* New York: Psychology Press, 1996.

Maxwell, John C. *Talent Is Never Enough: Discover the Choices That Will Take You Beyond Your Talent.* Nashville: Thomas Nelson, 2007.

Index